LEADING THE LEADERS

How to Enrich Your Style of Management
and Handle People Whose Style Is
Different from Yours

by
Ichak Kalderon Adizes, Ph.D.
Director of Professional Services and CEO of
the Adizes Institute

Library of Congress Cataloging-in-Publication Data

Adizes, Ichak.
  Leading the Leaders: how to enrich your style of management and handle people whose style is different from yours

Library of Congress Control Number: 2004092672

ISBN: 0-937120-05-7

Published by:
The Adizes Institute Publishing
2815 East Valley Road
Santa Barbara, CA, 93108
805-565-2901
www.adizes.com

Printed in China

For Nurit, who does not need this book to read people.

ACKNOWLEDGEMENTS

I want to thank Nan Goldberg who has diligently edited this book into a readable form and put up with my endless rewritings. Without her this book would not see the light of the day.

Zvonko Kuzmanovski labored on publishing this book and organized all that is needed for making it happen.

Martha Bright checked the spelling and did the copy editing.

Thank you all.

About the Author

Dr. Ichak Adizes is one of the world's leading experts in improving the performance of businesses and governments by making fundamental changes without the chaos and destructive conflict that plague many change efforts. Over the past 35 years, Dr. Ichak Adizes has worked with some of the largest commercial organizations in the world and has consulted to many heads of state. The methodology that bears his name has helped organizations in a variety of countries to achieve results and gain leadership positions in industries ranging from banking to food services, and in organizations as different as churches and governments. He is the Founder and CEO of the Adizes Institute. His work has been featured in *Inc. Magazine, Fortune, The New York Times, The London Financial Times, Investor Relations Daily, Nation's Business* and *World Digest.*

Dr. Adizes is also a noted lecturer and author. He lectures in four languages and has spoken in over 40 countries. He was tenured faculty at UCLA Anderson School of Management for 30 years and was a visiting Faculty at Stanford University, Columbia University and both Hebrew and Tel Aviv Universities. Dr. Adizes is the author of seven books that have been translated into 22 languages. His *Corporate Lifecycles: How Organizations Grow and Die and What to Do about It* (1988) is a well-regarded classic in management theory that was selected as one of the 10 Best Business Books by Library Journal. A revised edition was published under the title *Managing Corporate Lifecycles* in 1999. The list of all his works is at the of this book.

ichak@adizes.com

Contents

Preface.. 13
  Why This Book?.. 13
  Goals of This Book... 14
  The Premise.. 15
  Methodology and source of data................................... 16
  Organization and Presentation.................................... 17
  How to Read This Book.. 18
  A Note on Style.. 19
  A Request.. 20
Chapter 1: What Is Management?................................ 21
  The Functionalist View 23
  Why the Roles Are Incompatible................................... 25
  The Myth of the Perfect Manager.................................. 28
  Management vs. Mismanagement vs. Leadership...................... 31
  Management Training: The Big Fallacy............................. 32
  The Workable Solution: A Complementary Team...................... 33
  The Inevitability of Conflict.................................... 34
  Recognizing and Hiring a Good Manager............................ 35
Chapter 2: Management Styles.................................. 39
  A Raison D'Etre.. 40
  The (P)roducer (Paei).. 42
    Running the Railroad... 43
  The (A)dministrator (pAei)....................................... 44
  Seeing through the Fog... 46
  The Creative Contributor (paEi).................................. 47
  The (E)ntrepreneur (PaEi).. 48
    Getting Religion... 49
  The (I)ntegrator (paeI).. 52
  The (I) Role in Leadership....................................... 54
Chapter 3: Mismanagement Styles.............................. 57
  The Lone Ranger (P---)... 58
  The Bureaucrat (-A--).. 63

The Arsonist (--E-).. 70

The SuperFollower (---I)... 76

The Common Denominator.. 79

The Deadwood (----).. 80

Chapter 4: Prescriptions for the (P) Style........................... 85

Behavior... 85

Communication.. 90

Decision-making... 97

Implementing... 110

Team-building.. 112

Managing staff... 114

Managing Change.. 118

Top Ten Prescriptions for a Predominantly (P) Style........... 123

Chapter 5: (pAei) Prescriptions.................................... 125

Behavior.. 125

Communication... 128

Decision-making.. 134

Implementing... 143

Team-building.. 147

Managing Staff... 150

Managing Change.. 156

Top 10 Prescriptions for a (pAei)............................... 159

Chapter 6: (paEi) and (PaEi) Prescriptions........................ 161

Behavior.. 161

Communication... 168

Decision-making.. 173

Implementation... 182

Team-building.. 185

Managing Staff... 191

Managing Change.. 200

Top Ten Prescriptions for the Predominantly (E) Type....... 203

Chapter 7: (paeI) Prescriptions.................................... 205

Behavior.. 205

Communication... 208

Decision-making.. 211

Implementing.. 214

Team-building... 215

Managing Staff.. 217

Managing Change... 220

Top Prescriptions for an (I) Style........................... 222

Chapter 8: Management Style Comparisons........................ 223

Behavior Comparisons.. 223

Communication Comparisons................................. 226

Decision-making Comparisons............................... 229

Implementation Comparisons................................ 237

Team-building Comparisons.................................. 241

Managing Staff Comparisons................................. 246

Change Comparisons... 250

Chapter 9: Dealing with Other People............................ 255

Communicating... 257

Dealing with a (P) – a (P)roducer or Lone Ranger............ 259

Dealing with an (A) – an (A)dministrator or Bureaucrat.... 262

Dealing with an (E) – an (E)ntrepreneur or Arsonist......... 267

Dealing with an (I) - an (I)ntegrator or SuperFollower....... 273

Summing It Up... 274

Chapter 10: Prescriptions for Dealing with Others............. 277

Dealing with a (P).. 277

Dealing with an (A)... 281

Dealing with an (E)... 284

Dealing with an (I).. 295

Summary... 298

Afterword.. 301

Bibliography.. 302

Additional works by the author................................. 305

About the Adizes Institute....................................... 311

Preface

Why This Book?

I introduced my theory of management in one of my early books – *How to Solve the Mismanagement Crisis* (first published by Dow Jones Irwin in 1979 and subsequently reprinted several times by the Adizes Institute). The book was translated into 22 languages and became a bestseller in several countries. As I continued to work with hundreds of companies in 48 countries, my knowledge of the subject increased and I was able to expand each chapter of the original book into a book of its own. The chapter on corporate lifecycles became: *Corporate Lifecycles: Why Organizations Grow and Die and What to Do about It* (Paramus, N.J.: Prentice Hall, 1989), with subsequent enlarged and revised editions published by the Adizes Institute).

The chapter on how to keep an organization in its Prime condition of vitality became *The Pursuit of Prime* (Santa Monica, Calif.: Knowledge Exchange, 1997), and the chapter on how to manage change became *Mastering Change* (Santa Monica, Calif.: Adizes Institute, 1992).

More parts of that introductory book are being presented now in a series of three books. The first is: *The Ideal Executive: Why You Cannot Be One and What to Do about It*, in which I discuss why you can never become the perfect textbook executive that management development programs are attempting to produce.

The subject of management and mismanagement styles – and by this I am speaking of the styles of normal people, rather than a collage of perfect traits that no one actually possesses – I cover in the second book, *Management/Mismanagement Styles*.

This book, the third in the series, *Leading the Leaders – How Improve Your Style of Management and Handle Styles That Are Different from Your Own* – is meant to help you compensate for your own flaws and weaknesses, once you have discovered what your basic management style is; and also to help you handle other managers – your subordinates, peers, and those you report to – whose styles are different from yours. It is written in the form of "prescriptions" to follow – different prescriptions for each style. It is also directed to the emerging profession of corporate coaches, as it provides additional tools for coaching executives.

GOALS OF THIS BOOK

This book is not a survey of the literature, although I do include some references to illustrate that my experiences are not unique to me. Rather, these prescriptions are notes from the battleground, based on my experiences in coaching executives around the world. You might say that this book has been in the process of being written for more than thirty years.

It is important to note, however, that my prescriptions are not intended to change anyone, but rather, to enrich a manager's style. The word "change" is usually taken to mean a total transformation, such as a change of seasons from winter to summer. That kind of personality change is impossible to accomplish.

What can be done is to make the summer not so hot and the winter more bearable. Enriching a style does not mean a total change of personality and behavior. The purpose of coaching is to make managers, whatever their personal style, become more flexible, so that they can work with others whose styles are different.

Granted, it is more of a small, incremental, continuous improvement than a revolutionary change, a paradigm shift or a breakthrough. But that's life. I do not believe that people can change their innate character. That has been one of my continuing struggles with executives in many companies: "Why doesn't he change?" they ask me. "Can't you help us change him?"

My answer is: "People do not change, but since they can get worse they can also get better, and that might be all we need to be able to work with them."

In clarifying these definitions I am merely attempting to set appropriate expectations. Sometimes when companies hire a coach, there is the expectation that those who are being coached can become someone else entirely. We expect that in a marriage too, don't we? – until we realize that it does not and cannot happen. Making a fish into a bird is not something we should aim for – not in the time frame of one lifetime, anyway. But we can work on making people whose styles are different work better together nevertheless.

THE PREMISE

My premise, which I fully develop in *The Ideal Executive* and reiterate in Chapter 1 of this book, is that the ideal leader, manager, or executive does not and cannot exist. All the books and textbooks that try to teach us to be perfect managers, leaders, or executives are based on the erroneous assumption that such a goal is possible. No one can excel at all of the roles expected of leaders or managers. Every human being may excel in one or more roles, but never in all of them, forever and under all circumstances. We are all human and thus have strengths and weaknesses. The managerial task requires a perfection no one is able to provide since no one is perfect.

Thus, classic management theorists, including Howard Koontz, William H. Newman, and even Peter Drucker, present what the manager or executive should do – as if all managers have the same style and can be trained to manage the same way, ignoring the fact that different people organize, plan, motivate – in other words, manage – differently.

Since the "perfect," "ideal" executive, who excels in all roles, does not and cannot exist, does that mean that all organizations, by definition, will be mismanaged? The answer is: "Absolutely not!" What we need is a complementary team. But how can such different styles complement each other? How can they work together when they are so unlike each other?

The first step is to understand that the different styles speak different "languages" – in other words, they infer different meanings from different communication cues in word and in gesture. Conflict between the different styles is unavoidable; but by learning to speak the "language" of the people we are working with, we can build a complementary team and nourish it, thus preventing that conflict from becoming destructive.

You need to pay attention to how your behavior affects others. If you know your style, then you also know that your style of communicating is apt to be problematic for the other styles. If you know in what ways it is problematic, then you can compensate. And here is where we come to the purpose of this book: How to compensate for your style so you can work with others; and how to coach others so that they can work with each other.

METHODOLOGY AND SOURCE OF DATA

This book summarizes for the reader my insights based on thirty years of work in the field of organizational transformation ("consulting"). Since my work as an organizational transformationist and lecturer frequently takes me all over the globe, I have been able to compare notes and share my observations with executives around the world.

I have treated companies in 48 countries that range from $1 million to $15 billion in sales or $120 billion in assets, and employ from 80 to hundreds of thousands of people. They are involved in numerous technologies, including aircraft, insurance, banking, the performing arts, museums, and government agencies, in both the profit and not-for-profit sectors. I have also used my insights about leadership style to counsel several heads of state.

I've found that my insights on managerial styles are valid for all the countries in which I've lectured, including cultures as different from each other as those of Taiwan, Japan, Sweden, Mexico, Greece, Israel, England, and the United States. Managerial styles and behavior are independent of culture – although social culture, I have noted, tends to reinforce managerial behavior.

ORGANIZATION AND PRESENTATION

In Chapter 1, I sum up the first book in this series, *The Ideal Executive: Why You Cannot Be One and What to Do about It*. I define the concept of management, discuss the myth of the perfect manager, and briefly present my functional theory of management: the four roles – (**P**), (**A**), (**E**), and (**I**) – necessary to perform good management. Next, I explain why these four roles are incompatible and why they inevitably lead to conflict – and what you can do about it. Finally, I discuss the attributes of a good manager – in contrast to that mythical perfect manager who appears about as frequently as a unicorn.

Chapters 2 and 3 briefly review the contents of the second book in this series, *Management/Mismanagement Styles*, because it is impossible to understand this book without the information contained in the preceding book of the series. In Chapter 2, I describe the management style that results when one of the necessary (**PAEI**) management roles is performed with excellence and the others only adequately, creating archetypes that I have dubbed the (**P**)roducer, for a (**Paei**); the (**A**)dministrator, for a (**pAei**); the (**E**)ntrepreneur, for a (**PaEi**); and the (**I**)ntegrator, for a (**paeI**).

Chapter 3 contrasts the above management styles with the mismanagement style that results when all emphasis is placed on one role to the exclusion of the other three: the Lone Ranger, (**P---**); the Bureaucrat, (**-A--**); the Arsonist, (**--E-**); and the SuperFollower, (**---I**); and finally the Deadwood, (**----**) who does not perform any of the four (**PAEI**) roles.

(If you have already read *The Ideal Executive* and *Management/Mismanagement Styles*, you can skip those chapters.)

Chapters 4 through 7 contain my prescriptions for each of the four basic managerial styles. These are quick, easily grasped reminders that, once you have discovered your own style, will help you compensate for your weaknesses and communicate effectively with other management types.

Each style has its own chapter, and each chapter contains custom-made prescriptions divided into categories that reflect the five basic functions of every manager – decision-making, implementing, team-building, managing staff, and managing change – as well as behavior and communication. Within each category, there is no particular order or sequence to the pages. Each statement, each page stands on its own. Each prescription is followed by a brief discussion.

Chapter 8 contrasts the different styles' common managerial problems by placing the prescriptions in a comparative context, so that the characteristic failures of each style are juxtaposed. Reading these comparisons can make you wonder how any organization manages to function at all without imploding.

Chapters 9 and 10 focus on how to deal with a boss, employee, or colleague whose style is different from yours. (Theoretically, it should not matter what style you are, since how you communicate should depend on whom you are speaking to, not who is speaking.) The way to achieve influence over others is to master the style of communication that others respond to. And the more influence each manager has on the others, the better the quality of decision-making will become.

In Chapter 9, I offer clues to diagnosing another person's basic style (as opposed to your own), as well as some general tips on how to communicate with each style: What works and what doesn't work. Chapter 10 offers specific prescriptions for dealing with other people of each style in the areas of decision-making, implementation, team-building, managing staff, and managing change.

How to Read This Book

To get the full benefit from this book – particularly if you are still convinced that you can do the job all by yourself and don't need people who complement you – please read the first two books in this series before you start reading this one.

These prescriptions are meant for those who have an inclination to enrich themselves and are looking for encouragement, reminders, and direction. To get maximum benefit, you must be relaxed and open. Above all, do not be defensive about your own style or judgmental about someone else's. Remember that the prescriptions will not all be relevant – at least not all at the same moment in your career. Choose those that apply to you, based on your assessment of your own basic style.

When you get to the prescriptions, I suggest that you read no more than five or six at any one time. Each statement takes a page or more to explain and could take a whole book to elaborate. Reading too much too soon would overtax you, like reading a book of jokes: overexposure causes you to become bored and unappreciative.

On the other hand, I strongly suggest re-reading this book at intervals throughout your professional life – both to remind yourself of these tips and because as time passes and you have new experiences, statements that once had little or no relevance might become powerful and exciting. I personally re-read my own statements often, and even though they are my own I can find them banal or very illuminating, depending on when I read them and what my recent experience has been.

Everyone needs reminders. I, too, sometimes violate my own principles in communicating with people. I have found that the more tired or emotional I am, the more likely I am to forget to focus on the style of the person I am talking to, and to speak to him instead as if his style were identical to mine. When that happens, there is a good chance that I will start, or reinforce, a dysfunctional conflict.

I must make one important disclaimer: The prescriptions will not work for managers who have zeros, or dashes, in their code. I have found that when someone totally lacks the capability to perform a certain role, no prescription will help; it is beyond my capability to enrich his style. Thus, when I refer to someone as having the (P) style, assume that I am speaking about a (Paei) manager, not (P---); when I say (A), I mean a (pAei), not (-A--).

A NOTE ON STYLE

Throughout this book I have most often used the masculine gender, because I found it cumbersome to switch back and forth and inaccurate to assign one gender to any specific managerial style. My insights apply equally to female managers. When, occasionally, I use the female gender to refer to a managerial style, again I intend my comments to refer to both genders equally.

A REQUEST

I am extremely interested in your feedback. Do you have any disagreements? Do you have some experiences that confirm what I am saying or reject what I am saying? Let me hear from you.

I have learned from everyone who has cared to share their thoughts with me. If any reader wishes to communicate agreement, disagreement, experience or anecdotes, jokes or cartoons that illustrate my points, I would appreciate the feedback. Use the chat room at the Adizes Institute's website for that purpose (www.adizes.com), or write to me at the Adizes Institute, 2815 East Valley Road, Santa Barbara, CA 93108.

Better yet, send me an e-mail: Ichak@Adizes.com.

Thank you.

Ichak Kalderon Adizes
Santa Barbara, 2004

Chapter 1

What Is Management?

First, let's define our terms. What, exactly, do we mean by the word "manager," and what roles does the word "management" encompass?

From textbooks we learn that managers (also called administrators, executives, and leaders) plan, decide, lead, organize, control, and motivate.

However, there are organizations in which management does not perform some of those functions. Some years ago I studied the management of artistic organizations – opera, dance, theater, etc. – and I became aware that managers cannot manage artists as, let us say, one can manage workers.[1] They cannot plan, organize, and control as the textbooks prescribe. I noted the same phenomenon in the health and educational systems:[2] Administrators do not perform all the functions of management. They do not decide policy matters, for example, since physicians and educators usually have this as their prerogative.

Nor do all countries around the world practice the managerial process exactly as we define it. In fact, in some countries our form of management is prohibited by law. In Yugoslavia, for instance, during the Communist era of self-management, it was constitutionally prohibited to make decisions the way we do, *for* the organization. The manager's role was to suggest, present to, and convince the workers, who had the ultimate responsibility for deciding salaries, quotas of production, investments, etc.[3]

In other countries, management is socially discouraged. In the heyday of the Israeli kibbutzim, for instance, management was deliberately rotated every two or three years, so that nobody became what in the United States is called a professional manager: A person whose profession it is to tell other people what to do.

In certain languages, such as Swedish, French, Serbian, and Croatian, the word "manage" does not even have a literal translation. In those languages, words like "direct," "lead," or "administer" are often used instead. When they mean to say "manage" the way we use it in the United States, they usually use the English word.

In Spanish, the word *manejar*, the literal translation for "manage," means "to handle" and is used only when referring to horses or cars. When they want to say "to manage" in the American sense of the word, they use "direct" or "administer."

In an English thesaurus, synonyms for "manage" include: "decide," "operate," "plan," "control," "organize," "rule," "achieve goals," "lead," "motivate," "accomplish," "dominate," "govern," even "manipulate."

What is the common denominator shared by all these synonyms? They are all a one-way process. The managing person is telling the managed person what to do. Even the word "motivating" makes an assumption: that the motivator has decided already what to do, and in motivating is trying to convince a subordinate to do it.

Now let's look at the word "subordinate" – the one who is managed, who is supposed to carry out the manager's decisions. What does that word really mean? Listen to it: *Subordinate* – like *sub*-ordinary. Now listen to the word *supervisor* – it connotes superior vision. It connotes a fixed hierarchy of capabilities as well.

So the managerial process, as it is taught and practiced, is not a value-free process. It is not only a science and an art, but also an expression of sociopolitical values. All of the synonyms for "managing," to a greater or lesser degree, are a kind of manipulation.

So, then, what *is* management, if in some countries it's prohibited, in others it's socially discouraged, and in still others it doesn't even exist?

THE FUNCTIONALIST VIEW

Let us try to understand the meaning of management by understanding the function it performs: Why do we need it? What would happen if it did not exist?

The function should be value-free, without any sociopolitical or cultural biases. It should be the same whether we are managing ourselves, our families, a business, a not-for-profit organization, or even an entire nation. Whether we are speaking about managing, parenting, or governing, it should be one and the same process conceptually, differing only in the size and nature of the unit being managed.

What is the function of management? What is it supposed to do? Would you agree with me that it is to ensure a well-managed organization?

Now, what does "well-managed organization" mean? Would you agree with me that an organization is well managed if it is effective and efficient in the short and long run? Effective in the short run means that it satisfies the present needs of its present clients. Efficient in the short run means that it is operating with the minimum necessary resources. There is no unnecessary waste.

Effective in the long run means that it will satisfy the needs of its future clients. It means that the organization proacts to change. And efficient in the long run means that no one is indispensable in this organization. It can survive and adapt organically to internal changes as well.

The purpose of management, then, is to see to it that the organization is effective and efficient in the short and long run.

Please note that this definition is value-free. It applies to any organization of any size in any technology with any purpose in any country. It equally applies to running an organization of saints and, sorry to say it, to running a Nazi extermination camp. It applies to running a family, a business, a not-for-profit organization, or a country.

Thus it is a universal, functionalist theory of management.

How does management (parenting, leading or governing) accomplish this task?

Over more than 40 years of continuous research and testing, I've discovered that there are four roles that management must perform if an organization is going to be well managed in the short and in the long run. Management can be defined by these four roles, because each one of them is necessary and together they are sufficient for good management: In other words, if all four roles are performed, the organization will be effective and efficient in the short and long run.

What are those roles? Let me briefly define each.[4]

The first role that management must perform in any organization is to (**P**)roduce the desired results, making the organization effective in the short run. What are those results?

It is to satisfy the needs of the clients for which the organization exists. Why are people coming to you? Why do they need you? What is the service they want? The (**P**)roducer's job is to satisfy this need. One way of measuring client satisfaction is by how many people *come back* to buy your competitive products or services.

The second role, to (**A**)dminister, means to see to it that the organizational processes are systematized: that there are procedures and that events happen in the right sequence with the right intensity. It is the role of (**A**)dministration to ensure efficiency in the short run.

If you satisfy your clients' needs at a price that is higher than the cost of satisfying them (**P>A**), the organization will be profitable in the short run.

What about the long run?

For the long run, management must perform a visionary role, ensuring that the organization takes the direction it needs to take. This role requires the organization to proact to constant change and thus renders the company effective over the long run. This is the (**E**)ntrepreneur's role, which combines creativity with the willingness to take risks. If the organization performs this role well, it will have the future services and/or products that its future clients will want and seek.

Finally, management must (**I**)ntegrate, which means to build a climate and a system of values that motivates the individuals in the organization to work together so that no one is indispensable, rendering the company efficient in the long run.

In any organization of any size, in any technology, in any culture, these four roles are necessary for good management. Any time one or more of these roles is not being performed, there will be mismanagement. If the (**P**) role is not performed well, clients will not be satisfied and sales will decline. If the (**A**) role is not performed well, the organization will have unnecessary waste. If the (**E**) role is not performed well, the organization will be late to market with its products or have new products that fail; and if the organization is badly (**I**)ntegrated, then when a leader leaves the company, it will experience a seizure. And the pattern of mismanagement that will appear is a predictable, repetitive pattern all over the world, regardless of culture, regardless of technology, regardless of the size of the organization.

It is as if for organizational health, in the short and long run, we need four "vitamins": (**P**), (**A**), (**E**), and (**I**). Any time one of them is missing, a predictable and identifiable organizational "disease" will become evident. However, if one knows how to "inject" the missing "vitamin," the organization's performance can be improved and brought back to short- and long-term health.

For thirty years, I have used the (**PAEI**)[5] principles, among other tools that are covered in my other books, in my consulting work in companies around the globe – as have my associates, who are trained and certified in this methodology. It is a tested methodology for analyzing and solving problems and predicting behavior.

WHY THE ROLES ARE INCOMPATIBLE

Peter Drucker has recognized the complexity of the managerial task. "The top management tasks," Drucker writes, "require at least four different kinds of human being." Drucker identifies them as "the thought man," "the action man," "the people man," and "the front man." And Drucker also acknowledges, "Those four temperaments are almost never found in the same person."[6] But he does not go beyond saying that more than one style is necessary to manage any organization. Why those styles and not others? He neglects to say what those styles are and how they should interact in order to work together in spite of being so different. That is the gap I am trying to fill with my books.

Why is it that the perfect, all-encompassing (**PAEI**) manager does not exist?

The reason why no manager can be the perfect (**PAEI**) executive every organization needs is that the managerial (**PAEI**) roles are incompatible in the short run; in other words, they cannot be performed simultaneously. For example, (**P**) and (**I**) are incompatible. Have you ever attended a course or workshop where you were taught how to be a better (**I**): How to relate better to people and be a good communicator and a sensitive human being? Then there was a crisis, and time pressure, and you had to have a meeting in which you had to (**P**), then and there. There was no time to convince, explain, or motivate. What happened to your team orientation and ability to listen patiently?

When there is time pressure to (**P**)roduce results, it is normal to become rather "dictatorial" and assign a lower priority to (**I**)ntegration and teamwork. The (**P**) squeezes the (**I**) out.

Let us look more closely at the incompatibility of roles. We all know managers who are brilliant at conceptualizing plans and ideas but not very good at monitoring the details of implementation; or who are sensitive, empathic, and good at (**I**)ntegration, but just can't seem to make hard decisions.

The explanation is simple: The four roles are not mutually exclusive, but they are incompatible in the short run and thus mutually *inhibitive*: In other words, the ability to excel at one of the (**PAEI**) roles is likely to impede one's ability to perform another.

Any combination of the four roles is incompatible, not just (**P**) and (**I**). (**P**)roducing and (**E**)ntrepreneuring are incompatible too. How many times have you said, "I'm working so hard, I have no time to think"? In other words, the energy dedicated to satisfying present demands is so overwhelming that you have no time or energy to think about future opportunities. (**P**) actually endangers (**E**), because if you work very hard, day and night, focusing on short-run results, it is difficult if not impossible to also notice the changes that are coming your way. Your mind is like a camera: You can either focus on the close-up view, rendering the long view out of focus, or the opposite.

Conversely, (**E**) threatens (**P**): (**E**)ntrepreneuring means change, and that threatens the (**P**) role. People in Production often complain to the Engineering department, "If you guys don't stop changing things, we'll never get anything done!" At some point, you have to freeze the planning so you can proceed with the doing.

Now let's look at another combination: (**P**) and (**A**). They are also incompatible. When you want to be very effective, you have difficulty being efficient. That's why start-up companies, which are constantly putting out fires and dealing with unanticipated problems, are disorganized and inefficient. They accept the fact that organization and order – (**A**) – will have to wait.

The opposite is also true: If you are very efficient, you end up being less effective. That is the case with bureaucracies, in which every detail is planned and no variable is left uncontrolled. But the more control you insist upon, the more inflexible and non-responsive the system becomes, until it can no longer adapt to the changing needs of its clients.

Think of a tennis player who trains and trains until his hand and body movements are perfect. Then he announces to his opponent: "Send the ball *here!*" – to the spot on the court from which he knows he can return the ball in perfect form.

I call that being precisely wrong rather than approximately right. That is how bureaucracies work. The fact that the clients' needs have changed does not concern them. They just go through the motions as developed for maximum efficiency and control. It is efficient in the extreme, and extremely ineffective.

How are (**A**)dministration and (**E**)ntrepreneurship incompatible? As you freeze new ideas for the sake of efficiency, your ability to be proactive and effective in the long run will become limited. Policies, rules, and institutionalized behavior inhibit change. Thus (**A**) endangers (**E**). And vice versa: too much change hinders systematization, routinization, and order.

Let's look at (**A**)dministration/(**I**)ntegration incompatibility. Which country has the fewest lawyers per capita? Japan. Their need for (**A**)dministration, with its strict rules and policies, is low, and that is because their (**I**)ntegration is high. In Japan there is a great deal of loyalty and interdependence in business. Corporations offer lifetime employment and a family environment. They take care of each other; they are guided more by their culture than by their legal institutions.

Now, which country has the *most* lawyers per capita? The United States. (**A**) is very high and growing; our court system is overloaded. We rely on external intervention to solve our interdependency problems. Our (**I**) is low.

As a result of these compatibility issues, all managers have strengths and weaknesses in their ability to perform the four key roles. While a (**paEi**) manager may excel at activating change, he or she will be weak in (**A**)dministration. Another manager, a (**pAei**), may excel at organizing, but will show weakness at (**E**)ntrepreneuring. A (**paeI**) will excel at understanding people – but don't expect a high level of (**P**)roductivity, (**E**)ntrepreneurship, or (**A**)dministration from him.

And so on. Unfortunately, in any manager, a role can be completely missing, squeezed out, threatened into extinction, or never fully developed. When that happens we get mismanagers, which we will expand upon in the next chapter.

The Myth of the Perfect Manager

The New York Times once ran an article about me in which I was labeled "the corporate exorcist."[7] I go from company to company trying to purge management of its belief that it can do the impossible.

What is it they cannot do? They cannot find, or even train, the perfect manager, executive, or leader: one who can single-handedly create and maintain a well-managed organization by causing it to become effective and efficient in the short and long run.

Try the following exercise. Call all of your top managers into a room. Ask each of them to write down the company's top five problems. The rules are that, first, no names be mentioned; and second, that they not use the word "because" – no explanations for the problem are necessary.

Just ask them to note on a piece of paper, which they do not have to show to anyone, the company's top five most critical, significant problems, as manifested in undesired results or processes.

All of these problems must be *controllable* by the people in the room; it is not acceptable to define a problem as something "they" are not doing. Focus on what "you" – those in the room – are not doing. In other words, instead of saying: "Unpredictable interest rates" (this was a problem raised in a bank), they could write: "We do not have a plan for how to handle unpredictable interest rates," or, "Our strategy for handling unpredictable interest rates does not work," etc.

Now ask them: "How many of these problems did the company have last year?"

Do not look at what they have written. Do not let them share what they have written. Just ask them: "How many of the problems on your list did we also have last year?" The answer is usually: 90 to 100 percent.

What about two years ago?

Most of them, right?

How about three years ago?

Again, most of them!

Now, if this is true, then how many of these same problems are we likely to have three years from now?

Most, right?

But why?

Because look at your list of problems again. How many of them can *any individual* in the room *solve by himself*?

None!! Right? If they *could* have, they probably *would* have.

Now ask them: "How many of these problems would disappear if I gave you a magic pill that would permit you as a team to agree on the solution?"

All of them, right? If you followed my instructions correctly and only wrote down problems that can be solved by the people in the room, then it is true by definition that a solution is possible – if only the people in the room would agree to it.

So what is our problem?

The problem is that we usually have one executive or manager chasing ten problems, rather than ten managers chasing one problem at a time.

"The problem is not what you have on your list," I tell them. "What you have are *manifestations*. The problem is YOU!!! You do not know how to work together. *That* is the problem!!!!"

The business world is trapped by its misguided principles of individualistic management, which personify the whole management process in one individual who excels at all tasks – planning, organizing, training, developing, motivating, leading, organizing, disciplining, communicating, building a team, and making him- or herself dispensable – under all conditions in all organizations in the same way: in other words, a (**PAEI**) manager, executive, leader, tsar, sultan – or whatever else you want to call him.

But where on earth would you find this perfect animal? Forget it; you wouldn't! That's why I call this theoretical (**PAEI**) person "the textbook executive" – because he or she exists only in textbooks. In reality, such a manager does not and cannot exist – because what is expected cannot be achieved by a single individual.

How come?

The reason is that although all four (**PAEI**) roles are necessary, they can rarely if ever be performed by a single individual for each decision that that individual has to make. The total managerial process is far too complicated for one person to perform.

And why is that?

Because, as I demonstrated above, the (**P**), (**A**), (**E**), and (**I**) roles are incompatible. You cannot perform them simultaneously. No one can – not for every problem an organization might have.

Management vs. Mismanagement vs. Leadership

If the individual (**PAEI**) manager is nonexistent, is every manager necessarily a mismanager? Of course not. We have argued that each of four managerial roles is a necessary but not a sufficient part of a good managerial style; that managers should excel in one or more roles but not to the exclusion of the others. Thus, the (**P**)roducing manager should be a (**Paei**) rather than a (**P---**), the (**A**)dministrating manager should be a (**pAei**) rather than an (**-A--**), and so on. An (**-A--**) style is dysfunctional – not because it emphasizes only one role but because the other roles are totally absent.

Mismanagers lack the ability to perform certain roles. Managers must perform all the roles – to the degree of meeting the threshold needs of the task – and they must excel in one or more roles depending on the task – but they should not be expected to excel in all four. Not even the best corporate leaders excel in all four roles; as a rule, they excel in (**I**) plus one or two other roles. Whether their leadership is functional to the needs of the organization depends on their task at that stage of the organization's lifecycle.[8]

Thus the difference between managers, mismanagers, and leaders is one of degree and circumstance. A person with no dashes in his code – that is, a person who is capable of performing all four managerial roles even if he excels only in one of them – is a potentially good and useful manager without being perfect, as long as what is expected of him conforms to his ability to get the job done.

The purpose of managerial education, then, whether it is at programs for top executives or at schools that grant MBAs, should not be to create an ideal, perfect (**PAEI**) executive, manager, or leader, but to train normal human beings to accept their deficiencies and learn how to work with others who complement their strengths and weaknesses. Education should make each student aware of the roles he will need to perform and teach him how one can and should benefit from others' differences, instead of being threatened by them.

Management Training: The Big Fallacy

Unfortunately, management schools continue to focus on training the perfect individual manager. They make the same assumption that drives economic theory, which attempts to predict how a firm will behave: If you have one set of conditions, the firm will raise prices; if you have another, it will reduce prices. This theory personifies the group process of making a decision into an abstract entity called "the firm." It tries to analyze *why* decisions were made but neglects to explain *how* they were made.

Management theory, and management schools, suffer from the same type of perceptual limitation – nor do they differentiate among the different styles and the various ways each style thinks, acts, and communicates. Management theory, as a profession and a "science," is a 20th-century phenomenon that has resulted in a burgeoning of management training schools that attempt to equip the newcomer with the knowledge and skills necessary for good management, and assist the veteran in improving his managerial performance. These efforts are documented in textbooks, which are written by taking the best traits of the best managers and personifying this collage of characteristics in an individual who doesn't exist. (Books in which leaders of industry share their experiences do not meet the need either, because they tend to show you only their best practices. Where do they reveal their deficiencies, which all humans have, and how they were overcome?)

But how many people have you known who went to the best MBA schools in the country, the best programs, who know the textbooks by heart, and still go back and mismanage? Quite a few, right? Why? *Because no one can excel in everything.*

This is where I depart from traditional management theory. Traditional management theory talks about what managers *should* do, *although in reality they cannot do it.*

Thus, this kind of training is an exercise in futility, because by my definition we are *all* mismanagers, all of us. Even the management gurus.

I think it is very dangerous to believe in genius. I think it exists very, very seldom. When it does exist, it exists in terms of a man's personal or individual output, whether it be painting or music or whatever. It certainly does not exist in a corporation. Any corporation will be extraordinarily limited if it depends upon what any individual can do, even if you assume he is an outstandingly competent individual."

RALPH ABLON

THE WORKABLE SOLUTION: A COMPLEMENTARY TEAM

My belief is that for good management to occur, the four roles must be performed by several people. Managers who act and think differently need to be brought together. Instead of talking about a manager who plans, organizes, etc., we should be talking about the managerial *team* that performs these functions. The roles of (**P**)roducer, (**A**)dministrator, (**E**)ntrepreneur, and (**I**)ntegrator must be fulfilled by a *complementary* team, because no one person can perform them all.

"I have never met a person who was not my superior in some particular."

Ralph Waldo Emerson

I want to emphasize the word *complementary*, because normally when I say to a manager, "We need a team," he replies, "Yes, you are right. I am going to hire several more people who are like me."

That is not a team. That is cloning.

Look at your hand. What makes a hand a hand is that every finger is different and that they cooperate.

In the same way, we need a complementary team – a team in which the members of the team are different from each other, not similar to each other. That means acknowledging the differences in style and opinion. Each person's style should complement the others' by balancing their naturally biased judgments. *That* is a team.

Please note that I am not talking about the need for different kinds of know-how, such as having both an accountant and a marketing expert, for example. I am talking about having people on your team whose temperament, style, and behavior are different from the other members'. I am talking about diversity of styles.

Think of this as a kind of organizational ecology, in which diversity is acknowledged to be necessary for the organization's health in the short and the long run.

If it is so obvious, then why hasn't this theory been universally embraced? Because differences of style cause conflicts – and we do not know how to handle those conflicts well.

The Inevitability of Conflict

Since the (**PAEI**) roes are incompatible, then it follows that those who perform the different roles will be in conflict.

For example, the (**A**) style and (**E**) style are in conflict, because (**A**) is conservative and wants control, whereas (**E**) wants change. (**P**) and (**E**) are also in conflict, because (**P**) requires short-term feedback, whereas (**E**) needs time to develop his thoughts and looks to the long-term for feedback.

(**E**) and (**I**) are in conflict, because (**E**) prefers to discuss, whereas (**I**) wants only to listen. (And in any case, very few people can both talk and listen effectively – that is, communicate well.)

All styles are in conflict with each other because of misunderstandings, each style communicates differently, sometimes even speaking the same words but with opposite meanings.

One example is how the different styles express agreement and disagreement. If (**E**)ntrepreneurs disagree with an idea, they will usually be very expressive about it. They're expressive even when they *agree*. (**A**)dministrators, on the other hand, express disagreement by being silent. That discrepancy alone can cause tremendous misunderstanding and conflict.[9]

So how do we build managerial teams in which the team members are different from each other and yet can work together?

One essential goal is to recognize and accept conflict as an inevitable and even desirable facet of managing. To do that, one must learn how to deal with styles which are different from your own – a matter I start to cover in this book.

Recognizing and Hiring a Good Manager

If the ideal (**PAEI**) executive does not exist, then what kind of manager can be an effective leader of a complementary team?

There are nine important characteristics to look for:

Self-awareness: A good manager must be aware of what he is doing, aware of his style, his code.

Consciousness: He must understand the consequences and meaning of his actions, including the impact his behavior has on other people's behavior.

*"Make it thy business to know thyself, which
is the most difficult lesson in the world."*

Miguel de Cervantes

Well-rounded: no zeros in his (**PAEI**) code: Can he perform all four roles? The difference between a manager and a mismanager is that one is flexible, the other inflexible. What makes a mismanager inflexible is his inability to perform (and I did not say excel) – and therefore appreciate and respect – all the tasks required of a manager.

Knows strengths and weaknesses; knows his uniqueness: To be able to put together an effective team, a manager must have a balanced view of himself, so that he can find out what kind of people he'll need to complement himself.

Accepts strengths, weaknesses, and uniqueness: Accepting one's weaknesses is a condition for improving. We all have limited energy, and if a manager's energy is spent on rejecting who he is, there will be little or no energy left for adapting and changing himself into who he wants to be.

Can identify excellence and weaknesses in others: In particular he must be able to identify other people's strengths in areas in which he is weak. Unfortunately, many managers fear excellence in others. Will he hire and utilize and develop people who are different from him, instead of opting for the security of hiring people who are like himself?

Can accept and appreciate differences in others: Can he see beauty in difference? Can he accept, respect, and nourish it? Is he aware that since he cannot be superior in all four management roles, his subordinates will ideally be superior to him in some respects? Can he experience that without feeling threatened?

"I never learned from a man who agreed with me."

Robert A. Heinlein

Knows how to slow down and relax in difficult situations: On a basic level, being a good manager means knowing how to disagree without being disagreeable. I jokingly say that one way to recognize a good manager is by the depth of the scars on his tongue.

Creates a learning environment in which conflicts can be resolved, by both commanding and granting mutual trust and respect: How does one accept conflict, legitimize it, and harness it? A manager who cannot command and grant trust and respect cannot help resolve the conflicts that necessarily arise in a complementary team. We grow through disagreement, because you have points of view that I don't have. I might not like it, I might feel uncomfortable with it, but I'm learning.

This series is a step in the right direction. In *The Ideal Executive: Why You Cannot Be One and What to Do about It*,[10] I cover the material in this chapter in much more depth. In *Management/Mismanagement Styles*,[11] I cover the styles that emerge when one or more roles are performed, and when some roles are completely absent – a subject I also summarize briefly in the next chapter.

In this book, I offer specific advice for how to behave toward people whose styles are different. How do you become more rounded in your style so that you can work with others? In future books we will cover how to manage meetings when various people with various styles participate, how to structure the company correctly so that the different styles can coexist, how to reward people by recognizing their diverse needs.

So this book is just the beginning.

Let us now turn to the different styles that emerge when different roles are performed.

NOTES

1.   Adizes, Ichak, with Griffin, Patrick H.: *Managing the Performing Arts Organization: Founding Principles in the Management of the Arts* (Santa Monica, CA: The Adizes Institute, 1999).

2.   Adizes, Ichak and Zukin, P.: "A Management Approach to Health Planning in Developing Countries." *Health Care Management Review* 2, 1 (1977).

3.   Adizes, Ichak: *Industrial Democracy, Yugoslav Style: The Effect of Decentralization on Organizational Behavior* (New York: Free Press, 1971; reprinted by MDOR Institute, 1977, paper).

4.   For a more detailed discussion of this topic, see Book I of this series: Adizes, Ichak: *The Ideal Executive: Why You Cannot Be One and What to Do about It* (Santa Barbara, CA: The Adizes Institute, 2004), Ch. 1.

5.   For more details, see: Adizes, Ichak: *Managing Corporate Lifecycles* (Paramus, NJ: Prentice Hall Press, 1999), Ch. 12.

6.   Drucker, Peter F.: *Management: Tasks, Responsibilities, Practices* (New York: Harper & Row, 1973), p. 616.

7.   Fowler, Elizabeth M.: "The Team Approved at the Top," *The New York Times* (Business section, Sept. 16, 1977).

8.   Op. cit., *Managing Corporate Lifecycles*.

9.   Another source of conflict in managerial teams is divergent interests, which can lead to a lack of cooperation. That is the subject of *The Ideal Executive*.

10.   Op. cit., *The Ideal Executive*.

11.   Adizes, Ichak: *Management/Mismanagement Styles, How to Identify a Style and What to Do about It* (Santa Barbara, CA: The Adizes Institute, 2004).

Chapter 2

Management Styles

We've determined that in order to be effective and efficient in the short run and the long run, management has to perform four roles: (**P**)roducing, (**A**)dministrating, (**E**)ntrepreneuring, and (**I**)ntegrating.

INPUT	THROUGHPUT	OUTPUT	
The Roles	**Make the organization**	**To be**	**In the**
(**P**)roduce results	Functional	effective	short run
(**A**)dminister	Systematized	efficient	short run
(**E**)ntrepreneur	Proactive	effective	long run
(**I**)ntegrate	Organic	efficient	long run

Each role is *necessary* and the four together are *sufficient* for good management. By "necessary," I mean that if any one role is not performed, a certain pattern of mismanagement can be identified.

In problem-solving, each role focuses on a different imperative:

> (P): what?
> (A): how?
> (E): when?
> (I): who?

If all four questions are not answered before a decision is finalized, then that decision will be only "half baked."

If you both (**P**)roduce results and (**A**)dminister, you'll be effective and efficient in the short run. You will be profitable for the short run only. If you (**E**)ntrepreneur and (**I**)ntegrate only, you'll be effective and efficient in the long run, but you will suffer in the short run.

For a company to be profitable in the short and long run, it needs to perform all four roles well. If you do not happen to be in a for-profit business – if, for example, you manage a government agency, then by capably performing the four roles you will achieve, instead of profit, whatever results you're looking for: Service, political survival, etc.

Even parents must perform these roles, because a family is an organization and thus a system that requires all four roles to be performed. In the traditional family, the husband performs the (**E**) and (**P**) roles, building a career and bringing home the bacon. The wife is the (**A**) and the (**I**), transforming a house into a home and a group of adults and children into a family.

In contrast, look at what we call the modern, extended, two-career family. What do we have? Two (**P**)/(**E**)s – who need a maid to do the (**A**) child care and housework and a family therapist to do the (**I**) work.

This chapter describes the four roles in detail as well as the four basic styles that correspond to those roles. In the next chapter, we will discuss the types of mismanagement that result from an absence of some roles.

A RAISON D'ETRE

The first and most important role that management must perform in any organization is to (**P**)roduce the desired results for which the company or unit exists.

What does this mean? Every organization has its *raison d'etre*. It is not put together just to be put together. Some sociologists claim that the purpose of organizations is to survive. To me, that's not normal; that's a pathological phenomenon, like cancer. An organization must have a larger mission than survival, and that is to do something or make something for *someone else* or for a common purpose.

Let's use an analogy:

Five friends get together on a Friday night and have some beers. As they are drinking, someone suggests they go on a hike to the nearby lake the next morning. The rest of the group enthusiastically agrees.

The next day, the five friends follow a mountain path that leads to the lake. It's a very narrow path so they must walk single file. They have been walking on the path for hours. They're singing, whistling, joking, and laughing.

This group can be described as an organization; in other words, it has common goals that continually change and progress: First it was to get together Friday night. Second it was to have some beers. And the latest is to hike to the lake. A social scientist or psychologist would have a field day studying this primary group: their interactions, their style, their leadership, their communication. But there is no management in this organization – *until* this group of five people comes across a big rock that's blocking the path and that none of them *individually* can lift.

Organizational management is born when a task evolves that cannot be performed by one person alone. To lift the rock, they need to plan and organize and control and delegate. They may decide to move the rock, or they may decide to camp out right there instead of trying to reach the lake, or they may go back home and have a barbecue.

There is no management without a task, whether it is in the immediate term, the intermediate term (in which case it is called an "objective"), the long-term (which is called a "goal") or when it is more spiritual and continuous in nature (a "mission"). But no matter which word you use, there must always be a *telos*, which in Greek means "a purpose" and a necessary interdependence to achieve the purpose.

And what is the rock of a business organization? Why does it exist? What result is it supposed to give you?

Profit?

No.

We probably all know organizations that are extremely profitable and yet are going bankrupt – not *in spite of* but *because of.* Let me explain why. Constantly thinking about profit instead of about what the client needs is as futile as saying, "The purpose of my existence is to be happy." So every morning you get up and ask yourself, "Am I happy?" You can become quite miserable doing that.

You must concentrate first on these questions: Who needs this organization? What for? First, there must be a satisfied client who is willing to pay for the satisfaction of his or her needs. You have to provide that for which people come to you and thus have sales and thus revenues. Without revenues there can be no profits. If you produce that satisfaction efficiently, at a price that is lower than the client is willing to pay to satisfy his need, you are profitable. So the first role that needs to be performed is to provide client satisfaction, to (**P**)roduce.

THE (**P**)RODUCER (**Paei**)

Let's describe the style of a manager who excels in (**P**)roducing re-sults while also meeting the threshold needs of (**A**)dministration, (**E**)ntrepreneurship, and (**I**)ntegration. This manager, whose code is (**Paei**), I call a (**P**)roducer, or the (**P**) type.

In order to (**P**)roduce, as a manager you must possess two quali-ties. The first quality is you must know what the heck you're doing; you must know what people need and why they are coming to you. And that includes all managers in the organization. Your clients could be inside the organization; for example, Accounting has clients: they are all those in the company who need information.

Then – very important – you must know something about the technology of how to provide that for which they come to you.

Thus, it's not true to say, "To manage is to manage is to manage is to manage – you can manage anything if you are a professional manager." That is dangerously oversimplified, unless we add three more words: *After some time.* And what do you do during that time?

You try to learn the peculiarities of the organization that you are managing. Because there are no two rocks alike in the world.

Any time you move from one branch to another in a bank – the same bank! – the rock is going to be different. If you move from one department to another, the rock is different. So what does a good manager do before he starts doing anything else? He learns the rock. He learns what it is that people come to him for. If he's managing an accounting department, what is this accounting department supposed to do – because there are no two identical accounting departments in two different organizations, even in the same industry. Organizations are like men and women – everybody is different. You cannot treat them all alike. You have to know the particularities of what you are trying to manage, so that you can (**P**)roduce results.

But that's not enough. Some people, despite being very knowledgeable, do not (**P**)roduce results. They can give you a beautiful report, they know the technology, their judgment is correct – but they lack what the psychologists call "achievement motivation" – the urge to get in there and do it! Don't just talk about it – *do it!* This is the desire to see the finalization of a task, like a salesman who won't stop selling until he has the final signature on the dotted line.

For me, then, a manager, a (**P**)roducer of results, is a knowledgeable achiever.

RUNNING THE RAILROAD

Is (**P**)roducing results sufficient? No. What happens when the manager is an excellent (**P**)roducer of results: a knowledgeable achiever? This person is so good that we reward him with a promotion. But now, he is no longer merely a (**P**)roducer: He has to work with five or six or more people; he must coordinate and delegate and control and oversee; instead of (**P**)roducing by himself, he must make the *system* (**P**)roduce results. That is more difficult. That's why we need another role: To (**A**)dminister.

The (**A**) role is indispensable for good management. It is the role of (**A**)dministration to pay attention to details, to systematize the

(**P**)roduction process so that a wheel does not have to be reinvented each time a wheel is needed, and to ensure that staff follows those systems and routines. It ensures that the organization does what it was intended to do – efficiently. It moves the organization up the learning curve so it can capitalize on its memory and experience. It analyzes successes and programs so that they can be repeated.

If you (**P**)roduce results, the organization will be effective. If you also (**A**)dminister, your organization will be efficient. If you (**P**) and (**A**), the organization will be both effective and efficient in the short run.

An American analogy for management is "running the railroad." How do we run a railroad? First of all, we need the railroad engineer to (**P**)roduce results: that's transportation. The engineer takes the train from station A to station B. Then we need someone to manage the engineers, making sure they get the train from station A to station B, correctly and on time. The latter role, in companies, is called Operations.

If the railroad engineer does a bad job or if Operations does not perform, then the organization is going to be mismanaged. The trains will not run or will run ineffectively; thus the need for transportation will not be satisfied.

But "running the railroad" entails more than taking customers in trains from station A to station B. We need supplies and money, collection and payment, and we need universally communicated timetables to get the right train to the right town at the designated time. If the schedules are well coordinated, we are running a tight railroad. That is the role of (**A**)dministration.

The (A)dministrator (pAei)

This person is methodical and likes his environment to be well-thought-out and organized. When you have a business idea – especially a crazy one or one you are afraid *might* be crazy – you go to this manager to help cool your enthusiasm. He will think things through for you. He will ask you questions you had not thought of. He will see all the pitfalls you did not realize existed. Give him a business plan to read and he will tear it apart. And you will be grateful! It costs less and hurts less in the long run if problems are foreseen; either you can find ways to solve them before they become crises, or you can reject the plan as unworkable.

A good (**A**)dministrator, or (**A**) type, can foresee the problems inherent in an idea. People have told me, about such executives, "He can find a hair in an egg while it is still in its shell," and "He can smell a rat a mile away."

If you trust him, then if your idea passes his scrutiny, you know you can do it. And *should* do it. And if it does not pass his scrutiny and you decide to do it anyway, at least you know ahead of time what risks you are taking.

A good (**A**)dministrator always knows what is going on. He cannot sleep if he doesn't know what is going on. He keeps track of the details. He is well organized and concerned with follow-up and implementation. He has an excellent memory (or is fortified by systems, which means that he does not have to rely only on his memory), and he works to see that the system operates as it was designed to operate.

The (**A**)dministrator is good at worrying, but he worries *appropriately*. He worries about precision, about integrity of information. He worries that the organization will lose its memory, its database, or its intellectual property.

A lawyer who has a (**pAei**) style is the one you want to write up your contract. But do not ask him to be your trial lawyer. He will lose in court. He can write an agreement that is faultless, but if you have to sue, find a (**paEi**) lawyer who can interpret night as day and turn a liability into an asset.

The same is true for accountants. I need two: one to advise me on my taxes – the (**paEi**) type – and the other to *file* my taxes – the (**pAei**) type. If the (**E**) *files* the taxes, I will get in trouble for creative accounting. If the (**A**) *plans* my taxes, I will probably pay more than necessary.

A good (**A**)dministrator is indispensable to a growing organization. A young organization usually grows too fast and in too many directions, and can easily trip and fall on its face (i.e., go bankrupt) without even realizing that it's been bankrupt for quite a while.

A good (**A**)dministrator protects your back. He keeps the gates to the castle closed so that the enemy – chaos – cannot enter.

What he does *not* do is (**P**)roduce that for which the organization exists.

If you open a thesaurus and look for the word "administration," you will find that its synonym is "to serve." (**A**)dministration serves those who (**P**)roduce, or meet the needs of the market. One (**A**)dministers *for* someone, *for* something. In public service organizations, the government should (**A**)dminister for the public.[1]

Seeing through the Fog

Are (**P**)roducing and (**A**)dministrating enough? No. Beyond these tasks, an organization must also be capable of planning, deciding what direction it should take as it adapts to change. This is the role of (**E**)ntrepreneuring.

The (**E**) role analyzes changes in the environment as they affect the organization. Whereas (**A**) involves systemizing and implementing plans that have already been decided, (**E**) must generate a plan of action.

A metaphor I find useful for the (**E**) role is "the capability to see through the fog." The creative person will look into the fog and see pieces of information appearing and disappearing, and all at once something clicks. He says, "Aha! I think I know what's out there. I have an idea what it might be and what we might do about it."

The non-creative person waits until the fog lifts, until the sun is shining and it's totally clear, and then says, "Aha, *this* is what I think it might be!" But that person has not added any information or created anything. The creative person, using his imagination, fills in the blanks in the fog.

Returning to the "railroad" analogy I used above, it is the (**E**) role to decide which stations to close and which new stations to open, whether to add or subtract the number of cars on each line, and to determine how often the train should stop at each station. It is (**E**), in other words, that will guide the organization as it deals with changing realities.

(**E**)ntrepreneurship is not confined to the business world. In addition to business (**E**)ntrepreneurs, who try to exploit the monetary opportunities of the market, there are social (**E**)ntrepreneurs, who initiate change in the cultural and political sphere, and educational and artistic (**E**)ntrepreneurs, who initiate activities that satisfy aesthetic needs and generate new ones. All are of tremendous value to society.

Since change is inevitable and constant, the (**E**)ntrepreneurial role is also essential to good management. It makes the organization effective in the long run. If there is no one to perform the (**E**)ntrepreneurial role in an organization, that organization will eventually lag behind its competitors who are more creative and proactive toward change.

THE CREATIVE CONTRIBUTOR (**paEi**)

In my previous book *How to Solve the Mismanagement Crisis*,[2] where I first presented the (**PAEI**) model, I named the person who performs the (**E**) role, whose typical code is (**paEi**), the (**E**)ntrepreneur. That book was written exactly 30 years ago. Since then, in studying these codes in greater depth, I have changed my mind.

A (**paEi**) is not quite an (**E**)ntrepreneur. To be an (**E**)ntrepreneur, who creates organizations and develops them, one must be strong in the (**P**) role as well. A focus on (**E**) alone is not enough.

A person who focuses only on (**E**), whose (**P**) orientation is weak – (**P**) – I now call a Creative Contributor. This is the person who has plenty of ideas – some good, some bad. But he has lots of them, sometimes non-stop. He is like the kid in school whose hand goes up even before he hears the end of the question. He is the person in a meeting who does the most talking. Whatever solution we propose, he has another option.

This person adds energy to the meeting. He is not totally oblivious to what the discussion is about and what the goal is. He is not without some sensitivity to what others are saying (**I**) and he is capable of paying attention to details (**A**). But without a strong (**P**) focus, he is not the person to say: "Let *me* lead, let *me* do it."

Without a strong (**P**), he will not be able to build an organization. He will be constantly moving from one idea to the next, never finishing anything.

THE (E)NTREPRENEUR (**PaEi**)

To be (**E**)ntrepreneurial, a manager must have two major characteristics. He must first of all be creative, able to visualize new directions and devise strategies for adapting the organization to a perpetually changing environment. He has a feel for the organization's strengths and weaknesses, as well as the imagination and courage to identify strategies in response to such changes.[3]

Both qualities, creativity and willingness to take risks, are necessary for being an (**E**)ntrepreneur. If a manager is willing to take risks but lacks creativity, he may be more at ease in a Las Vegas casino than in the corporate world. If he is unable to take risks, but is creative, he may end up as a staff person, a consultant, or a business professor – someone who is capable of identifying a course of action but does not undertake it himself.

The (**E**)ntrepreneur knows what he wants and why he wants it. He is creative (**E**) but in the service of a purpose (**P**). He has an idea, a purpose, and he can translate that idea into reachable and achievable outcomes. His creativity is focused on how to make that outcome a reality. He is a no-nonsense person, focused and creative. Ideas without results annoy him, and results that are not born out of BIG ideas are a waste of time.

An even better (**E**)ntrepreneur would be a (**PaEI**), who also excels at the (**I**) role. The (**PaEI**) is a leader of change. He can visualize what needs to be done and why, *and* he can motivate people, (**I**)ntegrating them as a team in order to make those changes.

GETTING RELIGION

In the example of the five friends, their friendship and sense of belonging expressed itself in a need to do something together. First, that need was satisfied by drinking beer. Then it was satisfied by going on a hike to a lake. Then it was satisfied by working together, either to lift the rock or to come up with another plan.

The process of identifying a new need that satisfied that ultimate purpose – going on a hike rather than drinking beer – was (**E**)ntrepreneuring, the (**E**) role. The organizing of that hike – where to meet, what time, who would bring the picnic basket – belonged to the (**A**) role, or (**A**)dministrating. The actual act of drinking beer, hiking to a lake, or removing the rock that blocked the path, the act of doing whatever satisfied the purpose of the interrelationship at that moment, was (**P**)roducing, the (**P**) role.

What is the fourth role? Let's imagine a scenario. What would happen if your organization were managed by an executive who is an outstanding (**P**), (**A**), and (**E**)? This person is a knowledgeable, achievement-oriented, task-oriented, effective, no-nonsense (**P**)roducer; also an outstanding (**A**)dministrator who runs a tight ship: everything is efficient, correctly done at the right time. The organization is effective and efficient. In addition, he is an outstanding (**E**)ntrepreneur – constantly adapting and improving so that the organization is really moving and adjusting to its changing environment.

Now, what happens to this organization when this unique, unbelievably gifted manager dies?

The organization also dies.

Why? Because the (**P**), (**A**), and (**E**) roles are necessary, but they are not sufficient if the organization is to be effective and efficient *in the long run*. Organizations should be managed so that they can survive for thousands of years. Look at the Catholic Church, for example. It has existed for two thousand years and it could go for another two thousand. Why? Because it has a set of values that each individual in the organization can understand and identify with. And to do that, you need (**I**)ntegration.

(**I**)ntegration means nourishing this need for interdependence, feeding the need by sensing people's aspirations and needs, recognizing them and finding the tasks (**P**), the rituals (**A**), and the missions (**E**), that transform individuals into a community with a shared identity.[4] If the role of (**I**)ntegration is performed well, people will work as a team and not as individuals, and will be able to achieve or support any task that happens to be missing or deficient.

(**I**)ntegration builds a climate, a system of ethics and behavior, that encourages everyone to work together so that no one is indispensable. To (**I**)ntegrate means to change the consciousness of the organization from mechanistic to organic.

Mechanistic means: "I care only for my own interests; you care only for yours." Look at a chair. If one of the legs breaks, does the other leg care about it? Does it change position on its own to create a tripod so that the functionality of the chair can continue? Since there is no internal interdependency, where does the repair have to come from? Outside.

Now look at your hand. If one finger breaks, your whole body feels it. There is empathy. And not only that: When one finger breaks, the other four fingers on that hand will try to back it up, to compensate for the loss. That is organic consciousness. There is interdependency, there is cooperation; it's synergetic instead of being individualistic, independent, and frequently adversarial.

(**I**)ntegration is what you do in your family when the kids are fighting. You don't always give them a solution. You demand that they solve their own problems. You say, "Hey, you are brothers or sisters, you're supposed to be helping each other. I'm not going to be here forever." A family is more than a group of people; a hand is more than five fingers. There is interdependency. (**I**)ntegration involves making yourself dispensable so that the team can continue to function if anything happens to any individual member.

Look at a sports team. If you take a team of stars, each from a different team, and put them together to play against an above-average team without stars that has been together for a long time, who might win the first game? The average team. Why? Because the star team has not yet developed its team consciousness. The team members cannot yet predict: "If he does this, I can back him up by doing that." That sense of cooperating to reach a common goal is what we mean by teamwork.

(**I**)ntegration turns individual (**E**)ntrepreneurship into group (**E**)ntrepreneurship. If a manager does not (**I**)ntegrate, does not nourish group (**E**)ntrepreneurship, then in extreme cases the group will be unable to initiate action or determine goals in his absence. Thus, (**I**)ntegration is a necessary component to good management. Companies that rely on any one individual for continuous success in their operations inevitably will face a crisis if that individual leaves or dies. Even organizations that have been managed by a (**PAE-**) have found themselves in trouble if that manager leaves before a team feeling – an *esprit de corps* around an effective course of action – has been developed.

Since an organization's life span is longer than the life of any individual, effective long-range continuity depends on building a team of people who understand, trust, and respect each other, and who complement each other's abilities. (**I**)ntegration creates that effect.

When there is no (**I**)ntegration taking place, no one is focused primarily on the company's long-term interests. Instead, everybody is looking out for his own interests, often at the expense of the company. The stockholders are trying to milk the company. Management is trying to get maximum rewards for itself. Labor is trying to get the best salaries and the best security at work. Among such competing interests, it's possible to arrive at a working consensus in which everyone is working hard but the company is actually going bankrupt.

When I find a situation like this in the organizations I coach, I often dramatize the dilemma by bringing an empty chair to the table. I place the company name on the front of the chair and ask, "If someone were sitting in that chair, what would he say? What does *this company* want?" When I let the participants play out that scenario, I hear voices that have previously been silent. In this exercise, I am playing the (**I**)ntegrating role.

Interrelating is the ultimate purpose of our existence. There is nothing in this world that doesn't exist to serve something else by functionally interrelating to it. If it serves only itself, then it is a cancer and serves death.

The pen I write with is useless if it does not leave a mark on paper. Breathing has no meaning unless the oxygen feeds my body. Nothing in itself is functional. The ability of anything to function must be measured and evaluated by how it serves its clients. The final purpose of existence of any system is (**I**)ntegration, the (**I**) role. In fact, managers with the ability to perform that role have the potential to go beyond good management and become leaders.

The (I)ntegrator (**paeI**)

There are two types of (**I**)ntegration – passive and active – and three directions: upward, lateral, and downward.

A passive (**I**)ntegrator will (**I**)ntegrate himself into a group of people. An active (**I**)ntegrator can (**I**)ntegrate a group of people among themselves. Because in management (**I**)ntegration must be active, we will concern ourselves here only with active (**I**)ntegration.

Upward (**I**)ntegration is the ability to (**I**)ntegrate people who are higher in status, authority, rank, and so on. Lateral (**I**)ntegration is the ability to (**I**)ntegrate peers into a cohesive group. Downward (**I**)ntegration provides leadership by establishing cohesion among subordinates.

A very effective lateral (**I**)ntegrator may function poorly as a downward (**I**)ntegrator – tending to be arrogant with subordinates. In fact, it is unusual for a person to be an excellent (**I**)ntegrator in all directions.[5]

Let's talk about the characteristics that a good (**I**)ntegrator brings to an organization.

Perhaps surprisingly, the (**I**)ntegrator is the most creative of all the management types, since he must make decisions from a more diffused and less structured database. (**I**)ntegrating is even less programmable than (**E**)ntrepreneuring, because (**E**)ntrepreneuring does not necessarily deal with people, whereas (**I**)ntegrating involves uniting individuals with diverse interests and strengths behind a group decision.

In (**I**)ntegrating (**E**)ntrepreneurs, one has the additional burden of forging their individual creativities into a cohesive unity – to develop group risk-taking out of individual risk-taking, to fuse an *individual* sense of responsibility into a *group* sense of responsibility.

The (**I**)ntegrator clarifies issues by finding the common threads of deep – not just superficial – agreement, and by analyzing contrasting values, assumptions, and expectations.

A successful (**I**)ntegrator also must make himself dispensable. His subordinates must be trained to be capable of replacing him. Ideally, in a cohesive group almost any member should be able to initiate action, (**A**)dminister programs, and (**P**)roduce results. To take a military example, if any soldier in a squad can take the squad leader's place and be accepted by the squad when the leader is killed, this demonstrates that the leader was a good (**I**)ntegrator. If the squad scatters when the leader is killed, this shows that the (**I**)ntegration of the unit was insufficient, though the leader may have been a competent commander in other respects.

The (**I**)ntegrator is sensitive to others (i.e., empathetic), and he is capable of deductive thinking (i.e., able to infer what people really want to say from what they do say). He has few ego problems of his own, which enables him to hear and respond to other people's expectations, problems, and needs rather than his own.

The late Juscelino Kubitschek, former president of Brazil and founder of Brasilia, was very (**I**)-oriented. I was told that when asked whether he was for or against a certain political program, he replied: "I am neither for nor against it: I am above it."

The (I) Role in Leadership

The (**I**)ntegrator is unique in that he not only provides for future organizational continuity, but also enables the organization to function smoothly in the present. His role is essential for success, both in the short run and in the long run. Finally, his is the one role that must be present in order for leadership to occur.

Without (**I**), you can be a good manager. Managers can be strong in two or even three roles – (**PAei**), (**PaEi**), (**pAEi**), (**PAEi**) – but unless one of them is (**I**)ntegrating, they will not be leaders. For leadership to occur, the (**I**) role must enhance whatever other roles a manager excels at performing.

What, exactly, is leadership? What defines a leader?

Many people visualize leadership as a pointing finger: "Do this, do that!" But my definition is that leadership functions as a thumb. Why? The thumb is the only finger that both opposes the other elements of the hand and, by (**I**)ntegrating them, helps them work together as a hand.

A manager does not have to excel at (**I**)ntegration, or being a thumb. A leader, however, does. Without that ability to (**I**)ntegrate, there can be no leadership that makes four fingers perform like a hand.

Along with their other abilities, leaders must motivate, inspire, thus (**I**)ntegrate. There are three styles of leadership: (**PaeI**), (**pAeI**), and (**paEI**).

Whether the organization needs (**PaeI**) leadership, (**pAeI**) leadership, or (paEI) leadership depends on where the organization is in its lifecycle.[6] The appropriate leadership style must change as the organization grows and ages, just like parenting style has to change depending on the age of the child.

Now let us turn to describing the styles of mismanagement that occur when only one role is performed or even excelled at, but the other roles do not meet the threshold needs of the task.

NOTES

1. In government, the (P) and (A) functions are the same. In other words, the (A) actually (P)roduces what the organization exists for. Take a government agency that issues licenses or monitors the health and safety of food service establishments. Its (P) function is to (A). Of course, this organization will have its traditional (A) roles too: to organize, systematize, and monitor the system.

2. Adizes, Ichak: *How to Solve the Mismanagement Crisis* (Santa Monica, CA: Adizes Institute, 1979).

3. For a definition of entrepreneurship, see Schumpeter, Joseph: *Business Cycles* (New York: McGraw Hill, 1939), pp. 102-109; and Drucker, Peter F.: *Management: Tasks, Responsibilities, Practices* (New York: Harper & Row, 1973), Chapter 10.

4. On the role of integration, see Lawrence, P.R., and J. W. Lorsch, "New Managerial Job: The Integrator," *Harvard Business Review*, 45 (November 1967), pp. 142-51.

5. The (I) component, as has been pointed out, is essential to good management at all levels, because the manager must work through others to achieve organizational goals. Where management has succeeded in (I)ntegrating the individual members of an organization into a group, we may expect greater identification with the organization, more job satisfaction, and better performance. The importance of interpersonal relationships for the success of organizations has been repeatedly demonstrated in the literature. Chris Argyris found that the worker's skill and pride in his work were directly related to his on-the-job friendships. See Argyris, "The Fusion of an Individual with the Organization," *American Sociological Review*, 19 (1954), pp. 145–67; and "Personality vs. Organization," *Organizational Dynamics*, 3 (1974) no. 2, pp. 2–17.

    A similar association between level of competence and degree of (I)ntegration with the organization was reported by Peter M. Blau in a study of law enforcement agents. See Blau, "Patterns of Interaction among a Group of Officials in a Government Agency," *Human Relations*, 7 (1954), pp. 337-348.

6. See *Managing Corporate Lifecycles*, op. cit.

Chapter 3

Mismanagement Styles

If the (**PAEI**) roles are necessary and together they are sufficient for good management, then any time any of the four roles is not being performed, what will happen? Mismanagement – a predictable, repetitive pattern of mismanagement.

In order to simplify comparisons between managerial and mismanagerial behavior, I have chosen to profile five exaggerated archetypes of mismanagement. Why? The difference between normal and abnormal people is only one of degree. So you start by studying abnormal people, whose behavior is so acute that it's readily visible, in order to understand what is normal.

Thus, instead of seeing what happens when one role is missing, I'm going to do the opposite. I will ask what happens when *one* role is performed and *three* are missing.

These archetypes – the Lone Ranger, (**P**---); the Bureaucrat (-**A**--); the Arsonist, (--**E**-); the SuperFollower, (---**I**); and finally the Deadwood, who is missing all four roles (----) – represent mismanagers who exhibit none or only one of the four essential elements of management – (**P**)roducing, (**A**)dministrating, (**E**)ntrepreneuring, and (**I**)ntegrating – while failing to meet the threshold needs of the other elements.

Learning to recognize these patterns can be a significant tool in treating the "disease" of mismanagement. It can also help you to analyze the normal and abnormal problems that organizations have over time, guide you in resolving conflict in your organization, and evaluate whether your team is working well together.

The Lone Ranger (P---)

What happens when an organization has a manager who is an outstanding (**P**), who functions like the ideal railroad engineer — a knowledgeable achiever, a do-er? You show him the track, tell him what stations to go to, give him the train, and off he goes, full speed ahead – through walls if necessary. He is such a good doer, such a good achiever, so diligent, that naturally you promote him to a higher level of management.

That's when the problem arises: He's not an (**A**), not an (**E**), not an (**I**). I don't know why. It's irrelevant. I am only marginally interested in the why of behavior. I am mostly interested in *what* that behavior is and *what* to do about it. The fact is that he can't (**A**)dministrate: organize, coordinate, delegate, follow up, supervise, and control. He's not an (**E**)ntrepreneur: He doesn't come up with new ideas; he's not creative, he dislikes taking risks. And he's not an (**I**)ntegrator: He is not sensitive to interpersonal relations; he doesn't worry about group dynamics or personal feelings. He does not relate well to people. He does not build a team or develop the capabilities of others around him. He is too busy (**P**)roducing.

I call him the Lone Ranger. In Mexico he's called the Lonely Wolf. Why is he a manager? Because you promoted him to be a manager – because he was such a good (**P**).

Once he identifies a task, the Lone Ranger is a good soldier. And he will get the job done. That's his advantage: He's loyal, dedicated, and a compulsive doer – but because he overdoes one aspect or role of management to the exclusion of the other roles, he can become a liability.

What are the characteristics that typify a Lone Ranger?

The Lone Ranger focuses on the *what*, not the *how*, not the *who*, not even the *why*. "What do we need to do now? Come on, guys, let's go to it! Let's not waste any more time." He does not really care if he is doing the right thing, as long as he is doing *something*.

Does he work hard? Yes, very hard. Too hard. When does he come to work? First one in. When does he leave work? Last one out.

In fact, the Lone Ranger measures his success and his value to the organization by how hard he works. When you ask him, "How are you doing?" his typical answer might be, "I've been working till midnight lately." And "lately," in his case, might be his entire working life!

How is his desk: clean? Never. It's piled with papers, and somehow, although he's always working hard, he's always behind, always complaining that the day is too short. "The new week has already started, and I haven't even finished last week's work!"

Yet how would he feel if he came to work and found his desk clean and nothing to do? He would panic. Why? Because he's worried when he's not worried. He needs to be constantly doing something.

Over the years, I've discovered that the Lone Ranger is an addict, just like an alcoholic. He is a *work*aholic.

One of the characteristics of an alcoholic is that he's never far away from a bottle. Similarly, the Lone Ranger is never far away from work. It's 11 o'clock at night; what is he carrying home with him? A briefcase full of work – in case he can't sleep, at least he can do some work.

To a workaholic, going on vacation is a punishment. It's like saying to an alcoholic, "You must go to a dry island for two weeks." That's *scary*. So what will he pack for this vacation? A trunk full of work, like an alcoholic who hides a bottle in his suitcase.

If you say to an alcoholic, "I have a bottle of the best booze there is; what should I do with it?" he's going to say, "Give it to *me*." Similarly, if you go to a Lone Ranger and say, "I have a problem; what should I do with it?" he's going to say, "Put it on my desk." In fact, the more difficult the problem is, the more likely he is to say it.

Those tons of overdue paperwork and projects on the Lone Ranger's desk aren't work. They are all bottles. Bottles, bottles, bottles. Only when he's sure he cannot do a job by himself – only *then* will he delegate. But by then, of course, the problem is already a crisis.

The (**P---**) is the least sophisticated of the mismanagement styles. He's like a kid: "Let's go! What's next?" He has only a short-term attention span; he moves quickly from one thing to another, and if it doesn't work out he loses interest and goes on to the next thing. When a new problem is brought to his attention, he drops whatever he was doing and plunges indiscriminately into the new task. In fact, he is always rushing from task to task, from crisis to crisis. The more running around he does, the "better" he thinks he is working.

Also like a kid, the Lone Ranger takes things literally: "Yes" means yes, and "no" is no, even if that's not what other people really mean. Lone Rangers do not understand nuances. For them, everything is simple. Everything is literal. Give them a "yes" or a "no"; just don't give them a "maybe."

Lone Rangers hate to deal with uncertainty, with alternatives, with ambiguity. They see everything as either black or white; a (**P---**) is exceedingly uncomfortable with gray. They can't take the pain of sitting in a meeting, thinking things through. They cannot accept that it might take three days to solve a major problem. They want things simple and they want them *now*. Going full speed ahead makes the

(**P---**) feel good – even though he might be speeding directly into an abyss.

The Lone Ranger prefers doing the job himself to directing others. Let's take a (**P---**) architect as an example. He is such a good architect that eventually he heads his own firm and hires other architects and draftsmen to work for him. But when he comes to work, where do you think he drifts? Does he drift to the accounting department? No! He drifts to the design department. He watches his employees work for a little while; then he says, "OK, you're doing it wrong; move aside." And he sits down at the drafting table himself and starts drawing.

Why does the Lone Ranger prefer to do everything himself? One reason is that he wants to make sure things are done properly. "If you want to be sure it is done right, you'd better do it yourself," is one of his typical expressions.

Also, he hates being idle; it makes him feel like a parasite. The Lone Ranger measures himself by how hard he works – so if he were to delegate, what would be left for him to do? He needs to be indispensable, to have problems waiting in line for him. He is always rushed, and he likes it that way.

The Lone Ranger only delegates when it's too late or almost too late. He delegates today what should have been done two weeks ago. That's why he is always in a crisis. His subordinates are hanging around, waiting, coming in late, doing very little. Then all at once there's a crisis: everybody's running here and there, firefighting. That's why yet another nickname for the Lone Ranger is the Firefighter.

Lone Ranger types are like bulldogs; they get their teeth around the other dog's neck and lock their jaws and don't let go. They are so compulsive about getting the job done, no matter what, that it takes a tremendous effort to make them move on to something else.

And this is also how they treat others. If they want to make something happen, they do not touch, they hit. A (**P---**) will come down on others in an inappropriately dictatorial style, telling them what to do and when he wants them to do it – "You do it right *now*!" He overdoes it.

Managing, to the Lone Ranger, means managing the task, getting the job done. To him, other people are merely tools for serving that goal. As a result, the Lone Ranger is politically naive. He doesn't realize that people's judgments might be colored by their own needs and desires. He can make political blunders that lead you to seriously question his intelligence.

The ultimate do-it-yourselfer, the Lone Ranger hates meetings with a passion. If he is required to come to a meeting, he will come reluctantly.

What about staff meetings? Does the Lone Ranger have them? No: "There's too much work to do, I have to run the railroad, I have no time for meetings." If you tell him he is required to have meetings, what will he do? He'll initiate a conversation, one-to-one, very likely standing in the hallway on his way to somewhere else, and he'll call that a meeting.

The Lone Ranger's subordinates are the same everywhere, though their nicknames vary in different countries. In the television series "The Lone Ranger," the subordinate was called Tonto. In the United States, they are called gofers. In Mexico, they are called *inginiero ibeme*, which means, "Go bring me something." In Israel, they are called errand boys.

Such a manager's subordinates are hardly more than spectators at a performance. Since the Lone Ranger cannot do everything himself, he uses his subordinates as "expediters," who assist him with errands and short-term assignments but have no permanent long-term responsibilities. These people spend most of their time waiting to be summoned to deal with the next crisis – for which they generally have no experience or training. These gofers and errand boys are not always low-level managers. In many companies, top vice presidents are gofers for a Lone Ranger.

When do these gofers come to work? Late. When do they leave? Early. What do they do in the meantime? They wait.

Does the Lone Ranger delegate to his subordinates? No. When you ask him, "Why don't you delegate?" he responds, "They can't do it. They're not ready. They're not prepared."

"How long have they worked for you?"

"Twenty-five years."

"So why don't you train them?"

"I have no time to train them."

"Why don't you have time to train them?"

"Because I have no one to delegate to."

Because everything has to go through him, he becomes a bottleneck. Since he has limited time, not everything gets done and things get lost on his desk.

The Lone Ranger sees no value in the systematic *ex cathedra* classroom training of subordinates. He prefers the apprenticeship approach: subordinates learn how to perform a task by watching him do it himself. "In this business there aren't any secrets; just get the job done," the Lone Ranger insists. "If someone is willing to work hard, he should have no problem getting the job done."

The Lone Ranger's ability to see the horizon is primitive and limited.

He is typically an improviser – "All right, let's get going! Does it work? Done! *Finito!* Go! Next!" He won't take the time to pay attention to the larger questions: What is ultimately needed? What are the details that are necessary to make it work? His view of time is that it should be used to solve the immediate problems of the organization. He has no concern for "ten years down the pike."

Thus, he is always promising to plan later, "after I finish clearing my desk." But of course that never happens.

The organization that a Lone Ranger manages cannot grow, since *he* is not growing. He is inflexible and simpleminded. He can easily burn out and become obsolete. When he leaves a company, he leaves untrained people behind.

THE BUREAUCRAT (-A--)

What happens if a manager is exclusively (**A**)-oriented? Zero (**P**), zero (**E**), zero (I). An (-**A**--).

What is the (-**A**--) interested in? While the Lone Ranger – the (**P**---) – is exclusively interested in *what*, the (-**A**--) is only interested in *how*. That's why I call him a Bureaucrat: "Never mind *what* we do; it's *how* we do it that counts."

Bureaucrats tend to rise in their organizations by following the rules, often to the point of excess. A Bureaucrat may be the easiest to spot of the four mismanagement types. Certainly he is one of the easiest to satirize.

In literature, there's a great example of a Bureaucrat. Captain Queeg, in Herman Wouk's novel *The Caine Mutiny*, has risen through the ranks of the Navy, not because he was especially competent at leading a crew or running a ship, but because he followed the rules. He says so himself:

"Now, I'm a book man, as anyone who knows me will tell you," Queeg tells his sailors proudly. *"I believe the book is there for a purpose, and everything in it has been put in it for a purpose. When in doubt, remember we do things on this ship by the book. You go by the book and you'll get no argument from me. You deviate from the book and you better have a half dozen damn good reasons – and you'll still get a hell of an argument from me."*[1]

What are the characteristics that typify an (-**A**--) type, or Bureaucrat?

The Bureaucrat spends an *excessive* amount of time worrying about (**A**)dministrative details. He prefers to do things right rather than do the right things. In other words, he would rather be precisely wrong than approximately right.

Here's a joke that will illustrate this point: I was flying over Brazil some years ago. Sitting next to me was a leading accountant from a leading accounting firm, a big (-**A**--). We were looking through the window, and we saw the Amazon River. He said, "Dr. Adizes, did you know that this river is a billion years and seven months old?"

"How did you get a billion years and seven months old?" I asked, amazed.

"Well, seven months ago someone told me it was a billion years old."

Bureaucrats pay attention to the form, to the number to the very last digit – at the expense of the total picture. The Bureaucrat may be focused on the wrong market, the wrong product – the wrong *direction!* – but his reports always look very good because the numbers are calculated to the third decimal.

If you ask a Bureaucrat to give you a report analyzing whether your company should try to penetrate the New York market, he'll say, "Sure," and disappear for a while. He'll accumulate data and analyze it ad infinitum. But by the time he comes back with his recommendation, that market may already have been claimed by your competitor.

Why? Because the Bureaucrat prefers not to take risks. He does not want to be embarrassed by making the wrong decision. He wants everything safe and precise. He's precisely wrong because his timing can be off.

When does he come to work? On time. When does he leave work? On time. How is his desk? Clean, all in neat piles.

He wants everything to be perfect and under control, and he is capable of spending an inordinate amount of time and money on a marginal control that is really not worth it. Such demanding perfectionism can suffocate a company.

The Bureaucrat behaves as if he believes that form produces function. Now, sometimes that is true; military leaders assume that the form produces the function, that if you polish your shoes and shave exactly as required and hold your head exactly as required to salute and march exactly as required, when the time comes and they tell you to go and attack and sacrifice your life, you will run and do exactly as instructed. So the form will produce the function.

But here is the danger: Sometimes the form is so inflexible that it will not produce the function. That's why partisans and guerrilla forces invariably defeat organized establishment armies: They rely more on (**I**) than on (**A**) in asking people to put their lives on the line.

The Bureaucrat has an organizational chart readily accessible – if it is not on paper it is in his head. He has no trouble finding any of the organization's rules or procedures at a moment's notice. He manages by means of directives, usually in writing. Even when violations are necessary to produce the right results, he won't tolerate his subordinates' breaking the rules.

*"I'm sorry, dear, but you knew I was a bureucrat
when you married me."*

The Bureaucrat's free time is spent looking for new transgressions against the system. When he finds one, he designs a new form, a new report, or a new policy that will prevent the transgression from being repeated.

Like the Lone Ranger, the Bureaucrat is very literal-minded. An (-A--) needs to see something for himself in order to believe it. But because he is reluctant to take risks, he rarely learns anything new. An (E), for example, looking through the fog and seeing a big ear and a big leg and a big back, might say: "Aha, that must be an elephant." He fills the gaps with his imagination to come up with a conclusion. But an (-A--) will not infer anything. The big ear and the big leg and the big back do not add up to an elephant, until the fog rises. Then he'll go and touch the elephant and smell the elephant, and then – hesitantly – he might say, "Aha! *Maybe* it's an elephant."

(-A--)s are prone to what I call "manualitis": Everything is documented, processes are written, and the written word begins to dominate the organization's behavior.

People who are managed by an (-**A**--) spend an enormous amount of time reading memos and writing memos and filing memos and responding to memos. This cuts down efficiency tremendously. So while he tries to increase efficiency he de facto cuts it down by creating bureaucracy.

When you ask a Bureaucrat to diagnose a problem, he usually starts all the way back with Adam and Eve, and then takes you through the entire history of the problem – *first* what happened and *then* what happened and *then* what happened and *then* what happened. Given his 2,000-year perspective on the problem, a Bureaucrat naturally thinks it's going to take another 2,000 years to solve it. In the field of management this is called "paralysis from over-analysis."

A Bureaucrat knows the cost of everything but the value of nothing, for the following reason: The cost is for sure, the value is maybe. He will tell you, "We cannot do this, it's too expensive." But the truth is that very often the cost of *not* doing may be higher than the cost of doing. I'll give you an American expression that exemplifies this principle: "If you think education is expensive, think of the alternative."

But an (-**A**--) will prefer not to take the risk or spend the money. He will waste resources by asking for more information and more details and more justifications and more studies and more analyses – all to minimize risk. But time costs money, and meanwhile the opportunity will slip away.

The Bureaucrat can subvert the goals of the organization through his insistence on observing the letter of the law, even when departures from it are essential. His primary and often exclusive commitment is to the implementation of a plan, regardless of its wisdom or even its ethics.

At his 1961 trial in Jerusalem for implementing the genocide of European Jewry, Adolf Eichmann's defense was a morbid and extreme example of this type of behavior. Eichmann described his role in the Third Reich as having been "an administrator of trains." The fact that at one end of the railway line were the victims, and at the other end were the extermination camps, did not preoccupy him.

Bureaucrats frequently have difficulty revisiting a decision during the implementation phase. "We decided," he'll say. "We spent a lot of time on this decision. We spent a lot of money on it. We are not going to open this chapter again!" The world often changes even faster than you can implement a plan to adapt to the changes. A typical Bureaucrat resists such change.

While the Lone Ranger evaluates himself by how hard he works and by the results he achieves, the Bureaucrat evaluates himself by how well he *controls* the system and by his success in eliminating deviations and minimizing uncertainty. Because of this, he tends to be a crowning example of Parkinson's law.[2] He gets increasing numbers of subordinates to implement the same task, trying to control every detail, without achieving any apparent increase in productivity.

Bureaucrats are linear thinkers: A, B, C, D, E, F, G. They do not understand that sometimes G relates to H and H relates to A and A relates to J and J relates to B. They get very upset when they perceive a discussion as getting out of order. Discussions do need to be open to lots of different options, but an (-**A**--) can't see that.

The Bureaucrat hires people like himself – people who do as they are told and will not take initiative. They do not ask questions that challenge the status quo; they do not rock the boat.

I call the Bureaucrat's subordinates yes-yes men or office clerks. But although they have a clerk mentality, they are not necessarily clerks. They could be vice presidents earning $100,000 a year or more. Regardless, they have to come on time, leave on time, and do everything by the book.

There's even a joke about this kind of subordinate: A new person arrives in Hell and is sent to a bureaucratic department in Hell to work. When he gets there he finds that all the other workers are standing in fecal matter up to their lips. Horrified, he asks, "How do you work here?"

"Just don't make waves!" is the reply.

Why? Because the Bureaucrat's subordinates know that if they reveal that there are problems, the Bureaucrat is going to have to find out who did it, why, how, where and when. In a word, there is going to be a witch-hunt.

Does the Bureaucrat hold staff meetings? You bet your life: Every Monday and Friday from 9 to 12. Secretaries take minutes; the last meeting's conclusions are discussed and verified as to their implementation. There is order, and along with it there is boredom with the myriad details that the Bureaucrat insists on covering.

Does he have an agenda? Absolutely. In detail. Does the agenda deal with important subjects? Not necessarily. The company might be losing market share, even going bankrupt, but the Bureaucrat will be droning on about the need to fill out the necessary forms in duplicate and on time.

The Bureaucrat loves training. He wishes he could program everybody and make every process a routine.

What is an (-A--)'s typical answer when a subordinate asks for permission to do something different? "No." Before you even finish the sentence: "No." Here is a typical Bureaucrat on the phone (this is a Russian joke): "No. No. No. Yes. No. No. No."

"What was that one 'yes' about?" you ask him.

"He asked me if I heard him clearly."

Change, to a Bureaucrat, is a threat of major proportions. His ingenuity in finding reasons to discourage new projects makes him an obstructionist. The organization has to achieve its goals in spite of him, and those individuals in the organization who are committed to getting things done learn to bypass him in trying to implement change.

Under the Bureaucrat, strategic planning is at best an exercise in forecasting, and quite often it simply analyzes the past and projects it into the future.

So what is next year's budget or goal? "What we are sure we can achieve. How about some sure number above the one we reached last year?" is the Bureaucrat's typical approach.

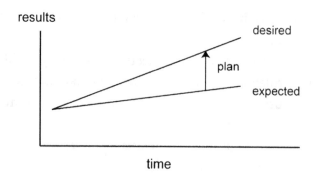

By the time the Bureaucrat is eliminated from an organization, that organization may have become so mired in regulations and rules that it will have difficulty adapting to long overdue changes, either internally or externally or both.

The Arsonist (--E-)

What happens if the (**E**)ntrepreneurial role is performed exclusively, and the other three roles are not? This manager's efforts would consist entirely of innovating, just charging at any target that appears on his organizational horizon.

This is the type of mismanager I am most familiar with, because I usually work with CEOs and company founders, who are strong in the (**E**) role. I call him the Arsonist.

What are the characteristics that typify an Arsonist?

What we do is not important. *How* we do it is not important either. The Arsonist is concerned with *why not*. Change. Ideas.

When does the Arsonist come to work? Who knows? When does he leave work? Who knows? When do his subordinates come to work? Before him; by the time he comes to work they'd better be there. When do they leave work? Right after him. I've seen vice presidents working for this type of mismanager – it's 7, 8, 9 o'clock at night; there's nothing to do, but they can't leave, because if they leave what might happen? The boss might call a meeting: "Drop everything you're doing. Everybody to the meeting room, now."

Do his meetings have an agenda? If they do, nobody knows what it is. And if there is an agenda he violates it anyway, moving from subject to subject at will. But he nevertheless expects people to be ready for the meeting.

Luckily for them, who does all the talking in these meetings? He does.

Meanwhile, what do the subordinates do? There is a joke that illustrates their behavior. It is an ethnic joke but I don't think it's in bad taste. I hope I am not offending anyone.

It is the First World War. The Italian soldiers are in the trenches, ready to attack. Out of the trenches emerges the captain – in a beautiful blue uniform with red sashes, all the decorations, golden epaulets, hat and feathers. He looks dashing. He pulls out his sword and shouts: "*Avaaaaaaaantiiiiiii!*"

What do the soldiers do? They clap hands and shout: "Bra-vooooooo!" But nobody gets out of the trenches.

Why? Because, like an Arsonist, the captain doesn't say, "Attack in *this* direction!" He says, "Attack in *this* direction, *that* direction, *that* other direction, and that *fourth* direction." All simultaneously.

So what can the soldiers do? They stay in the trenches and shout "Bravooooooo!" And when they're asked, "Are you attacking?" their typical answer is "We're working on it."

Here is another analogy: Picture an organization as an axle. There is a big wheel at one end (in English, "a big wheel" even has a corporate meaning) and a small wheel at the other end. When the big wheel makes one revolution, the small wheel must turn many times. If the big wheel is an Arsonist, he will frequently change direction while the smaller wheels are still in motion. Eventually the gears of the smaller wheels are stripped and the axle breaks down. The big wheel is left spinning alone.

But the (--E-) does not realize that he himself is responsible for the breakdown. Instead, he thinks, "Somebody must be undermining my efforts." He becomes paranoid and looks for someone to blame.

Still, the Arsonist is usually very likable, because he is stimulating, enterprising, and full of energy. Working for him can be exciting

– until you figure out that no matter what you do the Arsonist will find fault with it, because his priorities are continually changing; before you've completed one project, he wants to know why you haven't made any progress on a new one.

The Arsonist likes chaos: He loves to witness the furor that his initiatives cause. He seeks maximum short-run impact, and he obtains it by generating crises.

Under such managers, projects are always being completed under pressure. The staff is forced to work overtime and crucial details remain in a state of flux right up to the last minute.

Details are the Arsonist's Achilles' heel. The (--**E**-) tends to ignore details; he works with a big brush on a wide canvas, as if he were looking down from 40,000 feet at a topographical map. For an (--**E**-), a million is somewhere between 700,000 and a million and a half – while for an (-**A**--), 999,999 is not the same as a million. You can see why (**E**)s and (**A**)s don't usually get along.

Picture the (--**E**-) as an eagle, flying thousands of feet over the mountains and seeing the big picture but not the small details. From up there everything looks simple; with one movement of its wings it can fly from one boulder to another. The eagle cannot comprehend that down on the ground, in order to make the move from one location to the other, you have to go up and down mountains and canyons.

Arsonists act out of emotion and nervous energy; very often it's negative energy. They have a huge need to build something new, which often means destroying what's already in place. In order to "own" their idea, they feel they have to start from scratch or change what is there even if it is more than adequate already.

Because they create on the run, Arsonists often contradict themselves: the mouth is talking, the mind is working, but there isn't necessarily a connection. An (--**E**-) often says, "It's too late to disagree with me; I've already changed my mind." He starts with one angle, and changes to another angle and then a third angle, and eventually you can't follow what he's saying.

Yet not being understood upsets and offends Arsonists, and they can react with unbelievable hostility.

An Arsonist habitually works on the "why don't we?" principle: "Why don't we do this?" "Why don't we do that?" But what is a mere question for an (--**E**-) is assumed to be a decision by his subordinates, especially the (**P**)s. Sometimes the subordinates believe the boss has made a decision, so they begin to implement it and get penalized for acting without authorization. Then, the next time the (--**E**-) thinks out loud, his subordinates don't act, thinking that this, too, was just an idea. The Arsonist then becomes upset because the staff didn't implement his instructions.

Of all the four types, the (--**E**-) is the worst listener. Why? Because he's full of ideas and it's so easy to trigger more. Anything you say might trigger a chain of thought in him, and while he's developing the little seed you planted, he's so busy listening to himself that he doesn't hear what else you are saying.

In conversation, the Arsonist is emotional and expressive. He uses words like "never," "always," "impossible." He exaggerates and intimidates. In a company managed by an Arsonist, Monday mornings are dangerous, because over the weekend the Arsonist has had time to think – and guess what? New directions, new priorities, new goals, new objectives.

Ironically, however, not much happens in a company run by an Arsonist, because he doesn't like to finalize anything; even in mid-change he might change things again in yet another, "better" direction. Every idea leads to another idea. He does not understand that by adding an idea, he's diminishing the value of other ideas because there's a limit to how much one person or one company can handle.

Nor does he measure the cost of his plans against their value. The opposite of the Bureaucrat, the (--E-) "knows the value of everything, but the cost of nothing." An (--E-) is always talking about all the brilliant innovations he's going to make. But how much will they cost? "These are details," he'll shrug. This is why an Arsonist can build a big company and lose it overnight.

Because he is bored by details, the Arsonist's attitude and preferences are to decentralize. But it's equally important for him to maintain control of the decision-making process. The result is a catch-22 for his subordinates. They are *expected* to decide – as long as their decisions coincide with the decision he would have taken. But they don't know because he keeps changing his mind. For his subordinates, that decision is a moving target, and the result is paralysis.

Like the Bureaucrat, who is so focused on efficiency that he creates an inefficient bureaucracy, the Arsonist is so focused on change that by overdoing it he creates no change.

The Arsonist cares about the process, the novelty – not necessarily the results. He is interested in the *why not*, whereas the Lone Ranger is interested in the *what* and the Bureaucrat in the *how*. The Arsonist typically will develop fantastic ideas and then expect others to figure out how to implement them. If he is pressed for specifics, he gets annoyed.

Arsonists do not play well with others.

If you give an (--E-) an idea, he immediately says, "No, I don't agree with you," but then next week he will give you back the same idea, rephrased and with some small change, as if he'd thought of it himself. That makes people very upset.

Arsonists are often considered to be narcissistic, self-centered troublemakers. They always act like they know best. They are constantly giving advice and can hardly stand to take it. But the truth is, they need a tremendous amount of approval and applause.

It takes a very strong person to work with an Arsonist, and yet (--**E**-)s surround themselves with weak people. Why? Because an (--**E**-) has to win every argument, and weak subordinates will never challenge him.

If the Lone Ranger's subordinates are gofers and the subordinates of the Bureaucrat are yes-yes men, the typical subordinates of the Arsonist are claques. Claques (it's a French word; in Mexico they are called *palleros*) are the hired hands in opera houses who are paid to start clapping when a singer ends an aria, to encourage the rest of the audience to clap as well.

Claques are required to agree with the Arsonist's ideas, at least in public. The result is that the Arsonist invariably receives tumultuous applause, but it isn't real.

The Arsonist's subordinates learn not to reject his plans outright, because he will interpret a rejection of his ideas as a rejection of himself. Thus, the subordinates are forced to accept tasks that they already know are impractical. They come up with creative excuses instead, trying to appear cooperative without actually cooperating.

The Arsonist's typical complaint about his staff is, "Nobody understands me." No one is following the priorities; he feels he's surrounded by idiots. "It is difficult to soar with the eagles when you are surrounded by turkeys" is a typical (**E**) attitude.

Sometimes the Arsonist will go through successive stages of firing and bring in someone new. Then, for a little while, he thinks this new kid on the block is a genius: "Look at him! Look how good he is!" He walks on water – for a while. Six months later, the Arsonist has become convinced that this man does not understand his genius either – and he's as disappointing as the rest.

Still, (--**E**-)s dislike firing people. They prefer to get a hatchet man to do the firing or, more often, they'll make your life so miserable that you'll eventually resign. They demean you, put you down, criticize you in public, humiliate you. Until you resign. But they will not usually fire, as (**P**)s and (**A**)s will not hesitate to do.

For the Arsonist, planning does not mean committing the organization to a course of action. Planning means making long lists of ephemeral goals. Whereas the Lone Ranger rarely takes the time to plan at all, and the Bureaucrat derives next year's budget by adding some percentage to last year's results, the Arsonist may not even have a budget, and if he does it is usually unrealistic.

The Arsonist is usually so preoccupied with opportunities that he sees few if any threats. He can endanger an organization by recklessly trying to exploit too many opportunities at once and spreading himself and his organization too thin.

One might expect to find creativity throughout an organization managed by an Arsonist, but the opposite is usually true. An organization managed by an Arsonist is not a creative, flexible structure but a slave ship. The Arsonist sets the course, changes direction, ignores the suffering of his subordinates, and takes all the credit for successes.

When the (--**E**-) leaves, the organization is in a shambles and its people are exhausted. They're desperate for peace and quiet, for stability. As a result, they usually ask for and eventually get stuck with a Bureaucrat or a SuperFollower.

The SuperFollower (---**I**)

How would a manager function if he were deficient in the areas of (**P**)roducing, (**A**)dministrating, and (**E**)ntrepreneuring and were only capable of (**I**)ntegrating?

What is he mostly concerned about? He's concerned about *who*. He doesn't care *what* we agree about, nor *how* we agree about it, nor *why* we agree. The important thing is: "Do we agree?" I call him the SuperFollower.

What are the characteristics that typify a SuperFollower?

He's not a leader. He's the one who asks, "Where would you like to go? Let me lead you there."

An (---**I**) accommodates endlessly. He wants everything to run smoothly. He tries to find out what plan will be acceptable to the largest number of powerful people and then he gets behind that plan. That is, he does not really lead – he follows. That's why I call him a SuperFollower.

The SuperFollower is like a fish monitoring the undercurrent, always seeking the right tide to carry himself forward. He's like a cheap politician, always adapting his stand to the polls, trying to sense the undercurrent.

What is the difference between a politician and a statesman? The statesman worries about the next generation, while the politician worries about the next election. The SuperFollower is not concerned about the long-term future; he's concerned about the present political smoothness: "Do we agree?" He might be running a very happy disaster. He negotiates an *appearance* of agreement rather than resolving the deep-seated issues that cause conflict.

So, again we see the interesting inconsistency: The (**P**---) is so focused on effectiveness that he becomes organizationally ineffective, a bottleneck. The (-**A**--) is so exclusively focused on efficiency that in overdoing it he creates a bureaucracy – which is inefficient. The (--**E**-) wants change so badly that he produces chaos and thus no real change. And the (---**I**), whose role is to create and nurture long-term efficiency through (**I**)ntegration, is so exclusively (**I**)-oriented that he loses sight of the goals (**I**)ntegration is supposed to serve: he does not integrate around a mission (**E**), or around tasks (**P**), or for smoothness or implementation (**A**). He (**I**)ntegrates merely for the sake of (**I**)ntegration. But that kind of (**I**)ntegration is usually short-lived; any major change that calls for political courage – which an exclusive (**I**) does not possess – can destabilize the situation.

The SuperFollower welcomes any training – *if* it improves his ability to understand human nature or contributes to the appearance of unity.

If the SuperFollower has free time, he spends it listening to complaints or agreements. However, in doing so, the SuperFollower doesn't tell you what he thinks; he asks you what *you* think. He's noncommittal. He might say something like, "I have an idea, but I'm not so sure I agree with it," or, "I suggest we declare dividends, but I don't feel too strongly about it."

It's difficult to get a SuperFollower to commit to a point of view. In Mexico, they call this type of manager "the soapy fish," because you just can't catch him. He always has some way to slip away; he always wiggles out of your hands. His typical complaint is: "You didn't understand what I wanted to say…. What I *really* meant to say is…." You can't corner him. That's why he is usually able to remain in power for quite a long time: In any given conflict, he figures out which side is winning and adapts himself to that side.

The SuperFollower tends to avoid making decisions as long as he can. He has no ideas of his own that he would like to implement – no (**E**); no tangible results that he wants to achieve – no (**P**). Unlike an (-**A**--), he is indifferent to any particular system, as long as agreement is achieved or is seen to be achieved.

Because he does not have strong convictions, his mind can be changed quickly and easily. He sways along with popular opinion.

Sometimes a SuperFollower will postpone and postpone a decision until there's a consensus, but his procrastination can have a high price. While he waits, opportunities disappear.

Another thing the SuperFollower doesn't understand is that once people agree on a decision, that does not necessarily mean they are actually going to implement it.

At meetings, the SuperFollower is the one who is listening very attentively. Who is saying what? What does he *really* mean? What is *not* being said? Where does the power lie? Which way is the decision likely to go?

If the SuperFollower is chairing the meeting and a consensus cannot be achieved, he will probably postpone the decision by establishing a subcommittee to study the problem further.

An (---**I**) makes sure he is in control by being instrumental to the resolution of the conflict. If this is impossible, if he cannot resolve the conflict, he will simply not get involved. Thus, he is perfectly capable of watching Rome burn without lifting a finger to help.

The SuperFollower hires people like himself, who are politically intuitive; they have a good nose for how the political power base is moving. They are the first to identify it and to jump on the bandwagon. What do they spend their time on? "What's going on?" "Who said what?" "What did he say?" "What does it mean?" "Where is the power base?" I call them informers, or oilers.

Their main job is to keep the boss up-to-date and keep everybody happy. It is their duty to feed the boss the latest office "news"; no gossip is too insignificant to relate.

In his presence, the (---**I**)'s subordinates seem peaceful and accepting, remembering that their boss prefers people whom other people like. This often requires them to hide their true feelings from him, which can easily lead to their feeling manipulated and emotionally exploited.

A SuperFollower, being a politician, will not upset the short-term consensus in order to achieve long-term goals. He is not a statesman, who is willing to risk conflict in the short run because he sees the necessity of change over the long run.

The SuperFollower has no particular goal; or rather, the goal is whatever is most desired at a particular time by a consensus of his co-workers. This is, of course, a very limited attitude toward corporate goals, and as a result, short-range interest groups flourish under the SuperFollower.

When a SuperFollower leaves an organization, the superficial (**I**)ntegration he established will rapidly deteriorate. At that point, a (**P**)roducer is often called in to get some action. His solutions can be traumatic, as they are totally different from the accommodating style of the Super Follower. The organization is usually in shock.

THE COMMON DENOMINATOR

For all their differences, the four managerial styles – (**P**---), (-**A**--), (--**E**-), and (---**I**) – have one trait in common: They are all inflexible stereotypes. The managers who exhibit these styles have uni-dimensional, one-track minds. They have only a limited perception of who they are and of what they are supposed to do in life.[3] They are not well-rounded individuals.

All of them – and in fact anyone who exhibits an exclusive management style – is in danger of becoming a Deadwood (----).

The Deadwood (----)

When change happens, a manager can either adapt or "die" – that is, become Deadwood, with a (PAEI) code that looks like this: (----).

A Deadwood is agreeable, friendly, and non-threatening. He is liked, much as a friendly old uncle is liked, but he is not respected. People do not want to hurt him, so they endure him. In the meantime, the organization suffers.

The Deadwood is apathetic. He waits to be told what to do. He might work hard, like the Lone Ranger, but the results are never achieved. He does not get involved with power intrigues, as the SuperFollower does. Nor does he provide sparks, as does the Arsonist: if he has any good ideas or opinions, he keeps them to himself. And unlike the Bureaucrat, Deadwood cares about following the rules only insofar as doing so will help him survive until retirement.

DUNAGIN'S PEOPLE - By Ralph Dunagin

"And I remind you that I have served you for two terms without causing any harm."

His only goal is to keep intact the little world he has created. He knows that any change threatens his position. Thus, to maximize his chances for survival, he avoids change, by avoiding new jobs or projects.

However, he does not resist anything. Resisting would expose him and make him vulnerable. Instead, he cleverly agrees to everything and takes action on nothing.

In his free time, the Deadwood looks for successes that he can plausibly take credit for. He is usually out of the information network, but if he does get access to any information, he cherishes it and uses it at every conceivable opportunity, even when it's irrelevant – just to prove that he's still plugged in and kicking.

Four distinct characteristics mark a Deadwood as distinct from any other mismanagement style:

No. 1: "Low managerial metabolism"

Deadwood very likely started out as one of the other four types of mismanagers, and he still evinces his former dominant personality traits; one can still see in him traces of the enthusiastic Arsonist or the meticulous Bureaucrat. Nevertheless, by the time he becomes Deadwood, his most prominent characteristic is a "low managerial metabolism."

He smokes or drinks a lot. He coughs, hums, and nods his head in agreement ("Uh huh"; "Oh yes, sure"); he confides to you how well he is doing, or how well he did in the past, or how well he will do – *but nothing is happening*. He is only going through the motions.

No. 2: Deadwood has no complaints

Each of the other four mismanagers has a typical complaint: "The day is too short" (**P**); "It's not being done the way it should be done" (**A**); "The most urgent priorities are not being followed" (**E**); "They did not understand what I really wanted to say" (**I**).

Deadwood? If you ask him, "How is it going? Any problems?" he will tell you, "No, no! Everything is fine."

Now, we know that to be alive is to be always working on something. That is how you grow and develop. You're trying to resolve or improve something. If there are no problems, then there are no opportunities either.

But Deadwood thinks a complaint might reflect badly on him or set changes in motion that he cannot or prefers not to handle. He might actually, for instance, be asked to solve the problems he is complaining about. To avoid such threats to his existence, he never complains.

No. 3: No resistance to change

Each of the other styles will resist change for one reason or another. If you go to the Lone Ranger and say, "This item needs to move from here to there," what will he say? "I have no time. When am I going to do it? I'm already so busy. I'm falling apart!"

If you go to the Bureaucrat and say, "We need to move this item from here to there," he's going to yell "No!" before you even finish the sentence. He will tell you there is no way to move this item – "unless" – and that "unless" will be so complicated that you will either give up the effort, or do it behind his back.

Now let us go to the Arsonist. "We would like to move this item from here to there." What does the Arsonist say? "Interesting, but not good enough! You know what? While you're moving this item from here to there, why don't you move this other item as well from there to here, and also take this third item and put it over here, and then drop that building down...." His technique is to insist that if there is going to be change, it has to be his idea. And usually it isn't one idea but a succession of them.

Now we come to the SuperFollower: "We'd like to move this item from here to there."

"That is a great idea," he'll say. "I am really proud of you for coming up with that idea. But you know what? It's not the right time; people are not ready yet. Let's wait and see. Let us think about it a bit more."

In contrast, if you go to the Deadwood and say, "We would like to move New York to the Sahara," he'll say, "Sure. Great idea. Let's do it." He'll show *no* resistance.

A year later, if you ask him how the project to move New York to the Sahara is going, he will tell you, "We hired consultants. We have researched the subject; we have a study. We have a committee working on it."

Everything is being done except one thing: Not a pebble from New York has been moved anywhere.

The irony is, the person I'm describing is every manager's favorite subordinate! You say, "How's it going?" He says, "No problem; everything is fine." You give him an assignment; he says, "Sure." This is the person you always wanted, right? You don't want someone who says, "No, that can't be done," or "I have no time," or "That's the wrong thing to do." You want someone who says, "Fine," no matter what.

But think about it: Where is the quietest place in the city? The cemetery. Nothing is happening there. There are no more complaints.

No. 4: Deadwood's subordinates

All the above characteristics would not be so bad if it weren't for characteristic No. 4: Who works for the Deadwood?

Other Deadwood. The disease spreads.

Why? First of all, Deadwood's hiring practices reflect his strategy for survival. He favors not-so-bright subordinates, even to the point of promoting those who produce less than he does.

Also, any subordinates who wish to grow and develop are completely frustrated by a Deadwood manager. He does not grow, nor does he let anyone under him grow. Either the Deadwood's subordinates get out, or they mentally die in their jobs, becoming Deadwood too.

Even those who are not quite Deadwood themselves can create full-fledged Deadwood. The gofers who work for the Lone Ranger and the yes-yes clerks who work for the Bureaucrat become Deadwood. The claques who work for the Arsonist eventually learn to suppress their own aspirations. They learn to make lots of noise but do very little: they become Deadwood.

The SuperFollower's subordinates become Deadwood, too. They are never sure what really needs to be done, and they become sick and tired of the politics, so they give up and just follow. Where? Nowhere, since the SuperFollower gives no direction.

The worst disaster is to have Deadwood at the top of an organization. He no longer wants to change; he is happy with what he's previously accomplished. Although such management sometimes tries to disguise itself as conservative, it is in fact moribund.

Deadwood almost never leave an organization on their own; either they die on the job, or they retire or are fired. They aren't missed, but by the time they go the organization is usually dead as well. No purposeful activity, no creativity, no (I)ntegration of people is evident.

Now that we have described the styles, we proceed to prescriptions: what each style can do in order to work better with others. (For more details about management and mismanagement styles, please read Book 2 of this series: *Management/Mismanagement Styles.*)

NOTES

1.   Wouk, Herman: *The Caine Mutiny* (New York: Bantam Doubleday Dell, 1951), p. 131.

2.   "Work expands so as to fill the time available for its completion." C. Northcote Parkinson, Parkinson's Law: *The Pursuit of Progress* (London: John Murray, 1958).

3.   I am grateful to Bob Tannenbaum of UCLA for having directed my attention to this common characteristic.

Chapter 4

Prescriptions for the (P) Style

General note for coaches: If you coach, consult with, or lecture (**P**)s, it's crucial to provide what I call "deliverables" at regular intervals. By deliverables I mean advice that has immediate relevance and practical applications, with "take-home value," which they can use as soon as they leave you. For (**P**)s you will need to provide a "deliverable" every 15 minutes or so, otherwise the (**P**)s will not see any value in what you are saying; they will simply get annoyed and lose interest.

BEHAVIOR

Learn to say "no." Being indispensable makes you feel good, but it can also "kill you."

(**P**)s take pride in their competence and believe they do most things better than anyone else. That may even be true. However, there are dangers to trying to do everything yourself. First, everyone around you will become an "errand boy," just waiting around for you to take full responsibility for the task and do most if not all of it.

If you act this way, your subordinates will never grow, learn, or take more responsibility. That, in turn, means you will forever be doing everything yourself.

You don't have to work harder, but you do have to be more disciplined about what kind of work you do yourself and what you delegate to others.

Not everything that needs fixing is your responsibility. You must be capable of making priorities and sticking to them, which means sometimes saying "no" to tasks even though you know best how to do them. Even if you're sure you can do something faster and better than anyone else, if you say, "Yes, put it on my desk," too often, you will be spreading yourself too thin. You will not achieve your ultimate goals and eventually you may fail.

From now on, your mantra should be as follows: "I, [your name here], will do *only* those things that only [your name here] can do."

This means: Do *not* take care of everything you are best at. Do only those tasks that *no one else can do*. If someone else can do it, even if they're less accomplished than you are, let them do it. You need to be free to do the things that *only* you can do. And let me assure you, you will still have a full-time job. You won't be idle. You will not be irresponsible. You will not be considered a freeloader. You will not be a parasite.

As time goes by, there should be fewer and fewer tasks that *only* you can do, because you must train your staff to do them. By letting them do it and correcting them as they do it, you are allowing them to learn from experience. Again, this is like parenting: If you never let your kids hammer a nail because they might hit their fingers and because you can do it better anyway, then they will never learn to hammer nails.

Your being indispensable is ultimately destructive for your organization. Even though *not* being indispensable makes you feel insecure, it's necessary for becoming a better manager. Find your sense of security elsewhere: For example, rounding out your style by developing your (A) and (E) and (I) characteristics. The more well-rounded you become, the less you will feel the neurotic need to do everything yourself.

I realize that, like all really important things in life, this prescription sounds simple and easy while in reality it is extremely difficult to implement. That's because I am asking you to do what does not come naturally. It is natural to want to do that which you excel in. Asking a (P) to do (A) work feels like a punishment; who wants to do something they feel deficient at?

We all prefer to repeat what we know best, can do with ease, and get intrinsically rewarded for doing.

But please note: What makes a good manager, executive, parent, or leader, is flexibility: The ability to adapt to new situations, the ability to call upon elements of style that are necessary at that moment. A lack of flexibility in times of continuous and accelerated change is one sure prescription for eventual failure.

So work on your weaknesses. Imagine that you have a strong left hand and a very weak right hand. What is your doctor going to tell you: "Forget the right hand; use only your left"? No, he is going to say: "Leave your left hand alone for a while. Use only your right hand. Strengthen it."

True, it is going to be painful and difficult, and in the short run you will not be as effective. But you need to be able to use both hands or you will fail as a manager.

Do not be a field rat.

Native Americans have something they call the "medicine wheel," which makes animal analogies to archetypes of human personalities.[1] For instance, the description of the eagle on that wheel corresponds with an (**E**)-type personality. The buffalo is an (**A**) type.

A (**P**) personality is like a field rat. Why? The field rat is constantly running, collecting food here and there, never stopping. It's very short-term-oriented: Constantly doing, doing, doing, doing. Its vision is very close to the ground; it sees only what's directly in front of it. It is interested in the immediate, not in the long run.

Don't be a field rat. Raise your eyes above the ground; look around. Plan for the future. Take time to think.

Can you see how vulnerable you become when you keep your eyes low to the ground? You cannot see what is coming from above or from afar. Working so hard, you do not have time to work smart; being so busy making the small money, you have no time to make serious money.

If you cannot soar like an eagle, an (**E**), then you need to strategically align yourself with an eagle, who can monitor the horizon for you. Since you cannot be everything and do everything, you need to team up with people whose styles complement yours.

And in order to do that, you must learn to see the value of styles that are different from your own.

Can you see the forest from the trees?

(**E**)s can juggle many balls in the air; in fact, they will *create* balls to juggle, they will create problems – because juggling excites them.

(**P**)s, on the other hand, get very frustrated if they have more than one ball in the air. I have a (**P**)-type secretary, for instance. If I give her more than one task at a time, she just cannot handle it. An (**E**) likes to have fifteen things on his desk at a time, so he can move from one to the other and enjoy the diversity. But (**P**)s find it painful.

However, wanting to focus on one task at a time does not mean that a (**P**) will have a clean desk. On the contrary, his desk is piled with work and more work. As he methodically handles one task at a time, the problems pile up, the desk gets overcrowded, and eventually some problems will develop into crises. That is when they finally get the (**P**)'s attention.

That overburdened desk creates the immense pressure you feel to keep working without respite. Even scheduling a meeting with you becomes almost impossible: "A meeting? I can't take the time! Where will I find the time?"

Because you focus on one small task at a time, you habitually miss the big picture. In fact, it's not even accurate to say you miss the forest for the trees, because you aren't looking at the trees. You're *looking* at one tree at a time. You cannot see the forest because of the tree, not the *trees*.

Remember that sitting and thinking is not a waste of time. Being idle is not a waste of time. When you are idle, you start seeing and imagining things you could not see or realize when you were so busy working.

Idle time is necessary and indispensable for being a good manager, leader, or executive. Why? Because looking at the big picture helps you remember that there is, in fact, a forest, and that each tree, although it has its singular purpose, is not in itself the ultimate goal. To be able to see the forest, you must stop looking at the tree.

Stop worrying that "it" will not get done. Maybe "it" should not get done.

(**P**)s want to solve everything right now, today! They see a problem, and they want to fix it. They can't bear to leave a problem unattended.

But sometimes it may simply be too early to deal with a problem, and the most immediate solution may only *seem* to solve it. In fact, a quickie solution may actually disguise the problem, and thus contribute toward exacerbating it.

Let me give you an example. I've consulted with (**P**) clients who claim that "the problem" is that the staff is not working hard enough. This is, by the way, a typical complaint of all (**P**)s.

Why do they believe this? Because (**P**)s believe one should be paid for performance, and very often there is no incentive system in place that will pay by results. Therefore, a (**P**) will automatically blame the problem on the lack of incentives to work "hard enough."

A (**P**) solution, then, would be to set up such an incentive system. But taking that action might be premature, if the company had not yet been re-organized to accurately determine who *really* contributed results. Unless you know who is responsible and accountable for a particular result, you may be throwing money out the window by rewarding people who either did not actually contribute to the results, or did not know *how* they contributed. If an organization is badly organized, the wrong person can reap a windfall just by being in the right place at the right time, while the one who should get the credit does not.

You should organize the company so that people's achievements really reflect their contributions, taking the extra time to identify who causes which result. Otherwise, you're spending a lot of money and getting no benefit. Yes, it is very frustrating and tiresome to go through the process of organizing a company: to systematize it, to build information systems, and to synchronize strategies and information structure. But what is the alternative?

(**P**)s just want a simple solution: measure results and pay by results. Simple. But life is far from simple. Do not hurry to put something in place. It may not be the right system yet.

You might be running a railroad, but in the wrong direction.

A (**P**) puts his blinders on and pushes full speed ahead.

For example, if a (**P**)-type salesman isn't succeeding in making a sale, what does he do? He'll go in and visit the client two times, three times, four times, making a stronger appeal each time.

But maybe that strategy is wrong. He might be selling the wrong thing. In other words, he might be running a fast train, but in the wrong direction. He's working very hard, but on the wrong product in the wrong market. Instead of repeating and repeating, harder and harder, faster and faster, maybe what's needed is a new system, a new product, different clients.

Don't just repeat and repeat and repeat your strategy if it isn't working well. You shouldn't need an earthquake to tell you it's time to move on. A small tremor should be warning enough for you to reconsider: "Am I doing the right thing?"

Communication

The meaning of "yes" and "no" depends on who is saying it. It is not always as straightforward as it sounds.

(**P**)s interpret words literally. "Yes" for them means yes, and "no" is no. But other people understand and use those words very differently.

Imagine a horizontal continuum with small vertical points. On the left it says, "Do not know"; on the right, "Know."

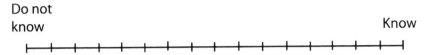

Do not know — Know

Suppose you ask a type (**A**) the question, "Should we change something?" If he doesn't feel he has enough information, is he going to say "yes" or "no"? He's going to say "no." So you keep trying to explain to him, and as you explain he will be moving across that horizontal line to the right, continuing to say "no," "no," "no" – until finally he has all the information he believes he needs to give an answer. At that point, he might very well say, "Oh, OK, yes."

Now take a type (**E**). He doesn't have enough information to make a decision about the change either, but if he is intrigued, he will say "yes," because the possibilities look interesting. The more you explain, the more he will keep repeating "yes," "yes," "yes" – but at the end, when he completely understands what is being suggested, he might say, "Ah, that's what you mean? No!"

So now, what do the words "yes" and "no" really mean? For a type (**A**), "no" means: "maybe; tell me more." "No" doesn't really mean "no." The fact is that ultimately the (**A**) may say "yes."

For a type (**E**), "yes" means "maybe." At the end, he may still say "no," so no matter how many times he repeats it, his "yes" does not really mean "yes" as you understand it.

SAYS		MEANS			
	Type	**P**	**A**	**E**	**I**
YES		Yes	Yes	Maybe	Maybe
NO		No	Maybe	No	Maybe

Here's an example: An (**E**)-type husband is married to an (**A**)-type wife. (This is a common and natural phenomenon: In effect, a marriage is a complementary team designed to raise healthy, well balanced children.)

The (**E**) husband comes home one night and says to his wife, "I'm so exhausted. We need a vacation."

She asks, "Do you really mean it?"

He says, "Yes."

What will an (**A**) immediately start doing, the moment she hears the word "yes"? She'll start organizing: Do they have the right clothes? Where is the suitcase? Who's going to water the plants in their absence? Who's going to take care of the dog? She's getting ready.

But her husband comes home the next night and says, "What on earth are you doing?"

"I'm organizing for our vacation."

"What do you mean, vacation? Don't you know how much work I have to do?"

"But you said 'yes,'" she replies, astonished.

"I did *not* say 'yes' [the word starting out pitched high and ending low – meaning yes]," he says, annoyed. I said 'yes' [starting out pitched low and ending high – meaning *maybe*]!"

You see, for an (**E**), a "yes" actually means "why not?" It is not a real "yes!" But for an (**A**), it is very difficult to say "yes" – it is practically like giving birth – so if he finally says "yes," he really means it.

This simple misunderstanding causes (**A**)s and (**E**)s to have difficulty communicating and getting along. In fact, the (**A**) often decides that the (**E**) is a liar, that his word is not to be trusted.

The meaning of "no" is also a source of miscommunication. An (**A**) may say, "no," "no," "no," but eventually he may say "yes." This means that "no" is not "no" – it is "maybe."

An (**E**), on the other hand, has difficulty saying "no" to opportunities, so if he finally does say "no," he really means it. And furthermore, an (**E**) gets very aggressive if you doubt his "no" – so if you dare to challenge him you may be putting your career on the line.

Now, for whom is "yes" literally "yes" and "no" literally "no"? A (**P**). He gets confused by (**A**)s and (**E**)s. He wants to keep everything simple – "Is it 'yes' or is it 'no'? What's going on here?"

In my consulting work, I train people to speak the (**P**) language in meetings when the time comes to make decisions: "Yes" means "yes," "no" means "no," and "maybe" means "maybe." If we don't all speak the same language, we cannot communicate effectively.

At all times, keep in mind that different people have different styles. Notice who is saying what, and particularly when dealing with an (**E**), make sure you have a "yes" that means "yes." You should even put his decision in writing (because he won't do it himself) and have it signed as soon as possible – before he changes his mind and claims that you misunderstood him.

Silence speaks.

Like "yes" and "no," silence has different meanings for different styles. For an (**E**), silence means agreement, whereas for an (**A**), silence means *dis*agreement.

Most of the time, a (**P**) ignores silence. He is too busy to pay attention to it, much less try to interpret it.

But in life, often what is *not* being said can provide a valuable source of information. You need to learn how to listen to silence. Pay attention to *who* is saying "yes" or "no." When there is silence, don't ignore it but try to interpret what it might mean: *What* is not being said? Why isn't it being said? How do those factors affect what is being said?

If you cannot develop this art, then form a strategic alliance with an (**I**). An (**I**) always knows perfectly well who did not say what and why he did not say it. He can interpret a whole meeting for you, providing you with subtexts and information you never even knew existed.

"Maybe" is sometimes better than "yes" or "no."

A (**P**) sees everything as either black or white. "Yes" means "yes" and "no" means "no," and "maybe" usually gets him very upset. But sometimes indecision, or saying "maybe," is better than "yes" or "no," because deciding "yes" or "no" could be premature.

You have to allow time for a situation to mature, to ripen. You are so eager for action and so worried when there is inaction that waiting is painful for you.

Give time the time to do its job. Hold back. Not every decision needs to be made right now. Wait before you act. Are you sure you've heard everything you need to hear in order to make the right decision?

"Maybe" might be a good enough answer – until the situation changes one way or another. Wait for the situation to be appropriate for the actions you want to take.

I constantly have to remind (P)s that good generals choose the time and the place for their battles. (P)s react so quickly to problems, they are so responsive, that I often have to tell them: "What you want to do is the right thing, but it's the wrong time and you are doing it at the wrong intensity"; or, "That is too much too early."

I have rarely seen (P)s or (E)s act too late. Being late is the domain of the (A)s and (I)s.

Easy does it. You do not need a two-by-four to change or be changed.

If a (P) wants to make something happen, he does not gently pressure you; he shoves. Why? Because (P)s are always dealing with some kind of crisis. It is as if they enjoy the adrenaline rush, so they create time pressures and crises to get that adrenaline going.

But there are consequences. When there is time pressure, there is a perceived need to act quickly. So a (P) may call people into a very short meeting and really give them hell, telling them what to do and when to do it in a dictatorial style; the more time pressure there is, the more dictatorial they become. In fact, (P)s are often accused of being "bicycle riders": They advance by stepping down on others. If they are short in height, they are also referred to (though not to their faces) as "Little Napoleons."

To use another parenting analogy: You don't have to actually hit your children in order to make a point. If you do hit them, the side effects – the emotional or physical scars you create – might be bigger than the problem you were trying to solve by hitting.

Take your time. Slow down. Not everything is a crisis, not everything needs to be a crisis. Is the situation *really* a crisis, or do you just want to get it over with as soon as possible? In other words, did your *behavior* make it a crisis?

Easy does it. You don't have to hit; touching is enough. You don't have to be so overbearing. The amount of energy you expend on getting people to act is way out of proportion.

How do you know when you're overdoing it? Use a little bit more (**I**), and you'll find that managing people will go more smoothly. Remember: The higher you go up the organizational ladder, the bigger your ears should be and the smaller your mouth should become. Speak less. Listen more. Also check yourself: Did you speak first or last? Remember that whoever speaks first usually loses the argument.

Conversely, you yourself should not have to be hit over the head with a two-by-four in order to change. But unfortunately, often the only way people can get *you* to listen and change is by coming at you very aggressively. You are always complaining that people overdo it with you – but your boss knows from experience that that's the only way that you will actually, finally hear him. You don't understand subtle hints. Suggestions are not good enough for you. The message must be very clear, and to be clear it has to be sharp and sometimes painful.

Here is a joke that makes this point:

There was once a brilliant engineer who did not take directions well. His boss would advise him and advise him to no avail. Finally the boss's boss said, "Let me handle it."

He called this engineer into his office. The meeting took no more than five minutes – and lo and behold! – from that time on the engineer followed instructions perfectly.

Seeing this, the engineer's direct boss asked him: "Why did you listen to him and not to me?"

"Well," the engineer replied, "he told me, 'Do it or you're fired.' It was never presented to me that way before!"

Slow down. Listen more. Ask for feedback. Give suggestions instead of orders. Encourage and reward cooperation and teamwork.

If you cannot do it, you already know the prescription: Get someone who can do it for you. Let someone else communicate bad news or unpleasant tasks to your workers. Find someone who will provide the necessary smoothness.

When the gut is engaged, the mouth should stay closed.

When a (**P**) gets emotional, his mind stops working. He just explodes into action. This characteristic is shared with (**E**)s, whose "action," however, is to attack someone.

But no matter what form your actions takes, having your mind, your mouth, and your gut in gear at the same time is a Molotov cocktail, a recipe for disaster.

If your gut is activated – meaning you've got butterflies in your stomach or feel tense – you are too emotional to know what you are saying. Thus it is too early to say anything.

Ask your mind to interpret for you what your gut is feeling. It's OK for the gut and mind to be active together. But stop there: the moment your *gut* starts working, your *mouth* should stop working. If you're emotional, then shut up, wait, stop. Think about what you feel, but don't talk about it yet. Wait till your gut is calm and your mind is at ease before you say anything.

When you are emotional, write down your ideas and feelings for contemplation later. Analyze them; sleep on it. Once you calm down, you can share them with those involved if you think that would be helpful.

So the rule is: Mind and gut together, yes; gut and mouth together, no.

It's fine to have mind and mouth active at the same time. That is called "thinking aloud." It is good for you to think from time to time and also to let other people see that you are thinking. But the moment you feel your gut starting to act up, stop! You are moving too fast – and probably in the wrong direction. Learn to be extremely careful when you free-associate. That is the domain of the (**E**)s.

An (**I**)-style manager can speak even when he is emotional about a subject, without getting burned. Why? Because whatever he says is a "maybe" anyway; he does not like to commit to anything.

You are different. As a (**P**) executive, every word you say is taken literally and carries weight. Often it is interpreted literally by others as a decision. Thus, if you are confused and communicate your confusion, it can be fatal to the organization.

For the same reason, you should not think aloud (mind and mouth together) unless you tell people up front that your words do not signify decisions. Your staff is not used to seeing you deliberating rather than deciding, so you have to tell them, "I'm just thinking out loud."

Decision-making

The squeakiest wheel is not always the most important one. And some problems can wait.

A (**P**) is crisis-oriented, meaning that what gets a (**P**)'s attention is the squeaking wheel. If something is not (yet) a crisis, he won't deal with it.

This is because (**P**)s are reactive, not proactive. They don't set priorities well. (**P**)s can get over-involved in small things, losing track of the big picture. They get caught up in tactical decisions and thus miss the strategic decisions.

But not every squeaking wheel has to be addressed right there and then. Sometimes waiting can be the right thing to do. Why? Because there are bigger fish to fry.

Leaping to fix the squeakiest wheel is not managing; it's *being* managed. Good managers do not let themselves be managed by their problems; they are not Firefighters. Make your priorities and stick to them.

Don't get involved in small things, losing track of the big picture. Sometimes you must choose to ignore a problem in favor of working out a larger problem. Let it wait. I know it is annoying you, I know it is bothering you, but just control yourself and let it be, because you have a limited amount of energy. Hold your fire. Stop. Look at the big picture. Prioritize.

Look at the whole gamut of issues. The squeaky wheel may not be the problem; it may be only a symptom of the problem. Be prepared to look around, discuss, and analyze before deciding. This is what makes you a good manager.

Remember: A good manager is known by the depth of the scars on his tongue.

Sometimes the harder you go forward, the further behind you get. The result is that you are going full speed backward.

A (**P**) typically confuses quantity with quality, not realizing that quality is a totally different kind of measurement. He thinks that when he works longer and harder he is doing better, when what he really needs to do is work less but smarter.

Because of that, the by-products of his actions might be to create a larger problem than the one he was trying to solve.

In diagnosing a problem, a (**P**) is likely to come up with a solution that is "bigger and harder"; for example, if sales are faltering he will recommend, "Let's sell more advertising." Not necessarily *better* advertising, just *more*. More ads, more money spent, as if more will invariably create better results.

Or, facing a problem, a (**P**) might decide, "We have to work harder," although working too hard can also have side effects that are undesirable.

So the harder you go forward, the more backward you might get. What do I mean by backward? You're working harder and harder, which means spending the company's resources and going full speed ahead – while at the same time the company is going backward because it's not satisfying the market and is losing market share. Perhaps you really need to change your product line, or lower your prices, or streamline your distribution. Doing what you're already doing, but doing it harder and faster, is not going to solve these problems. To get more you need to get things to be better. Better is more, while in some cases more and more is less and less.

Before you decide that *more* and *harder* are the answers, take the time to look around and see what's going on. This is difficult for you, I know. Whenever I tell a (**P**) that he needs to put aside a day for a meeting, he goes wild: "A day? I can't take a day! Where will I find a day's time?"

Always overburdened and overcommitted, he believes that sitting and thinking is a waste of time.

Remember that improving quality can improve quantity.

Not to know is to know something very important.

(**P**)s feel very uncomfortable when they don't know something. For example, in a meeting, if they are not sure exactly where the discussion is headed, they will say, "Dr.Adizes, where the heck are you taking us?" It's very frustrating for a (**P**) to hear, "I don't know. I'm still exploring. I'm taking one step at a time."

Problem-solving is like stepping into a maze. We must think before we take each step, and sometimes we have to go back and re-find our way.

It's OK that we don't know everything up front. It's also OK that the process of exploring is not very effective or efficient in the short run. You make many false starts. You waste a lot of time eliminating alternatives. But it isn't really a waste. You actually learn something during this process: You learn that something is not applicable or appropriate.

For a (**P**), the time-consuming process of decision-making "foreplay" is extremely frustrating. There is a joke about a (**P**) about to make love to his wife: "Honey, start on your own," he tells her. "When you're ready for the orgasm, call me."

Explore. Learn. Find out what you do not know. At least then you'll know that you don't know. That's very important.

Then cool it; stay calm in the face of uncertainty. We've found out that we don't know something; now let's find out what we need to know.

You do not know what you do not know until you know it.

A (**P**) is like a train engineer: You show him the track, give him the train, and off he goes, full speed ahead. In the pursuit of results he just plunges ahead through any barriers.

Engineers, in fact, are often (**P**) types: Most are trained to rely on formulas for the answer to a problem. That's how they work things out: they plug in the formula and they're done with it. They can't take the pain of sitting in a meeting, thinking things through. They hate to deal with uncertainty, with alternatives, with ambiguity. A (**P**) always wants to know *already*. The process of looking for something, studying, is abhorrent to him. He wants that formula.

Slow down. You won't know what you need to know until you finish exploring. Furthermore, you won't know if you were right until you see the results.

Take the time to think about what you're doing, rather than just doing it.

To make this discussion short you might have to take the long route.

A (**P**) is always looking for the simplest solution or a shortcut. Because of this tendency, he can inadvertently make a situation more complicated, because the remedy he comes up with may be so flawed that it's worse than the disease he's trying to cure.

Complex problems are like a tangled ball of string. How do you untie it? Carefully. Slowly. You have to think about interdependencies and boundaries. You pull gently on one string until there is resistance. Then you loosen the string that is obstructing the first one. Then you return to the first string and continue loosening it, etc.

(**P**)s find such methodical slowness disturbing. They are impatient. When they encounter resistance, they simply pull harder. And what happens? Pulling on the strings only twists them together more tightly. Sometimes they give up and cut the string apart with a knife; they just whack at it – finished! (**P**)s are not called "hatchet men" for nothing.

I tell my (**P**) clients that there is a short-long way, and a long-short way. For example, if I am in unknown territory, and there is a normal route to follow although it is long, taking the long route can be shorter, time-wise, than trying to find a shortcut and getting lost.

In the same way, what may appear to be a long discussion is really going to produce a decision that can be easily and quickly implemented. A slow process may result in a good decision and fast implementation, while a quick decision, made without sufficient attention to detail, can produce a long and arduous implementation.

Use time; don't abuse it.

All of the mismanagement types abuse time, but each one does it differently.

An (**E**) abuses time by killing any decision that he does not see as his own. But he never really says no to it; an (**E**) hates to say no to anyone, because one day, God forbid, that person may be in a position to say no to him. Instead, he says: "Maybe, maybe – let me think about it."

Now, when an (**E**) says "maybe," he really means "no." But since people do not necessarily understand that, they don't know how to react and they end up doing nothing. Meanwhile, the (**E**) has allowed the decision to sit neglected on his desk until it becomes outdated and obsolete.

An (**I**) procrastinates until he's sure everybody will support a decision: "Let's wait until we know what people think." "Let's wait until the company expresses itself." In the meantime, a situation might be getting worse and worse, but the (**I**) will only act on it when it's become such a crisis that he will lose political power if he does not act.

An (**A**) will abuse time by asking for more information and more details and more justifications and more studies and more analyses – all in order to minimize the risk. But time costs money, so while he is doing all this costly research and analysis, the opportunity can slip away.

Now, how does a (**P**) abuse time? He wants to do everything *right now*. His view of time is that it should be used to solve the immediate problems of an organization. As a result, he never learns how to set priorities, and he avoids long-range planning. He has no concern for problems that are "five years down the pike."

But the truth is that not everything has to be done immediately. Priorities need to be set before action is taken.

Here is a lesson for a (**P**):

There was once a Crusader who was attacked by three different saber-holding enemies simultaneously. He realized that he could not fight all three together, but he *could* run faster. So he turned around and started running.

The other three began to chase him, but they did not all run at the same speed – some went faster, some went slower, and soon they were separated by distance. At that point, the Crusader turned and fought them one by one by one and killed them all.

You can do the same thing with problems. If there are too many begging for your attention, pull back, give yourself a little bit of distance, and prioritize. You decide which one to deal with first. Don't try to fight them all at once.

Focus on the process, not just on the solution.

A (**P**) focuses on the end result: Did we win or did we lose? If we won we celebrate, and if we lost we hide our faces. I saw this very clearly when I consulted with sports teams. For a typical (**P**) coach, the only thing that counts is winning.

Try rewarding the team based *not* on whether they won or lost the game but on how they played.

It's a lot more promising if the team played outstandingly well and lost than if they played badly and won. If they played badly and won, that was only luck, and you can't rely on luck every time. That victory cannot necessarily be repeated. But if the team played extremely well against a tough opponent and lost, then they had a tremendous opportunity for learning and becoming better. And eventually they will win.

If you look only at results, you are like a child trying to learn a new musical instrument who insists on playing fast, even though playing too fast before you've mastered the form – the notes, the fingering, the chords – involves making lots of mistakes.

Again, slow down. Learn to play it right first – learn the form. The function – playing at the appropriate speed – will inevitably follow.

For a (**P**), function is all-important. "Let us play," he insists, even before he's learned the basic form.

Whether it's learning to play a sport or learning to play a musical instrument, you must always focus initially on the form: Slow down, learn how to do it right. That's called process. Once the form is mastered, you can begin to focus on results.

In other words, do not focus only on the solution. Focus on the process of arriving at a solution. The right solution using the wrong process, in the long run, is worse than the wrong solution arrived at by the right process. The right solution using the wrong process is only luck – not repeatable – whereas the right process will eventually bring the right result.

If you stay in one place long enough I might be able to tell you something you should hear, although you might not want to hear it.

The (**P**) is a field rat, constantly moving, never standing still in one place. He is always searching for something to do, and because he's so busy searching, running from here to there, putting out fires and grabbing all the available work, he is never in one place long enough to hear what others are trying to tell him. As a result, he misses signals, is oblivious of market changes, and does not comprehend the necessity of adapting to new realities.

(**P**)s hate meetings, for instance. They will not come to a meeting if they have a choice about it; they will only attend if forced. Even then, they fidget, or occupy themselves with other tasks instead of listening and participating in the process. For them, discussion is painful; only action – the quicker the better – satisfies a (**P**).

One reason they can't stay in one place for too long is because they lack patience for any kind of slow, thoughtful analysis. A (**P**) wants to *do*; it is only when he is active – performing an immediate task – that he feels comfortable.

Another reason is that the (**P**) personality is uncomfortable and unhappy with alternatives, with ambiguity, with uncertainty.

In Hebrew, there are three words that derive from the root letters SVL: "tolerance" (*SoVLanut*), "patience" (*SaVLanut*), and "pain" (*SeVeL*). Sharing the same root (in other words, the consonants for all three words are the same; only the vowels are different) signals that the meanings of these words are related. But how? Think about it: There cannot be tolerance without patience. But to be tolerant of other people's opinions, and patient enough to listen to them, is painful.

A (**P**) has little tolerance for intellectual pain, the pain of thinking. He is very literal and simpleminded, very black and white. Because he doesn't want to wait for the best solution, I often have to work much harder and longer in my consulting work in order to compel a (**P**) to come to a solution that works. He prefers the quickest solution, even if the quickest solution will lead to delays and mistakes in the long run. The long run is beyond his ability to visualize.

But listen: If you stay in one place long enough, I might be able to tell you something you should hear. I know you might not want to hear it. That's not because you do not want to know; it's because you don't want to spend time listening. It's about impatience.

I know it's hard for you to believe this, but spending the extra time now will almost certainly speed up the implementation of your decisions later. You must make time to stop and listen; otherwise, you will end up wasting incalculable amounts of time compensating for all the mistakes you will make because you didn't have sufficient information to come to an informed decision. Stop! Stand still and listen.

You cannot manage if you cannot take the pain of listening to others. If you avoid pain, you ultimately cannot show patience or tolerance for what others have to say. So you isolate yourself from the information you need to make a good decision. In a small company, you might be an acceptable manager even if you lack patience and tolerance for a diversity of opinions. But if you want to grow and you want your company to grow, you must learn to bite your tongue and open your ears.

Focus on who is speaking and why he is saying what he's saying, rather than exclusively focusing on what is being said.

(**P**)s are not politically oriented or sensitive. They don't realize that what a person is saying might be colored by his or her own needs and desires.

A (**P**) focuses almost exclusively on *what* to do, but sometimes what to do depends on *who* is doing it. What needs, what personal agenda, is driving the decision?

Try to be more politically oriented. If you pay attention to who is saying something, and try to figure out *why* he is saying it, you will gain insight that will help you work together with others to get what *you* want.

If you are in pain with the decision-making process, become more – not less – engaged with it.

(**P**)s sit in a meeting and it drives them absolutely nuts. They fidget, they try to escape, they constantly check in with their staff. They will use any pretext they can find to disengage from the decision-making process. Why? Because they are in pain. Ambiguity tortures them. Indecision makes them feel as if they're wasting time.

Either they don't come to meetings at all, or if they are forced to come they bring other work to do: Checks to write, papers to sign, other material to read.

If doing other work has been forbidden, they sit in their chairs and twitch. It's sometimes comical to watch. You can almost see the thought bubble above their heads: "Why is this taking so long? I could have made this decision in two seconds: Here's how to do it; bingo! That's it! Why are these people wasting my time?"

But the reality is, the only way to avoid the pain is to engage! Say what you think. Express your opinions. In engaging with the process, you will feel busy, and when you are busy the pain will recede.

Here is a sailing analogy: Let's say you are in a boat out in the ocean, and the waves are so high that you feel nauseated. There are two things you can do to feel better. One is to put your hands on the wheel; the other one is to look at the horizon. The feeling of nausea will diminish.

Why? Because by putting your hands on the wheel, you feel more in control. And when you're looking at the horizon, you have more of a sense of stability and direction than if you were watching the waves move up and down and up again.

The same is true in a meeting. It's rocky: There are many different opinions; the discussion is going up and down, this way and that way. What should you do? The more disengaged you are, the more nauseated you will be. You feel like you need to throw up, but what you really need to do is to get engaged, which is like putting your hands on the steering wheel, setting the direction.

Look at the horizon: Ask questions. "Why are we having this discussion? What are we really trying to solve here?" Once you can see where you are going, you will feel more secure and less uncomfortable.

Stop shooting from the hip; think before you act.

There is a Hebrew expression from the Old Testament: *Na ase ve nish-ma*, which means: "Let's do it and *then* we'll talk about it."

That's typical (**P**) thinking. A (**P**) will sit in a meeting, and when it gets complicated and difficult, he'll say, "All right, we're wasting time. We need to act; we need to be decisive. Here's what we should do; now let's go and do it. We'll talk later." That's what I call the *na ase ve nishma* syndrome.

This can be very dangerous, because quick, un-thought-out decisions can become tremendous fiascos. But thinking things through and playing out scenarios does not come naturally to a (**P**). In fact, a (**P**) has to work very hard to overcome his resistance to prolonged analysis.

I remember being in an important meeting with a client. The problem was how to handle certain investors who were pressuring the company for money. In the middle of the discussion, emotions were running high, so I suggested a ten-minute break. At that point the president, a (**P**) type, disappeared for thirty or forty minutes.

I said to one of the other corporate officers, "I bet I know what he's doing. He's already on the phone, starting to act on the half-baked decision we made." And I was right. When the president returned, I asked him: "Where were you?"

"I was on the phone with our investors. I wanted to know if they would accept what we discussed," he replied.

I sometimes jokingly call this an "intellectual premature ejaculation."

The point is: Slow down. Slow down. Take your time to decide. Taking the time to make a thoughtful decision causes you pain, so you prefer to run away from it. But this weakness will hurt you and your decisions in the long run.

"Leave it on my desk" is not a solution.

If you go to a big (**P**) and say, "I have a problem; what should I do with it?" what do you think he's going to say?

"Put it on my desk."

The (**P**) assumes he will eventually get to "it," whatever "it" is. But the result is that everything piles up on that desk, and many of the time-sensitive problems don't get solved in time, or turn from problems into crises.

Only when he's sure he cannot do it by himself – only then will he delegate. But by then, it's often too late to find an optimal solution.

Why does he behave this way?

I am not a psychologist, but I can make some experience-based guesses.

For a really big (**P**), a Lone Ranger, work is an addiction. The tons of overdue paperwork and projects you find on his desk are just like hoarded liquor bottles to an alcoholic. The Lone Ranger's disorganized, paper-strewn desk signifies an addiction to work, exactly like an alcoholic's addiction to liquor.

That's one explanation. Another is that a (**P**) is quite sure he can handle any task better than his subordinates (which could easily be true, since he rarely trains them properly), and he wants to be sure it is done properly. A typical (**P**) expression is, "If you want to be sure something is done right, you'd better do it yourself."

Yet another explanation: He hates being idle. He measures his worth by how hard he works; if he delegates, he will feel less busy, and if he feels less busy, he fears he is becoming a parasite, just sitting around and watching others work.

A (**P**) needs to feel indispensable, to have problems waiting in line for him. He is always rushed, and he likes it that way. Delegation would take all the thrill out of his job.

Last but not least, the (**P**) truly loves what he is doing. He is totally devoted to the task. Take an architect. He really loves to design. When he is promoted and takes charge of a large architectural firm, he feels lousy. Instead of designing, he is spending all his time on (**A**)dministration, giving work to others that he would prefer to do himself.

So delegating, to a (**P**) type, is giving up the best part of his job. He would gladly delegate (**A**)dministration and business development; the problem is that the higher up you go in the organizational pyramid, the less (**P**) work there is to do, and the more (**E**) and (**A**) and eventually (**I**) work needs to be done. This transition is very painful for a (**P**).

"Put it on my desk" is a bad managerial solution. Problems get parked there and evolve into crises, and some of them may be fatal to the organization.

If you fit the above description, then you have become a bottleneck. You are the reason why the company cannot grow and change. It is essential that you learn to delegate and to prioritize.

Learn which tasks belong to you and which to assign to others. Your managerial job is not to manage the task but to manage those who should implement the task. You must, and can, learn to feel secure by excelling at your managerial responsibilities, instead of remaining stuck at the level of merely (**P**)roducing. You must develop your (**A**), (**E**), and (**I**) capabilities. You must evolve. You should do only that which by all accounts *only* you can do.

Do not micro-manage. There are not enough days in a year and hours in a day to do everything that needs to be done. Set policies and goals for others to achieve, and then let them do it. If they do not produce the expected results, or if they violate the policies, it is your job to find out why and make the changes necessary to ensure success the next time.

That is called managing. What you were doing before was not managing. It was just working very hard.

IMPLEMENTING

To get overcommitted to any task can be expensive.

(**P**)s don't really have long-term goals; instead, they have short-term tasks, and they sometimes become obsessed with these tasks, putting too much effort into a job that does not justify in value what it costs. In other words, the marginal value of another incremental effort is not necessarily worth it.

This is called sub-optimizing. It's as if a (**P**) has blinders on: he sees only the task directly in front of him, forgetting the context of the task and the ultimate goal the organization is trying to achieve. He overdoes the effort on one piece of the whole, and ends up sub-optimizing the totality.

For example, a (**P**)-type production manager might be so committed to making his quota that he cannot see that to (**P**)roduce more efficiently, he needs to make changes in the (**P**)roduction process. This myopia is dangerous. Ignoring the market and its changing needs may mean that the (**P**) manager obstructs the organization's flexibility, its ability to change the product line in response to changing circumstances. The cost of this reluctance to change can be much higher, eventually, than the cost of the change itself.

Sometimes being committed exclusively to any single task, right to the bitter end, is actually overdoing it. It may not be truly functional and does not serve you well. It's easy to subvert and undermine the final goal by being inflexible and overcommitted to one single thing at a time.

What you might see as commitment and loyalty to achieving a goal, might be seen by others as sabotaging and undermining the total effort.

Lift your head and look around. Check the horizon. What's the ultimate purpose of your task? How does it fit into the totality? Is it worth the effort you're giving it, or could you be more effective doing something else? Make sure that the effort you're making serves the company's mission instead of just giving you the personal satisfaction of a job well done. The wrong job, however well done, is still, ultimately, a failure.

Taking on more tasks than you can do might result in doing less than you can do.

A joke I've often heard is that (**E**)s give ulcers; (**P**)s get them. While (**E**) shoots in all directions, (**P**) compulsively addresses each problem and assignment personally. He ends up biting off more than he can chew. He prides himself on his competence, but ultimately he does only a mediocre job because his abilities are spread too thin.

Going in too many directions simultaneously means not doing any one thing particularly well, and probably burning out.

Thus, in the long run, it's better to do 100 percent of 80 percent than 80 percent of 100 percent. What does this mean? If you choose only 80 percent of the available tasks, but give 100 percent effort to each of them, you'll be much more successful than if you try to do everything but give each task only 80 percent of your attention and expertise.

Remember: For sustainable success, doing more will not make it better, but doing it better will eventually produce more.

Sometimes it takes time to get quality. Slow down, if you want to get things done right.

(**P**)s are very shortsighted, like that field rat: They just want something now – *bing, bing, bing, bang!* Their typical reaction to a demand for better quality is to push harder and faster.

But quantity is not quality. Sometimes slowing down and looking at the details is what creates quality.

In Arabic there is an expression: "The devil is in the details." Christians say, "God is in the details." Both of them are right. If you do not pay attention to the details, the devil is in the details. If you pay attention to the details, God is in the details. So it's up to you whether the details are godlike or demonic. Because (**P**)s do not like to pay attention to the details, they usually end up with hell.

The details can destroy you. You're always trying to do everything harder, faster, better, as if faster were better, as if harder were better.

You don't realize that that's not necessarily true. In fact, sometimes just the opposite is true. Losing track of the details may cause you to lose quality.

You can be very competent as a (**P**)roducer, and yet be less than competent as a manager. You have the discipline and the expertise, but you hate to stop working in order to plan a better strategy. You prefer to improvise: "If it works, fine! That's it. Boom! Let's go!"

Take some time to think things through. The fastest way may not be the best way.

Team-building

Telling people what to do does not mean you have a team.

The (**P**) is not sensitive to interpersonal relations; he doesn't worry about group dynamics or individuals' feelings. He does not relate well to people. He does not build a team or develop the capabilities of others around him; he is too busy (**P**)roducing.

He believes that managing means managing the task, getting the job done. People are merely instruments for getting the job done. He does not solicit others' opinions. He gives orders in a dictatorial style and yet believes he is participating in teamwork: "I talked to them, didn't I?"

If you tell a (**P**), "You need to be working as a team," he says, "Sure. That's what I'm doing. I called them in, I told them what to do. We have a team!"

But to have a team you have to listen. And, like an (**E**), you hate to listen. You are always in the telling mode.

For you, a disagreement is painful because you feel it's a digression and a waste of your time: You already *know* what should be done; let's just go and do it. If someone disagrees with you, you feel he is holding you back.

But watch it: There is much to learn from people who disagree with you. Maybe someone is trying to tell you upfront what problems you're going to have with the implementation of your idea. It's better to find out that it's not going to work *before* you try it out in the field.

Meetings do have a purpose.

(**P**)s do not grasp the concept of interdependency. They just want things to happen. Since a (**P**) likes to do everything himself, he cannot see the point of meetings and regards them as a waste of time.

But people do have to work with each other, to be coordinated and motivated and communicated with. The purpose of meetings is to communicate, to clarify, and to finally reach a consensus in which everyone "owns" the solution so that it can be implemented with full commitment.

I once worked with a company to analyze its problems. Everyone contributed. I usually put people into teams to diagnose the problems, identify the patterns and decide on a plan of action.

In this organization, the president was a typical (**P**). Before the exercise had been completed, he interrupted and said, "Give me all the problems." They were already written on index cards, so he put them all in front of him, and one by one he analyzed each card and decided what should be done. Meanwhile, thirty people stood behind him, watching him do it. Instead of delegating the problem-solving to his staff, or working with his staff, he was solving each problem by himself.

"A good manager creates an environment in which the most desirable thing will most probably happen," Ralph Ablon, the chairman of Ogden Corporation, once said. This company president was not doing that. That's why (**P**)s are dangerous: When they die, the company often dies with them, because they were doing it all and no one had been trained to take over. Once again, it's like good parenting: if you do everything for your kids, your kids will never grow up.

Meetings and discussion lend validity to a decision when it's made – even if some participants totally disagree with the ultimate decision.

If someone who is important to the implementation of a decision disagrees with that decision, you must listen to and deal with his objections before starting to implement. If you ignore him, you risk the possibility that he may sabotage the process.

On the other hand, I have found that even when people continue to disagree, as long as they feel they have been heard, they will not sabotage later. Thus, meetings are an essential part of an organization's progress.

Not having meetings forces people to have meetings in the corridors.

This is a corollary to the above prescription. Because (**P**)s hate meetings, they tend to avoid them.

But the truth is that not having meetings doesn't mean there are going to be no meetings. Instead, the meetings are going to be in the corridors, because people do need each other; there are interdependencies throughout the organization, and discussions are necessary.

But if they're meeting without you, that really is wasting time, for several reasons: You will be out of the loop, you will have no input if you are not there to participate, and you also will be encouraging secrecy and paranoia among your team.

Bite the bullet: Schedule and participate in the meetings, understanding that they *will* happen – with or without you.

MANAGING STAFF

Do not be a bicycle rider.

The (**P**) has a tendency to be very short with people and to dictate. He might not be at all cognizant of his staff's desires and aspirations, and does not necessarily incorporate their feelings into his scheme of things.

The most extreme (**P**) is the one I call a "bicycle rider."

How does a bicycle rider move forward? By stepping down on the pedal – but in this case "the pedal" is people: Subordinates, colleagues, everybody. He's only paying attention to the task, forgetting to consider the needs and feelings of others.

His subordinates say he's inconsiderate, insensitive, a dictator, and a taskmaster, but his intentions are not malevolent. He simply doesn't realize how he comes across. He orders people around, often unintentionally humiliating them, and he does not see that at all.

Do not be a bicycle rider. Try to develop your (I) abilities, or hire an (I) type to do it for you – and listen to his advice. An (I)ntegrator is necessary to good management, because he is able to divine what people's aspirations and needs are and align them in the direction of fulfilling a goal. He seeks consensus, and you will find that being more of an (I)ntegrator, or at least having one around, will reduce the conflict and bad feeling in your relations with your staff.

Do not hire and promote people because of their performance, in spite of their personality.

A (P) is always watching *what* people do, not how they do it or even *why* they do it. But having a good team requires people with different yet compatible styles who can work together and command respect and trust.

It's not enough to pay attention to performance. Personality plays a key role in whether someone can successfully do a job or not. Can he get along with others? Does he disagree for the sake of disagreeing? Does he like to make waves, promote conflict and turbulence, even when it isn't necessary to get the job done? *What* he does is important; *how* he does it might be equally important.

When you hire, remember to consider the *how;* otherwise what you might get is a high-performance team that doesn't get along. Then, when you retire or die, the whole enterprise will collapse.

Surrounding yourself with errand boys (gofers) is not going to free you.

Each of the four types has a typical subordinate. The (**E**), for example, has claques – people who clap and yell "Bravo!" The (**P**) has errand boys, messengers, or gofers.

Why are they just errand boys? Because they are untrained, unprepared, and uninformed. They are always being sent to tend to some errand or crisis – often without having had the necessary training – and then they come back and wait for the next task.

A (**P**) is always saying, "I need more people to work for me. I'm working too hard. I need to delegate." So what does he do? He hires yet another errand boy, which means that now there's even more work for him to do because there are more errand boys to manage.

You must hire people who are willing and able to be delegated to – and you have to delegate to them if you want to be free. Errand boys will not free you. You should hire (**A**)s, (**E**)s, and (**I**)s to complement yourself. Then you must learn to treat them with trust and respect despite the fact that their styles are different from yours.

Not everyone who works hard is necessarily doing the right thing.

A (**P**) measures himself by how hard he works. Working hard, to a (**P**) type, is synonymous with (**P**)roducing.

When a (**P**) has a problem, his diagnosis will often be: "We are not working hard enough."

I have worked with companies headed by a (**P**) president who tells me, "The problem with this company is that people are not working hard enough. If the staff came in earlier and stayed longer, we wouldn't have this problem." That's a typical (**P**) answer – very simple, very black and white. "If they work hard enough, they'll be successful; that's all there is to it. They need to get off their butts and just do it!"

But your subordinates could be working very hard – on the wrong things. How would you know? Do you monitor their work? Do you have regular meetings to talk about it? Do you stop to diagnose problems, or do you simply dictate the quickest, most convenient solution?

Stop urging your staff to work harder; instead, start thinking about ways they can work smarter. Harder is not necessarily better.

"Do as I do" is not a training practice. Hire someone who will train for you.

The desire to do everything himself can be seen both in a (**P**)'s disinclination to train others and also in the training methods he uses. He is not inclined to do systematic training of subordinates. "Too much time," he might say. "We'll do that later. For now, let us just *do*, and through experience the person will learn."

Thus, he prefers the apprenticeship approach, in which subordinates learn by imitating him: "Come and watch me do it. Now do you know what to do? Repeat what I'm doing. OK. Now you're trained."

"Why don't they take some initiative?" the (**P**) often complains. "Who trained me? Nobody! I learned by myself! Why don't they learn? In this business there aren't any secrets; just get the job done. If someone is willing to work hard, he should have no problem getting the job done."

Nor does he like to attend training himself. He'll avoid it. He doesn't believe he has time to go to training, so he will constantly postpone it, as often as he is allowed to: Tomorrow, tomorrow, tomorrow. He will only go for training when actually ordered to do so.

What is proper training? Proper training is to systematize. First you identify the ingredients of success; then you teach people to systematically create those ingredients.

Unfortunately, an apprentice does not know the ingredients for success, or why he is performing the tasks he is performing. He's merely copying: Monkey sees, monkey copies.

The best way to streamline an organization so that it is effective and efficient is to systematize. When you refuse to have people trained, you are losing the opportunity to run an efficient organization.

Hire someone who can systematize the work you do. Then train your workers so that their jobs are systematized and well defined. Finally, delegate some of your work to them. If you pursue this goal systematically, you will eventually be free to pursue the tasks that *only* you can accomplish.

Managing Change

What is, is not necessarily what should be.

The (**P**) is very reality-oriented; he understands what is, and that's all that interests him. He is not concerned with what *should* be or what somebody might *want*. If this is the way it is, then this is how he *wants* it and this is how it *should* be. Is equals *want* equals *should* – period: They are all the same. He is proud of the fact that his feet are planted solidly on the ground, and that his decisions are practical, based on what is and not on what isn't.

But reality is not always so simple. Sometimes what is, is not what *should* be. Sometimes change is necessary; what is must move toward what *should* be.

Let's define *is*, *want*, and *should*. What is, is reality: what is going on right now. What you *want* is in your heart, while *should* is in your head: what your conscience or your sense of obligation dictates. These correspond to Freud's theory of the ego *(is)*, id *(want)* and superego *(should)*.

Often there is a conflict among the three. You *want* to eat this whole box of cookies, but you *are* overweight and you *should* be on a diet. The question is, what will you do? Which of the two will drive your present *(is)* behavior: What you *want* to do or what you *should* do?

It's important to pay attention to *all* the scenarios: *is*, *want*, and *should*. You know there is a reality – OK, fine. That's a good starting point. But it's only a starting point. Now you must ask yourself: What do I *want*? Next, ask yourself: In light of what *is* and what you *want*, what *should* you do?

At each step, you have to compromise. You cannot get everything you *want*, because you must take into account the *is* reality. Furthermore, you must decide whether you *should* proceed, given the costs versus the value of what you want to do.

Ultimately, however, you will have a strategy that is realistic, the real costs and value of which you understand and accept, and which reflects what you *want*. Now go and do it.

To take into account *is*, *want*, and *should*, you need a complementary team. Why? Your focus as a (**P**) is naturally on reality: What *is*, *is*. The (**E**) usually provides the *want* elements for the discussion, and the (**A**) reminds everyone of the *should* elements. (**I**)ntegrated and motivated by the (**I**), you will be able to reach a strategy that is based on reality, reflects what you *want* and takes into account what you *should* do as well.

"Do not say 'tomorrow,' for tomorrow might never happen" (from the Old Testament)

A typical (**P**) hates to go to training, so he always says: "I'll go tomorrow," or, "Not now; I'll go as soon as I have time." But that hardly ever happens, because there is always some crisis du jour.

Let me give you an insight about the human mind: It only works in the present tense. It is like a computer. It takes what you say literally.

For example, let's say you tell yourself, "I will start my diet *tomorrow*."

Now, when you wake up in the morning, your mind asks you, "Is today *tomorrow*?" The answer is, "No. Today is today." So – you will not start your diet. In fact, you will *never* start your diet, unless you make the commitment to do it *now, now, now*.

And that is also true for planning. Planning is *not* what we are going to do tomorrow. It is what we are going to do *today* in light of what we expect to happen tomorrow.

Did you know that some languages do not have a present tense? Why? Think about it. *Is* there really a present time? Barely. It is a split second in passing, an infinitely small, micro-split-second. It barely exists. It is only the transition point between the past and future.

For an (**A**), the present is a continuation of the past. For others – typically (**E**)s – the present is the beginning of the future. ("All I remember is the future," Ted Turner, the founder of CNN, once said.) The expression "Today is the first day of the rest of your life" was probably coined by an (**E**) type.

The (**P**) lives in the *now* only, in a continuous present. But without a future, your present is nothing more than a reaction to the past. You are driving forward while looking into the back mirror.

And if you don't pay attention to tomorrow, by the time tomorrow becomes today, it will be too late to do anything about it.

You must train yourself to plan and deal with the future today. Please note that this is complicated. You are supposed to act today – something you are prone to do anyway – but you must do it with your face to the future.

Training is your preparation for tomorrow. If you don't have time for training, that's the best sign that you need the training.

Not every decision is necessarily a final one.

Once he makes a decision, a (**P**) hates to change it, even when it needs to change. "But we already made this decision! We spent a lot of time on it! Why do we have to change it again?" This resistance to change can be dangerous, because the situation might have changed and might need reevaluating.

But a (**P**), like the field rat with his nose close to the ground, may not realize that the world has changed. Maybe the original solution is no longer applicable; maybe it's outdated.

For an (**E**), change is no problem. But a (**P**) gets extremely annoyed and insists on holding onto a decision once it's made, as if every decision is forever, as if change never happens. Once a decision is finalized, a (**P**) doesn't want to think about it again and won't discuss it anymore. It's been chiseled in stone.

When you make a decision, remind yourself that your decision is "subject to further elaboration and changes." Maintain your flexibility. No decision is a hundred percent. Every decision is "80 percent decided; 20 percent keep-your-eyes-open."

The road to Rome will not necessarily take you there.

Maybe the road's been diverted since the last sign was erected. Or Rome itself may have moved.

What do I mean? Let's take the example of a high-tech company whose success so far has been in developing the latest, fastest, most advanced technology.

But at some point, the market may hit a technological ceiling – meaning that its customers don't have the technical knowledge that's needed to go to the next level. They may not even have caught up with the current level.

What happens then? The market changes. That's when I say Rome has moved. If in the past, "Rome" meant more and more sophisticated machines and higher capabilities, now "Rome" means something else, perhaps machinery that is cheaper, faster, and more reliable.

This requires that the high-tech company change strategies and take a totally different road. Instead of rewarding the genius engineers with stock options and bonuses, for example, it might be necessary to reward the quality assurance people, or those who manage the supply chain. That's a major cultural change for a company. It is a revolution.

In other words, a (**P**) needs to understand that the solution is not always more of the same. You have to be able to see when the road has been diverted and where the new destination is. A typical (**P**) could easily be on the wrong road – Rome may have moved – but continue to believe that if only he can travel faster, he will get there sooner. In reality, he will only reach the wrong destination faster.

Periodically, check and recheck the purpose of your actions. If your efforts are no longer working, you may be on the wrong road. While your head was down, concentrating on doing the same old task the same old way, someone might have built a superhighway next door. Instead of going further and further along the same road, stop walking and look around to see if there's a different and better way.

There is a story about a tourist who got lost. At an intersection he stopped an old man and asked him: "How do I get to such and such city?"

"If I were you," the old man said, "I would not start from here!"

Proact, don't just react.

"If it ain't broke, don't fix it" is a typical (**P**) mantra. (**P**)s wait until something is broken before they make the effort to improve the situation; that's why they invariably find themselves dealing with crises instead of problems. And that is very expensive.

The better idea is to pay attention to small movements and small deviations; then you will only need to take small corrective actions instead of the big, painful changes you would have had to make down the road. It's not necessary to wait till things fall apart before you notice them. Don't just be reactive. Preventive medicine is best.

People who work too hard have no time to make serious money.

(**P**)s work so hard that they never have time to look around and notice better opportunities. They work so hard that they end up selling their sweat, their physical prowess, rather than their brain power. That's why opportunities to make serious money pass them by.

I know you don't think that thinking is doing. Thinking feels like inaction to you, like a waste of time. You hate to take time for it.

But you need to work smarter, not harder, if you want to make it big. Just working hard will put bread on the table, but not much more. Stop doing so much. Instead, start thinking about *what* you're doing. Think about the different imperatives, identify the different choices and pick out the best ones. Test each until you find one that works. The formulas you are using may be in need of improvement or change.

No one knows better than you what needs to change, and – if you take the time to think about it – *how* to change it. Try selling your knowledge rather than your time; you can charge five dollars for hitting the nail, but two hundred dollars for knowing where to hit the nail.

If you feel insecure or embarrassed about charging for solutions and their value rather than for your time, hire an (**E**) who will gladly do it for you. An (**E**) knows quite well what ideas are worth.

TOP TEN PRESCRIPTIONS FOR A PREDOMINANTLY (P) STYLE

1. Do not be a field rat.
2. Focus on *who* is speaking and *why* he is saying what he is saying, rather than exclusively focusing on *what* is being said.
3. "Maybe" is sometimes better than "yes" or "no."
4. Easy does it. You do not need a two-by-four to change or be changed.
5. The squeakiest wheel is not always the most important one. And some problems *can* wait.
6. Focus on the process, not just on the solution.
7. If you are in pain with the decision-making process, become more, not less engaged with it.
8. "Leave it on my desk" is not a solution.
9. Surrounding yourself with errand boys (gofers) is not going to free you.
10. What *is*, is not necessarily what should be.

NOTES

1. Storm, H.: *Seven Arrows* (New York: Harper & Row, 1972).

Chapter 5

(pAei) Prescriptions

BEHAVIOR

Form does not necessarily produce function.

I call this the Captain Queeg syndrome: In *The Caine Mutiny*, by Herman Wouk, there is a war on, but what is the captain spending all his time doing? A comprehensive investigation into who took strawberries from the ship's refrigerator without asking permission.[1]

Sometimes following the form with absolute obedience works; that's why they do it at boot camp. But sometimes the form is so inflexible that it works against the function; that's why partisans and guerrilla forces usually have an advantage over organized, established armies. And when the form undermines the function, that means the form is dysfunctional to the function.

There's a joke from the 1973 Yom Kippur war, in which Israel was battling Egypt in the Sinai. At one point the Egyptians had advanced and were winning; then they stopped moving forward. Why? According to the joke, it was because the Egyptians were trained by the Russians, whose manuals advised using "the Kutuzov strategy," based on General Kutuzov's victory against Napoleon in 1812. It was simple: "Advance, then dig in and wait for the snow to fall."

How can you tell when form is dysfunctional and when it isn't? When you follow the form, and it doesn't produce the results you anticipated, check the *how* part of the process. Maybe *what* you are doing and *why* you are doing it are fine; while the *how* is undermining your results.

Sound simple? It does seem to be, and yet it is not. I wish I myself could follow this "simple" rule in my personal life, in my relations with my children, my spouse, my co-workers. Yes, it sounds simple; but it's precisely our long-established habits – our *hows* – that are the most difficult to change. The *how* also depends on one's personal style, which is almost impossible to change, especially when one is under stress.

Try to remember that form does not necessarily produce the desired results. Check and validate whether the form you have chosen is actually working. If it is not, then you must change it, or be doomed.

To rephrase Pareto's law: 100 percent of 100 percent is sometimes less than 80 percent of 100 percent.

More than a hundred years ago, Vilfred Pareto discovered a statistical relationship that is still unexplained, but is regularly seen in large systems. It's known as "the Eighty-Twenty Rule." In a business, 80 percent of the profits are produced by 20 percent of the products. In a police force, 80 percent of the arrests are made by 20 percent of the officers.

Or, phrased conversely: 20 percent of a business's customers create 80 percent of its problems; 20 percent of your clients give you 80 percent of your revenue.

How does this apply to an (**A**)?

He ignores Pareto's law.

An (**A**) wants perfect control and can spend an enormous amount of time and money trying to attain it.

For example: To get 100 percent of market share can be extremely prohibitive; trying to get that last guy out there to buy from you can cost you more than that customer could ever be worth. So it's not efficient. You have to know when to stop.

The same thing is true for controls. Trying to get 100 percent control can be enormously expensive. I have met quality assurance people who want everything so perfectly controlled that the cost of establishing such controls exceeds the value they get in return.

Despite the fact that you're cost-conscious, you have trouble computing potential value. In other words, you are apt to justify spending money on controls for the sake of controls, not realizing that you're wasting money and suffocating the company.

Learn to do the math first: How much will it cost to increase quality by another 20 percent, and how much will it be worth?

Ambiguity is not the worst evil.

An (**E**) "smells" a market, a trend, a direction, and he wants to jump on it: "We have to move – now!" An (**A**), on the other hand, will usually respond, "I don't feel we're ready for that yet. I don't think the market has expressed itself yet. Let's wait; there's too much risk now."

One reason for this is that an (**A**), like a (**P**), abhors ambiguity. But while a (**P**) will do anything, even the wrong thing, rather than wait for clarity, an (**A**) will wait forever, not comprehending that inaction in times of change can be worse than ambiguity. Unlike an (**E**)ntrepreneur, an (**A**) does not sense a trend, cannot interpret clues in the fog. He will always prefer to hold out for certainty. The danger, of course, is that by the time a trend becomes certain, the opportunity may have been lost. That's why (**A**)s never start companies; only (**E**)s start companies.

Your reluctance to risk changes makes you an obstructionist to new ideas, and that means that the organization must achieve its goals in spite of you. The individuals in the organization who are committed to getting things done learn to bypass you in trying to implement change.

Try to understand that computing risk does not mean rejecting it altogether. Uncertainty is part of the process; you have to learn to live with it and even to welcome it. Without risk, there is no opportunity. Without opportunity, there is no chance of success.

If ambiguity is not the worst evil, then what is? Without a doubt, for you it is inaction in times of change.

The fact that you don't know about something does not mean it isn't happening.

The (**A**) always wants to be sure. An (**A**) is capable of saying, "Zebras don't exist." Why not? "Because I've never seen one." Even if somebody describes a zebra to an (**A**), he still may not believe it, because unless he sees it for himself, he doesn't know it for sure.

But just because you haven't seen it, that doesn't mean it doesn't exist.

You have to trust and respect others and their perceptions and experience. You also have to learn to explore, extrapolate, guess! It's OK to say, "I'm not so sure, but it appears to me...." That's easy for an (**E**), but difficult for you. In order to say it, you must first overcome your style biases and understand that sometimes it really is appropriate!

When someone tells you something is happening, even though you don't know about it and you haven't seen it yourself, go and explore it. Be open.

COMMUNICATION

Not everything must be written into manuals and codified.

(**A**)s have a disease called "manualitis": Everything must be documented; all processes must be written out step by step. Because of that, the written word becomes the dominant determiner of organizational behavior.

Any government bureaucracy, or the United States military, will manifest this disease. For better efficiency, everything goes into a manual, in a language codified with acronyms that you have to be able to decode in order to know what's going on.

But sometimes in real life, you may have to violate some of your efficiency rules in order to respond quickly and be effective in unusual situations. You must be willing to be flexible, to allow for deviations from the norm, to take some shortcuts.

Here is one way I help organizations become more flexible without losing control: I divide an organization's documentation into "policies," "rules," and "guidelines."

"Guidelines" are instructions that can be ignored at will. They are the accumulation of a body of knowledge and experience, written down – for organizational memory – but the implementation is at the discretion of the manager in charge. This freedom is granted because "on the battleground" conditions may be atypical and thus past experience may not apply. That's why they're called *guide*lines.

"Rules" are instructions that a manager in the field *can* violate if he judges that the situation constitutes an exception to the rule.

However, if he does violate a rule, the manager must inform his superior of the violation, because it might call for damage control – or, if the consequences of breaking the rule turn out to be negligible, the supervisor may want to reconsider the wisdom of having such a rule. He may decide that the rule should really be a "guideline."

What is a "policy"? A policy cannot be violated without getting an approval *upfront*. They are decisions that you as a manager want to be sure no one violates without your express prior permission.

An organization should have very few policies. That's why the Bible has only ten commandments, no more, because more would be too difficult to follow. Even ten are too many for some people.

Everyone in the company should know which decisions are policies, which are guidelines, and which are rules.

But when I work with companies, especially global companies in the aging stages of the organizational lifecycle, I often find that the employees are confused about what is a rule, what is a policy and what is a guideline.

When I consult with these companies, I propose that policies, rules, and guidelines should appear on different-colored paper. Guidelines are on white paper, rules are on baby-blue paper, and policies are on rose or pink paper.

Now, when you look at that manual, what should you expect to see? There should be lots of white, less blue, and only a few pages of pink.

There is nothing wrong with having a manual with lots of guidelines, as long as you *call* them guidelines.

But if you do not distinguish among them in an organized fashion, here's what will happen: For the big (-A--)s in your organization, everything will be a rule or a policy. For an (--E-), because he changes his mind all the time, everything will become a guideline by default. A (P) will be totally confused. If he works for an (A) he will become paralyzed, and if he works for an (E) he will get so frustrated he'll lose confidence in his decisions.

Another danger is that if you have too many manuals – too many rules, too many policies – the organization ages rapidly. The difference between a young organization and an old one is that in a young organization, everything is allowed unless specifically forbidden. In an old organization, everything is forbidden unless specifically permitted. When there are too many policy manuals, at a certain point the organizational culture changes. Employees start to assume that everything they want to do must be forbidden somewhere – unless it's specifically permitted. So everybody asks for permission instead of forgiveness. Eventually, the climate becomes so moribund that people decide, "I'd better not do this unless I get specific permission, because somewhere there is probably a rule prohibiting it."

In a very large bureaucratic organization, nobody moves unless they get permission from somebody in their department – and it better be in writing! (This is called CYA: "Cover your ass.")

In your company, do you know which category each decision belongs in? If not, you should straighten it out. Write them all down and categorize them.

If you don't say it, how will they know it?

An (**A**) always keeps his mouth shut; he doesn't disclose what he thinks. Like an (**I**), he's very closed-mouthed.

People always know what a (**P**) is thinking because he will tell you, as does an (**E**), who likes to think out loud and will tell you what he thinks even if you haven't asked him. So in a meeting, the (**E**)s go back and forth, changing their minds constantly; the (**P**)s fidget in their seats; the (**I**)s listen; and the (**A**)s take notes. It's comical to watch.

But holding back does not always work to an (**A**)'s advantage: If you don't speak up and share your thoughts with others, how will people know what you're thinking?

On the one hand, your mysterious silence gives you a lot of power. Why? Because information is power. When people don't know what you know, they fear you because of what you know. So it's true that the more you share information the less power you have.

On the other hand, you leave yourself open to lots of misinterpretation and ambiguity. People have to guess at the meaning of your silence; and of course, they can easily guess wrong.

I know it is difficult for you to share information, because you don't like to speak until your ideas are all clear and organized, logical, defensible, and protected, so you won't get into trouble. But you can get into just as much trouble by remaining silent. Your co-workers can imagine that you think the opposite of what you really think.

So say what you think; then add, if necessary: "It's just a thought."

Speak first. Think more later.

This relates to the prescription above.

Watch an (**E**), who thinks aloud. In a meeting, the (**E**)s are having a field day: They're all shouting at each other, talking over each other, interrupting each other.

Meanwhile, you, an (**A**), are most probably sitting quietly and therefore being ignored. The (**E**)s and (**P**)s think there's something wrong with you – "Why isn't he speaking? Doesn't he have *any* ideas?" – when in fact you are very intelligent but don't like to join the fray until you're absolutely sure what you want to say.

Furthermore, since you usually participate only to ask questions about details and about risk, you may be viewed as an obstructionist, obsessed with minutiae, who must be ignored if anything is ever going to change in the company.

So being silent is not necessarily a good thing, especially in an environment where others are speaking their minds. By not participating, you are abstaining from the complementary decision-making process.

It's OK to contribute an idea for discussion, even when you're not sure you're committed to it yet. Say, "Look, this is just an idea." All the I's can be dotted and T's can be crossed later.

Item (C) does not necessarily have to follow item (B). It depends on what one wants to say.

(A)s are very linear thinkers – they are only comfortable proceeding from A to B to C to D to E to F to G.

But sometimes G relates to A and A relates to Y and Y relates to J and J relates to B. Sometimes A, B, C, D is the correct sequence, but sometimes it's D, E, M, A.

If you look at a business holistically, you can see that many elements are interdependent. Who is involved? How is the situation changing? What is the driving force? Sometimes it's the market, sometimes it's the product, sometimes it's the technology, sometimes it's something else altogether. So the discussion will roam, depending on the sequence of the facts that are being considered.

Most (A)s – and also (P)s, by the way – hate this nonlinear progression; they don't understand this kind of discussion and are sure it's illogical and a waste of time.

But it's important to learn to listen to an argument from many different directions. The fact that it doesn't follow a linear progress doesn't mean that the discussion is illogical.

Stay calm. Like they say, happiness is not a destination but a journey. It's the same thing here: Join the journey. The team is exploring different alternatives and possibilities. Nothing has been decided yet. We are just kissing; we are not getting married. So what's the worry?

Slower is not clearer.

An (**A**) interprets speed as lack of quality. He moves slowly, ponderously. He punctuates everything he says; he takes his time. He thinks about each detail; then he thinks again.

When an (**A**) senses confusion, he slows down his speech still further. Why? He believes if he goes slower, what he's saying will become clearer.

But slower doesn't mean clearer. In any case, it may not be confusion you're sensing. It may be disagreement. It may even be frustration with your lack of speed.

Being precise can be very imprecise.

For an (A), $999,999.50 is not a million; 8:31 is not 8:30. They're very precise, very literal.

An (**A**) will bring you a budget of $300,150,178.96 – and he isn't joking! He pays attention to the number to the very last digit – at the expense of the total picture. He may be focused on the wrong market, the wrong product – the wrong direction! – but his numbers are calculated to the third decimal.

Why this detail orientation? Because he prefers not to take risks. He wants everything safe and precise. And that obsession with being precise can ultimately cause him to fail big-time.

I've seen (**A**)s who will do strategic planning, pages and pages and pages of charts and curves and tables – and entirely miss the big picture. They can describe each tree down to the roots, but they cannot tell you what the forest looks like or where it is. This is a disease I call "overheaditis" or "Powerpointitis": Too many PowerPoint presentations, too many overheads. The lights are down, it's dark in the room, and as (**A**)s go through pages and pages and pages of details, trying to prove a point, a participant may wonder exactly what the point is.

To force yourself to see the big picture, it helps to begin by writing a one-page summary. Start from the end. Start with the conclusions and then substantiate your points with the tables and charts.

I repeat. *Start from the end* – don't start from the beginning and hope that the participants will derive the same conclusions as you have.

When you don't know for sure, say you don't know for sure. That's OK, as long as you pay attention to the direction you're going in. The budget doesn't have to be precise as long as it's in the right direction.

DECISION-MAKING

You might know the cost of everything, but do you know the value of anything?

This is the curse of an (**A**). He usually does not pay attention to the value of a thing, for the following reason: The cost is for sure, the value is maybe.

For example, if the organization is trying to decide whether to penetrate a certain market, an (**A**) will say, "Can we afford it?"

But that's before there has been any discussion of the potential return from that market. This makes the marketing people – usually (**E**) types – very angry.

It's true that the value is less certain than the costs. But that does not necessarily make the value less important. Unless you spend some money, you're not going to make money. Unless you pay attention to the value, you risk allowing little if anything to happen around you.

*You can't expect to hit the jackpot if you don't
put a few nickels in the machine.*

FLIP WILSON

Evaluate the risk, certainly. Then evaluate the probability of success, and then compare the two. You must learn to give weight to value.

It is better to be approximately right than precisely wrong.

An (**A**) spends an excessive amount of time worrying about (**A**)dministrative details. He prefers to do things right rather than do the right things. In other words, he would rather be precisely wrong than approximately right. To use a tennis analogy: An (**A**) would probably prefer to wait until he knows exactly where the ball is going to land before he goes to hit it. But by that time, of course, it's too late.

An (**E**) manager, on the other hand, will proact. He will try to imagine where the ball is going to go, and he'll go there and get ready to hit it.

Sometimes an educated guess is better than a minutely researched fact. There is nothing wrong with acting based on your intuition, hypothesis, or reasonable assumptions. If you can prove your hypothesis, great. But you can't always wait for proof.

Try to guess where the ball is going to land; then get over there and hit it. You *might* be wrong. Nevertheless, waiting for the ball to land *before* you go to hit it is *precisely* wrong. You're making the right movement in the right direction; you go there, but you hit nothing. The process is perfect – except you were totally ineffective.

The fact that a problem has a long history does not mean there must be a long process of solving it.

When you ask an (**A**), "What is the problem?" he usually starts back with Adam and Eve – "In the beginning ..." – and gives you the whole history of the problem.

Having this 2000+ years perspective of the problem, how long does he think it will take to solve it? Another few thousand years, of course.

An (**A**) perceives every problem as very complicated, very big and overwhelming; he sees the problem in the past and the solution somewhere vaguely in the future. And it takes forever to make anything happen. I call this "paralysis from over-analysis."

An (**E**), in contrast, sees the problem in the future; and "the problem" is usually defined as the opportunities we are not exploiting. He gets very upset about the future and hardly remembers the problems that need to be dealt with now. In fact, when confronted with problems he often asks, "Why haven't we solved this *already?*" In other words, it's the solution (**E**)s see that should have been done already in the past.

That's why (**A**)s and (**E**)s are often in conflict. The (**A**) starts to explain "the problem" by beginning in the ancient past, and the (**E**), who has a short attention span, says, "Stop! That's not what the problem is," and starts talking about the future. They are like trains passing in the night. The (**A**) says: "It will take some serious time to deal with this issue," and the (**E**) says: "Why haven't you done it *already*!!!"

A (**P**), on the other hand, just wants to know, "What do we need to do now?" And the (**I**) is watching the back-and-forth like a tennis game, complaining, "Why can't we communicate? Why don't we understand each other?"

I know that you, as an (**A**), think that since the problem is so deeply imbedded, the solution has to be complicated.

Absolutely not.

Even a longtime problem with deep roots may not need a big, complicated solution. In fact, sometimes, to gain time, it makes sense to alleviate some of the symptoms quickly, and deal with the longer-term stuff later on.

Not everything that is broken needs to be fixed.

I once worked with an executive who ran a company with a very strong, uncooperative union. One day I was following him up a flight of stairs, and I noticed that the stairs were quite dirty. I asked him, "Why don't you do something about it?"

"Because I have bigger fish to fry," he said. "If I use my political clout on this, there will be other, much bigger things that I would have to let go. You have to know when to use your political power wisely. You have to learn to live with some stuff you don't like."

An (**A**) wants everything to be in tip-top shape at all times. But the political cost of fixing everything could be prohibitive. You may not have enough political capital to control absolutely everything. It's important to set priorities.

Don't forget the future.

An (**A**) often takes power in a company when the company is already in trouble financially. He is hired specifically because the board of directors believes he will bring some "law and order" and cost control to the organization.

So, following his mandate, the (**A**) pays attention to every cent and slashes costs ruthlessly.

Unfortunately, an (**A**) doesn't know much about how to increase sales; all he knows how to do is cut costs. Meanwhile, the (**E**)ntrepreneur, who may have built the company, has paid no attention to costs, so the two are immediately at each other's throats. "All he knows how to do is turn out the lights at the end of the day, so no energy is wasted," the (**E**)ntrepreneur complains. And the (**A**) feels that the (**E**) is an unguided missile, charging heedlessly at every moving target and wasting the company's money.

In the short run, of course, cutting costs will make the company look very profitable. But don't over-cut. It's easy to cut costs and look very good very fast, but if you cut expenses that are necessary for increasing sales, your company can look profitable while it is actually going bankrupt, because there is a time lag between cost-cutting and the decline of sales.

Remember the long run. Balance value against costs if you want both efficiency *and* effectiveness. Remember what happened to Apple Computers after Steve Jobs was squeezed out of the company: If you squeeze the (**E**) out, your organization might be better organized and run more smoothly, but you might also lose the source of the ideas that built your company and that are necessary for its future survival.

Stop thinking that everything is prohibited unless it is specifically permitted.

(**A**)s like to maintain maximum efficiency, so they make lots and lots of policies and rules and put them into manuals.

But this obsession with efficiency can be detrimental to effectiveness and cause an organization to age prematurely. If every single action is codified, people start to assume that unless something is specifically permitted, it must be prohibited. They will feel they have to ask for permission each time they want to take some initiative.

If you're so efficient that you've got every possible scenario written down with rules, your employees' spontaneity and ability to react quickly to change will be compromised and perhaps paralyzed.

Establish a limited number of necessary rules and policies. Don't worry about the guidelines. Then, any time people violate the rules, re-examine them yourself: Maybe they shouldn't be rules; maybe they should be guidelines instead. Or maybe a policy should be a rule. Test everything continually to see whether it works well for the organization. Keep in mind that all policies and rules should be evaluated in terms of whether they serve (**P**) and (**E**). If they merely serve (**A**) purposes, watch out: You might be bureaucratizing the company unnecessarily.

Something else to remember: If your staff has to ask permission for everything, that means you have to be on the premises all the time.

Besides, you don't have enough time in the day to give permission for everything. The company will suffocate and become stymied. It's important to give yourself and others permission to take initiative and make mistakes; in other words, it should be OK to ask forgiveness. Asking forgiveness can be more effective – and in the long run, more efficient – than asking permission.

A solution does not have to have precedents.

An (**A**), when presented with a solution, will usually want to know: "Who else has done it that way?" "Where else has it been success-ful?"

This makes a company a follower rather than a leader.

Of course, if there really is some precedent, if there is some proof that the proposed solution has already worked somewhere else, then it's always nice to learn from others' experience.

But if not, why shouldn't your organization be the first one to try it? If you try it and it succeeds, you have an advantage over ev-erybody else, because you've accumulated knowledge and experience that nobody else has as yet.

If it is similar, it is not totally different. But it is similar.

Often, when an (**A**) hears the team discussing two alternative solu-tions that are very close, he cannot see the similarities. An (**A**) will automatically widen the differences. An (**A**) looks at cracks, and every crack looks like the Grand Canyon.

He will argue, "No, these alternatives are totally different."

In my organizational therapy, I try to show that the word "or" is sometimes a barrier to team problem-solving. It's not either/or. It doesn't have to be A or B. It's possible to have both – A *and* B – by choosing the best qualities of A and the best qualities of B and thus creating an alternative, C, that capitalizes on both A and B.

But for an (**A**), that's very difficult to do. For him, A is different from B and that's it.

"But they are similar," I tell (**A**)s. "You can unite them. The fact that they are similar doesn't mean that they are different. They are similar. So maybe we can find something in between."

Try to find the similarities in the various options under discussion, instead of only looking at the differences. (**I**)ntegration occurs when a consensus can be created by compromise, and compromise usually means taking the best of one plan, and the best of another plan, and more from a third. This is possible when you look at the big picture instead of the tiny details. If you take a more global view, there will almost always be something universal in all the various proposals.

Stop worrying about what should be and pay more attention to what is.

Is, want, and *should* are very different perspectives that create a lot of conflict and frustration in human life, because we often confuse one for another.

For instance, right *now* (the *is* perspective), you *are* reading this book. While you are reading this book, it might cross your mind that what you *should* be doing is some paperwork that has been waiting a long time for your attention. And at the same time, while you are reading this book and thinking that you *should* be doing something else, what you really *want* to do is go on vacation and leave all these problems behind.

(**A**) types tend to focus on the *should* scenario. An (**A**)'s reasoning is: "It *should* be a certain way; therefore that's how I *want* it; therefore it is. I *want* things to be the way they *should* be."

An (**E**), on the other hand, thinks: "I *want* it; therefore it *should* be; therefore it is. Since I *want* it this way, then this is how it *should* be."

But what is the reality? What is the *is*?

Here is one example from my work with organizations: About ten years ago a company in Brazil, a third-generation family business, asked me to come in and try to solve the disputes among the owners. They were fighting for control but no faction had enough votes to overrule the others.

I came and analyzed the company, and what I found *was* that during the heyday of the Brazilian economy, when economic conditions were very promising, this company had taken large loans with American banks, in dollars. Then the economy soured, the Brazilian rate of exchange went south, and all at once these dollar loans were putting tremendous pressure on the company's finances; 95 percent of its earnings had to be paid in finance charges to the American banks.

So I called a meeting of the third-generation owners, all 35 of them, and asked them: "Who owns the company?"

They said, "We do. We own the stock; it was given to us by our parents and grandparents. We own the company. Everybody has shares."

And I replied: "I know you *should* and *want* to own the company, but if 95 percent of the profits and the earnings go to the banks, who *actually* benefits from this company?

"What *does* it mean to own an asset that gives you nothing in return? You've got a piece of paper while the money is going to the banks. So in reality you really *don't* own any benefits of your ownership and it will remain so as long as you fight among yourselves. As it is right now, you might inherit zero at the end of the day. What you *want* and *should* have will not truly be yours until you *work together* to change the condition the company is in."

The same syndrome is evident in the Middle East. A Palestinian state will eventually be established, because it reflects reality. It is not what some Israelis believe *should* happen; however, millions of Palestinians *are* not going to disappear overnight. And for the militant Palestinians, Israel's existence *is* also a reality they will eventually have to accept, because millions of Israeli Jews are not going to disappear overnight either. They *are* there to stay.

But for this *Realpolitik* to take hold, the sequence of reasoning must be reversed: *is > want > should*, instead of *should > want > is*.

Notice that the *should > want > is thinking* – whether it's Islamic Jihad or Hamas on one side, or the religious, militant Jews on the other – is (-**A**--) reasoning: You do what the Torah or the Koran says you *should* do. These extremists all try to force the *is* to become the way they think it *should* be, and in doing so they cause thousands of innocent people to die.

To test your understanding of the *is/want/should* confusion, ana-lyze this statement by House Majority Whip Tom DeLay, R-Texas, as quoted in *USA Today* on Aug. 22, 2002. DeLay was responding to criticism of how President Bush was handling Saddam Hussein:

"Every generation must summon the courage to disregard the timid counsel of those who would mortgage our security to the false promises of wishful thinking and appeasement. ... The question is not whether to go to war, for war already has been thrust upon us."

What is the *is/want/should* sequence in his reasoning and in those he is criticizing? (Hint: They are not presented in the normal sequence.) The answer is below, at the end of this entry.

So the real question is always: What is the reality, not what *should* it be? People of different styles reason differently. The (**P**) thinks that whatever is happening is what *should* be happening; an (**E**) thinks that whatever he *wants* is what *should* happen. You, an (**A**), are so focused on what *should* happen that you cannot see what is.

Forget the *should* for a few minutes. Analyze what *is* going on. Listen to what the (**P**) is saying and what the (**E**) *is* saying.

Now put the two arguments together, and ask yourself: After taking *reality* into account, what do I *want?*

Then add cost and implementation considerations and think about what you *should* do.

Your final decision should reflect the *is, want,* and *should* elements in the right sequence. To reach a valid decision, your thought process must be disciplined, and you need to listen to others whose style and preferences are different from your own.

Can you do it?

If not, your decisions will be faulty and sooner or later your organization is going to be stymied.

Answer to Tom DeLay question: DeLay's reasoning is: What *is*, is what we *should* do (is=should):

"Every generation must *[should]* summon the courage to disregard the counsel of those who would mortgage our security.... The question is not whether to go to war, for war already has been thrust upon us *[is]*." In other words, we *should* accept what is. This is (**P**) thinking.

Those who "mortgage our security to the false promises of wishful thinking and appeasement," according to DeLay, apparently believe that *what* they want is what *should* be (*want=should*). This is (**E**) thinking.

IMPLEMENTING

The more you write it down, the less chance it will get done as written.

There is a Sephardic expression – *Todu que es demasiadu no valle* – that means: "All that is extreme, all that is exaggerated, is no good."

I had dinner once with a very famous professor of medicine. I asked him, "If you could summarize the whole field of medicine in one word, what would that word be?"

"Moderation," he said without hesitation. In other words, if you sleep too much it's no good; if you don't sleep at all it's no good. If you eat too much it's no good; if you don't eat at all it's no good.

It's the same thing here. An (-**A**--) is an extreme, just like an (--**E**-) is an extreme. Both need to develop moderation if they are going to work together, and they must work together since the organization needs them both. (By the same line of reasoning, you also have to work on your marriage, with your spouse, whose style I'd bet is 180 degrees different from yours. Your styles, however, are complimentary, and that is probably why you married her or him in the first place – so your offspring would grow up well rounded and emotionally healthy. You must find a way to make your differences in style enrich rather than threaten each other.

For an (**E**), I recommend writing everything down. But for an (**A**) I suggest the opposite. Don't *write* it all down. If you write it all down, what's going to happen? Everybody's going to waste time trying to cover their butts. How? By making sure there's a record of what was said and when it was said and how it was said, and having it all filed away so they can produce it on short notice to protect themselves. And time spent doing that can suffocate the company. Every word gets analyzed to death, and people spend more time comparing and interpreting notes than actually implementing the decisions that were communicated in the notes in the first place.

No decision is permanent.

An (**A**) hates change. He's the opposite of an (E), who lives to make changes. A typical (**A**) will say, "We did research, we spent money, we analyzed, and we decided what to do. So we are not going to revisit this decision anymore."

But why not? Everything is a study in progress. Environments change, and thus whatever you decided might *have* to change down the road. In fact, it is the process of implementation that often causes the change, because as you're implementing you might discover that some of your decisions were impractical for reasons that couldn't have been foreseen.

Don't make a decision and walk away from it: "We've decided, that's it, goodbye." Watch closely as your decision is implemented; keep your eyes open because you never know for sure what the future will bring.

It's like watching your toddlers grow. You can't let them move around without supervision, because you don't know what's going to happen next. You have to constantly watch. In the same way, decisions may need to change as implementation occurs – not always, but with a high rate of change it is a real probability.

Of course, you also have to make prudent decisions, looking at the cost of the change versus the value of the change. Either way can be very expensive: Too much flexibility versus not enough. The real answer is somewhere in between the two, which is why (**A**)s and (**E**)s need to work together. Then the right amount of change is going to happen.

Controls mushroom. Sometimes, success depends on how much you can let go.

When the new president of SAS, Jan Carlzon, took over about twenty years ago, he called a meeting and publicly discarded all of the company's manuals. Then he said, "Let's start from the beginning."

Why? Because he knew that controls reproduce themselves. I'll explain. Let us say that you are trying to control something. So you write some rules. Naturally, you will soon find some deviations or exceptions, right? So in order to control the deviations, you create more rules, more manuals. That's going to lead to finding even more deviations.

The manuals become more and more detailed, more and more minute, until no one will be able to make a move without consulting a manual. There will be bottlenecks everywhere you look, and you will have effectively suffocated the company.

Holding tightly to the rules won't make the situation better. You're merely confusing quantity with quality. If you increase the number of reports, details, and forms for people to fill out, you're holding very tightly to the controls. But that doesn't mean quality will improve. It might actually worsen, because people will be spending most of their time reading and writing reports instead of doing their jobs.

Don't become a bottleneck, and don't create them. Maybe the answer is to throw out some of those forms. To succeed, you may have to let go. How much can you let go? How much can you relax?

When there's a choice, do the right things instead of just doing things right.

This is a major difference between an (**E**) and an (**A**). An (**E**) often does the right things in the wrong way, while the (**A**) will do the wrong things, but using the precisely right method.

Who does the right things right? Saints, but unfortunately there are very few of them. Doing the wrong things wrong is for schlemiels, and they are not qualified to be managers.

So what do we need? A complementary team. The (**E**) decides what are the right things to do, and the (**A**) decides how to do them right. Then the (**P**) goes and *does* it. The organization gets the right things done right. Everyone should be happy.

"Why, this broth we made is magnificient"

Drawing by Dana Fradon; © 1976
The New Yorker Magazine, Inc.

Some time ago, I had an acquaintance who wanted to open a restaurant. She was a highly qualified chef, but was inexperienced in business. I told her, "Look for an (**A**) first. If you find one you like and appreciate and trust and want as your partner, then start looking for investors and a location. Otherwise, go take a cold shower." In other words, you are a great cook: You can prepare the dishes and present them beautifully. Look for an (**A**) who can manage your cost controls and accounting; otherwise you're going to lose your life savings.

Whenever I counsel an (**E**), I tell him to work with an (**A**); whenever I coach an (**A**) I ask if he has an (**E**). Every organization needs a complementary team.

There is more than one way.

An (**A**) designs a system, he spends money on the system, and he stays with the system. If someone suggests that there is an alternative system, that will upset him. Even the question of whether there is another way *is* a call to arms for an (**A**).

This is also true for a (**P**): The road he's on is the right road to be on. That is what he thinks, and he is too busy walking on that road to even talk to you about alternatives. He won't consider moving to a different road because he's too busy running to start changing.

If you ask an (**E**) whether there is another way, he will say, "Yes, sure, easy!" and suggest a few. But if you ask him, "Which is the *best* way?" he has difficulty. (**E**)s want to have flexibility and freedom, so they avoid committing themselves to one particular plan. They like all alternatives for different reasons.

As an (**A**), you are very good at analyzing why a particular road has deficiencies. But when you are asked, "Do you have an alternative road?" you have difficulty coming up with one.

So, use an (**E**) to generate alternatives for you. Then select the best of them. If you do not like any of the alternatives, tell the (**E**) more precisely what you're looking for and guess what? He will deliver more alternatives for your consideration.

Do not get stymied by your own style deficiencies. Use others to complement you so that you can make better decisions.

Team-building

Stop being naive. Not everybody agrees with you.

When an (**A**) runs a meeting, it is a very well-controlled disaster. The agenda is organized. Everyone honors the timetable. The meeting is very efficient. But the real problems are not discussed. There is an American expression – "the dead moose syndrome" – that is an analogy to some huge issue that everyone is aware of but no one is willing to discuss. In an (**A**)'s department, the dead moose is lying right in the middle of the conference room, rotting and stinking, while everyone keeps talking about small details of implementation and pretending the moose isn't there.

Why do they ignore the dead moose? Because if someone brought it up, the (**A**) would immediately appoint a committee to investigate who was at fault and who is going to pay the price. It's political suicide to open the door to this discussion. So people avoid it. "Everything is fine" is their motto. They just keep quiet. The company is going broke, but on time.

So watch it: the fact that people don't speak up doesn't mean that they agree with you. They're just intimidated and scared.

One helpful technique is to let someone else run your meetings. You can understand much more from the sidelines than you do sitting in the hot seat.

To have a team, you must let people disagree with each other — and with you.

An (**A**) wants to control, so he expects everyone to agree, agree, agree. Most people sense that and will avoid arguing. As a result, the (**A**) thinks, "OK, we have teamwork."

No! Teamwork does not mean that everyone surrenders or simply acquiesces. To have teamwork, you must have disagreements. Why? Because as we disagree, we learn from each other and enrich each other. A learning environment is created and nourished.

The reason Jewish people tend to be very smart, for example, is because they disagree with each other all the time. On absolutely anything. They even disagree that they are disagreeing. But argument forces people to think.

While disagreements can be enlightening if handled appropriately, all four mismanagement types hate disagreement. An (--**E**-) perceives disagreement as a personal attack on him. (He loves to disagree with others, however.) A (**P**---) believes that disagreements are a waste of time: "Let's just get our act together and get to work." For an (---**I**), disagreement means conflict, and conflict must be prevented at all costs. For an (-**A**--), who believes that disagreements could lead to change and loss of control, disagreements are simply taboo.

I believe that disagreements are natural and healthy. It is through disagreement and conflict that we can make better, more informed decisions.

Also, as the Zen expression says: "If all people agree on everything, none of them is thinking too hard." Or, to put it another way: "If two people agree on everything, one of them is unnecessary."

Start your meetings by telling everyone, "At the end of the day I'm going to make the decision. But first, I want to hear what you have to say, and I would appreciate hearing your disagreements so I can make a well-judged, well-articulated decision."

If you start off by saying that, you won't have to worry that a disagreement might undermine the solution, or that you will lose control. You *are* in control, so relax and let people disagree. Listen to them. Disagreement does not threaten you. In fact, it does the opposite: If you allow disagreements to emerge in front of you, you will find out where the opposition is coming from. On the other hand, if you try to implement a decision *without* knowing where the disagreements are, you might encounter a lot of resistance without being able to pinpoint its source.

Don't forget: *You* are always in control, because at the end of the day *you* are the one who will make the final decision. Listening to people's disagreements won't change that.

Teams must have flexibility.

(**A**)s like to manage everything "by the book." But the fastest way to kill a creative team session is to set the agenda so inflexibly that every item for discussion is limited to a specific number of minutes.

Setting a specific time frame for each item is actually a very good technique for reviewing decisions already taken, or for sharing information. But it's the kiss of death for meetings that are meant for brainstorming, for designing, creating, or diagnosing.

The fact is that you can never tell how long the creative process is going to take. So you must maintain flexibility and the freedom to think aloud. Let the meeting be inefficient if you want it to be effective.

MANAGING STAFF

Fewer meetings will get more things done.

(**A**)s schedule an inordinate number of meetings and spend them obsessively trying to control details. The time devoted to all these meetings and details can be prohibitively expensive.

You don't need to have this many meetings, and it is not efficient to gather a team together merely to work out small details. If you had a clock that could calculate hours and minutes in dollars, and you could see the cost per hour for each person sitting in one of your meetings, you would be shocked at how much money you spend on meetings.

Stop managing by memos.

This is a symptom of the disease I've mentioned before: manualitis. An (**A**) incessantly devises new policies and rules; everything goes into a manual or into memos. Now that we have e-mail and voice mail, an (**A**) can be even more dangerous: He will suffocate his staff with instructions. An (**A**)'s subordinates typically spend an enormous amount of time reading, writing, and filing memos, documenting every move they make.

You believe that by holding tightly to the controls and forcing conformity to the rules, you will improve efficiency. But at the same time, you are curbing your effectiveness. It may look to you like you're running a very efficient organization, because everything is documented, but if you look at your organization's effectiveness instead, you'll be shocked and disappointed.

Try, instead, to manage by results. Tell your staff what results you expect, and let them find their own way to get there. Give them a few policies – what not to do – to be sure that something critical is not violated. Give them some rules. Then stop! Everything else should be merely a guideline. You may be surprised to find that you've improved effectiveness without losing efficiency.

Arriving and leaving right on time does not mean your staff is doing the right things in between.

An (**A**) arrives on time and leaves on time. His subordinates will also tend to come on time and leave on time. They grasp very quickly that what they do in between is not important; as long as they show up on time and leave on time they will have the (**A**)'s approval.

Once again, that's putting form ahead of function. It's good that people arrive and leave on time, but what really matters is what they're doing while they're there. Don't assume they're doing the right things.

On the other hand, don't assume that if someone is late to arrive or to leave, he is being negligent. Listen to his explanations if he is late; there might be a good reason. And most important, watch what people actually do while they're at work.

"Yes–yes" men do "no–no" behind your back.

"No," to an (**A**), is a challenge. This is also true of an (**E**). People who like control, like (**A**)s and (**E**)s, tend to surround themselves with "yes-yes men." The Bureaucrat, or (-**A**--), likes to surround himself with people who have the mentality of office clerks: they always agree with him, and they are almost religiously guided by the rulebook. Thus, an organization managed by an (-**A**--) will look organized and clean and perfect – until someone decides to lift the carpet, where he uncovers an unbelievable mess.

Why? Because an (**A**)'s subordinates learn never to acknowledge problems or show deviations from the rule. When asked: "How is it going?" their stock answer is, "Everything is under control" – when in reality they are frantically stuffing problem after problem under the carpet.

Why this denial? In a word: Fear. If the Bureaucrat's subordinates present him with a problem, they know he will appoint a committee to look for the perpetrator – and who knows where the witch hunt will end? Eventually, it might reach out with its octopus arms and entangle the person who originally made the complaint. Better to be quiet....

As an (**A**), you prefer to hire people who are compliant and don't make waves. But be very careful: It is often the people who say "Yes, yes" in front of you who are whispering "No, no," behind your back in the corridors. And if you react negatively to problems and disagreements, you are in effect encouraging them to hide the facts from you.

With subordinates of this type, you will never know whether you are truly in control. You won't know where the opposition lies and where the subversion is occurring. On the surface it all looks good, but underneath it's rotten.

Encourage your staff to voice their objections directly to you instead of to each other behind your back. That way, you'll know what those objections are and where they come from, and even more important, you can deal with them as they arise instead of discovering them when they begin to fester.

But to effectively convince your staff to confide in you, you will have to somehow convince them that shooting the messenger is not part of your plan, nor is retribution going to be your focus.

When you hire, put those tests aside. Does it feel right?

An (**A**) is very mechanistic. He likes everything documented, fully supported, and easily defensible. Thus, he likes to use a lot of tests and examinations before deciding whether to hire someone.

Unfortunately, a test can't tell you everything you need to know. Sometimes all the answers are right and the person looks right on paper, but your gut is telling you something's wrong.

Often, you will hire the person anyway, only to find out later that your gut was right and the tests were wrong.

By relying on tests alone, you deny your own feelings and intuition, which are really the accumulated knowledge of your past. That's a mistake. Use the tests, but then put the test results aside and ask your heart, ask your guts: How does it feel? Don't ignore your past experiences; let them speak to you. Otherwise you could turn out to be, again, precisely wrong.

Delegation is not synonymous with decentralization. In order to decentralize, freedom to make non-programmed decisions must be granted.

Let's define our terms: When I delegate, I tell you what to do. When I decentralize, I only tell you what not to do; in other words, I give you boundaries, and you decide what to do, being mindful of those boundaries.

Decentralizing creates an environment that encourages (**E**)ntrepreneurship, commitment, enthusiasm, ownership, and loyalty from the staff. Delegating creates a different environment altogether.

Because an (**A**) is afraid of losing control, his tendency is to delegate rather than decentralize. He also confuses the two and believes that by delegating he's decentralizing. Then he cannot understand why the desired environment and results never occur.

I had a client, an executive, who told me a story about his prior career in the Israeli air force. An airplane – a MiG – from Egypt crossed the border into Israel, and my client, a pilot, was sent to intercept it and possibly shoot it down. He was in radio contact with the chief of the air force during the entire incident.

Now, an Israeli air force policy is that pilots may never cross into enemy air space during a dog fight. So while my client was chasing the MiG, his commander in chief, worried that he might cross into Egyptian air space, told him, "Disengage." My client responded, "I hear you," and continued chasing the MiG. The commander told him again to disengage. My client ignored him, continued the chase, and eventually shot the MiG down without crossing the Egyptian line.

I asked my client, "Didn't you get court-martialed? You got explicit orders from the chief of staff to disengage."

"Oh no, I got a commendation," he told me.

In the Israeli air force, if you are in the field and you get an order that you believe is wrong, you can ignore it, because it is assumed that the person in the field knows best. But you'd better be right. Had my client crossed into enemy territory, he might have been court-martialed. But he succeeded in shooting the MiG down in Israeli territory, without violating international borders, so instead he was commended.

In this example, it was not the form but the function that counted. Had it been an air force policy to obey an order regardless of results, if the form rather than the function were the driving force, then my client would have been court-martialed for violating orders, regardless of what happened to the enemy MiG.

When you decentralize, don't go overboard deciding which policies and rules to keep. You need only a few policies, a few more rules – and a lot of guidelines. Don't let the form take over.

Then, measure by results. Negotiate with your staff to set goals they should achieve, and allow them to improvise. As long as they clearly understand the policies, the rules, and the expected results, they can aim for those goals within the boundaries you've set.

And what is your job? You monitor them, making sure they aren't violating any policies or rules, and making your expertise available to help them achieve the agreed-upon results.

You hate to hear complaints, but silence can equal apathy – one step away from death.

When an (**A**) asks his subordinates how things are going, they usually answer, "Just fine," and the reason for that, as we discussed above, is because they fear the (**A**) will react to problems by becoming even more controlling. If there is a problem, the (**A**) will call a meeting and conduct a witch hunt. He will devise lots of new policies and rules to prevent a repetition of the problem.

That makes life even tougher for the (**A**)'s subordinates, so naturally they avoid the predicament by simply being silent about problems.

The trouble is that the (**A**) has absolutely no way of knowing what, if anything, is happening beneath that silence. A tornado could be brewing; or even worse, total apathy may have set in – "yes-yes men" gradually becoming Deadwood. I know a fairy tale that illustrates this very well:

There was once a king who told his ministers to raise the taxes. The ministers went out to tell the people, and when they returned they said, "Your majesty, the people are screaming, the people are crying, the taxes are too high." And the king said, "Increase the taxes."

The ministers increased the taxes again, and came back saying, "Your majesty, the people are crying even harder, crying to the skies, to heaven – the taxes are too high." But the king told his ministers to increase the taxes even more.

The ministers did so. This time when they returned, they reported, "Everything is fine now, Your majesty. The people are very quiet." And the king said, "Oh my God! Quick! Reduce the taxes!"

When people are silent, apathy has taken over. Productivity is zero. Innovation is zero. Eventually there will be no revenues to tax.

As long as there is noise, you know what is going on. Silence can mean anything, and usually this "anything" is not what you want. Maybe your staff has given up in frustration and don't want to work anymore. Or maybe they're hoarding their energies for a revolution.

If everything looks fine and under control, be very careful. The situation might actually be the opposite: Nothing is fine and nothing is under control.

Managing Change

Does the organization have to achieve its goals in spite of you?

In a bureaucracy, the employees know that the way to get anything done is to bypass the bottleneck, the big Bureaucrat at the top. This happens in the military, in government, and also in companies.

An extreme (-A--) is so controlling that most people will ignore him, ignore the rules, in order to do their jobs.

I heard a story recently about a newspaper editor, a big (-A--), the new chief of the copy desk. As soon as she arrived, she decreed a mandatory dinner hour for each shift of copy editors. The evening shift's dinner break was 7 p.m.

The problem was that the press deadline was 8 p.m., and the hour between 7 and 8 was the busiest hour of the day. But when the staff brought this to her attention, she stood firm: A policy is a policy.

What happened? Each night at 7, the copy editors obediently left their desks and went down to the cafeteria. A few minutes later, when the copy chief herself took her break, everybody sneaked back upstairs to their computers in order to make the deadline.

The most important thing you can do as a manager is open yourself up to listen. Don't tell, listen. Listen to problems. Listen when people need your help. Try to help them achieve their goals. This is called leadership by serving: "How can I help you achieve your goals?"

Don't lose sight of the ultimate goal in your pursuit of efficiency and standardization. Identify the goals, and then fire people up by listening and offering your help. Remember that your job is to serve them, not just to control them.

Problems or threats can actually be opportunities; conversely, not every opportunity is a problem.

In the Chinese language, the word for "problem" is also the word for "opportunity." I think that makes perfect sense. A similar view is implicit in the English expression: "Anything that doesn't kill you makes you stronger."

What does this mean? In solving problems, you have the opportunity to learn from them – even if you fail. You develop new capabilities.

So whether something is a problem or an opportunity depends on your attitude and approach. For an (**E**), every problem is an opportunity. For an (**A**), every opportunity is a problem. That's why (**A**)s and (**E**)s do not like working for each other.

Try a little attitude adjustment next time a problem presents itself. Ask yourself: What can I learn from this? There will always be something new to learn.

Forecasting is not planning.

An (**A**) "plans" by adding some percentage of growth to last year's results. "How much did we do last year? What is our forecast for next year? Ten percent better than last year: That's our plan."

An (**E**), by contrast, thinks that planning is stating the desirable: "Our plan is that we are going to be the leaders of the industry!"

A (**P**) doesn't plan at all: "My plan is to keep doing what I'm doing. Done!!!" An (**I**) doesn't have a plan either: "Whatever we agree on, that's the plan."

Here is my definition of planning: Trying to close the gap between what is possible and what is desirable. An effective plan is a combination of (**A**) and (**E**). In other words: "What do we forecast? Is that enough; is it what we desire? If not, then how can we make the forecast comply as closely as possible to what is desirable?"

This is difficult for an (**A**). But a plan is not a linear progression, a fixed percentage over last year's results. A plan involves thinking about what changes we need to make.

If there are no changes, then you don't have a plan. You might have a forecast, or a program, or a project, but you don't have a plan. Why? Because there are always changes in the environment; planning means figuring out how you're going to adapt and react to those changes. Do not react in a programmed way to altered situations that call for a new approach. Accept change.

Planning is not deciding what to do tomorrow. It is deciding what to do today in light of what you expect and want tomorrow to be.

Learn to say "yes" to change.

It's as hard as giving birth for an (**A**) to say the word "yes." They suffer from "the watch syndrome"; there's a joke about it:

A young man and an old man are on a train. The young man asks the old man, "Sir, what time is it?" The old man doesn't answer. So the young man asks again, "What time is it, sir?" The old man doesn't answer.

Now the young man is getting annoyed. He says, "Sir, why won't you tell me what time it is? I know you speak English because I saw you speak with the conductor. I see you have a watch on your wrist. Why can't you tell me what time it is?"

Finally, the old man responds: "Because, young man, I'm going to tell you what time it is, and I see you're a very intelligent young man, and we're going to get into a conversation, and I'm going to enjoy this conversation, and then we're going to get off at the same railroad station, and because we had such an interesting conversation, I'm going to invite you home for dinner. And I have a daughter who's very beautiful, and my beautiful daughter is going to fall in love with you. And I do not want my daughter to fall in love with a guy who doesn't have a watch!"

That's a typical (**A**): If someone even asks you a question, you extrapolate and decide, "I'm losing control." But the truth is, he is just asking you what time it is. It doesn't mean he's going to marry your daughter.

So when it's appropriate, say, "Yes, let us talk more. Let me hear more." Reserve your decision for later on.

The same is not necessarily better or cheaper.

An (**A**) tries to standardize everything; efficiency is his slogan.

But whatever is more efficient is also less effective. You can't have both. You have to decide which is more important for your company right now: To be more effective or more efficient.

Which is the driving force? If being effective is more important, than you'll have to accept becoming less efficient. And if efficiency is more important, then ease up on your standards for effectiveness.

Usually in a growing company, effectiveness is the more important issue. In the adolescent stage of the lifecycle, efficiency becomes more vital: The company must pay attention to profitability and not only to market share.

In general, as an industry ages, innovation becomes less important than cost of ownership. Supply chain management and cost control become more important.

Do you know where your company is in its lifecycle and what it needs now?

We will stop encountering problems only when there is no more change, and that will happen only when we are dead.

An (**A**) wants to have no problems. He wants everything clean, neat, and under control.

But problems inevitably occur, because change inevitably occurs. You will have no problems only when there's no change, and when will that happen? When you're either dead or almost dead.

So you might be killing the company with your extreme reactions to problems. People are going to hide problems from you instead of bringing them to your attention; thus you might not learn about them until it's too late. That's why companies like Enron implode: Everything looked good, even great, on the outside, and then boom! Everything fell apart, because nobody had dared to speak out.

Top 10 Prescriptions for a (pAei)

1. Form does not necessarily produce function.
2. Not everything must be written into manuals and codified.
3. Speak first. Think more later.
4. You might know the cost of everything, but do you know the value of anything?

5. Stop thinking that everything is prohibited unless it is specifically permitted.

6. Stop worrying about what should be and pay more attention to what is.

7. Controls mushroom. Sometimes, success depends on how much you can let go.

8. When there's a choice, do the right things instead of just doing things right.

9. Fewer meetings will get more things done.

10. Learn to say "yes" to change.

NOTES

1. Wouk, Herman: *The Caine Mutiny* (New York: Bantam Doubleday Dell, 1951).

Chapter 6

(paEi) and (PaEi) Prescriptions

BEHAVIOR

To start living you must accept death. Be here now!

In *The Denial of Death*, by Ernest Becker, Becker theorizes that "the idea of death, the fear of it, haunts the human animal like nothing else; it is a mainspring of human activity – activity designed largely to avoid the fatality of death, to overcome it by denying in some way that it is the final destiny of man."[1]

According to Becker, the repression of this terror of death – what Henry James called "the worm at the core" of life, and that T.S. Eliot, in his poem "Whispers of Immortality," called "the skull beneath the skin" – "is not simply a negative force opposing life energies; it lives on life energies and uses them creatively. … the organism works actively against its own fragility by seeking to expand and perpetuate itself in living experience."[2]

When we try to coach any manager, of any style, about how to manage better, we should start with what motivates him. I believe that each of the four styles has a particular overwhelming need. The (**P**) has what David McClelland, the famous Harvard psychologist, calls N/Ach – a need for achievement. The (**A**) needs control: N/power. The (**I**) has a need for affiliation, N/Aff.[3] To the best of my knowledge, McClelland does not cover what drives the (**E**) style. But I suggest that an (**E**) is driven by the fear of death. He wants to leave something after his death that will ensure his immortality. This is why he is constantly, obsessively, thinking and creating. More than any other type, the (**E**) fears that he will be forgotten. What he wants is immortality. He spends his whole life building "a statue," something that will survive his death. He wants to build whatever. I find that it is not money that motivates him, although he could be fighting for money furiously. "But what will you do with more money?" I ask. "You have so much already." "I do not know" is the answer. "Why do people climb mountains?" Because they are there. So I build this empire because it is there to be built."

If you are an (**E**) type, you will start living – which means enjoying life – only when you accept that someday you are going to die. No matter what you do, it cannot buy you immortality. Everything in life is subject to change, including everything you've built. Nothing is forever.

Did Jesus attain his goal for this world? Did Moses or Muhammad? I think all of them, if they knew how their ideas had been interpreted, would be turning in their graves or in Heaven.

As long as you spend all your time building immortality, you will never be free to live life fully and enjoy it in the present. Five minutes before you die, you're going to wonder, "Where did my life go?"

Can you accept that living in the future means ignoring the present?

How does one learn to live in the present?

Meditate. Learn to breathe slowly and deeply. Try some yoga; it will help you find a quality of life you've never even dreamed of. I recommend yoga and meditation to all my (**E**)-style executives. It does wonders to bring their focus into the present and away from focusing exclusively on the future.

In yoga, you learn to take pain instead of only giving it. You learn to listen to your body, which indirectly suggests that you also must listen to the whole organization, not only to your mind. The mind – especially the mind of an (**E**) – can push the body until it has gone beyond its capacity and begins to break down. An (**E**) can ruin a company he has built by pushing and pushing the envelope to a point beyond return.

What do I mean by "the mind" of an organization? First let's talk about the human mind. The right side of the brain, where we create and feel, is where (**E**) and (**I**) activity takes place. The left brain is where we act and think, or where the (**P**) and (**A**) roles take place. Another way to look at it is that emotions are (**E**), mind and thoughts are (**A**); body is (**P**) and spirit is (**I**).

In meditation and yoga, the mind is also called "the terrorist." In yoga you learn to balance the mind with the body. You learn not to demand more than the body can perform, to listen, "hear," and accept the pain that the body is experiencing, and not reject it by being judgmental about it. It is your body speaking to you, signaling its limits. You learn to accept your body's boundaries, to understand that your mind may be asking the impossible of your body. In addition, you learn your effect on others by becoming aware of what you do to yourself, to your own body.

In yoga you learn to direct your breath to where it hurts. Breath is your (**I**), and (**I**) is also love because love (**I**)ntegrates all and soothes pain. There is no sustainable change without love. Hate actually slows down change, because the energy that is necessary to make change happen is subsumed by hate. In love there is openness and the energy to make change happen. (I once made this point to President Fernando Enrique Cardozo of Brazil, who subsequently told me that of everything we talked about, this point has stayed with him most vividly.)

(**E**)s have to learn how to seduce rather than rape an organization by pushing and pushing without listening to what the "body" wants and needs. Yoga can teach them that experientially.

In the early 1980s I was hired to change the culture and the abysmal financial performance of Bank of America. To this day, I am known as the consultant who made the Bank of America top executives stand on their heads. I was later told that the executives got the most insights about management by experiencing their bodies. (**E**)s hate to experience pain but love to give it. Yoga teaches them to feel it and also not to give it too excessively.

(E)s easily get attached to any new idea. One lesson they must learn in order to work in concert with others, who may absorb ideas more slowly, is: "Observe but do not get attached, no matter how great the idea is." Meditation experientially teaches them that.

It is professionally dangerous to tell an (E), "You have to change how you behave as an executive." You might get fired (although he will often let someone else do the hatchet job). Or he might decide to ignore you or make your life miserable. The point is that as far as he is concerned, he does not feel or think that he needs to change. It is everybody else that needs to change.

(E)s love themselves so much that if you offer even a mild criticism of his idea, even if it involves one of your own departments, the (E) will perceive this as a gratuitous personal attack; in response, they will disconnect and disengage. They do not want to change. They want everyone else to change.

But if you tell them: "You can learn something really good and beneficial by doing just one session of yoga and one session of meditation," they will give you the benefit of the doubt and do it once. "I always try everything new at least once" is an expression that an (E) must have coined. They love to learn something new, so they will say, "OK, let's try it once." Then, during the yoga class, I explain that the body is analogous to the organization and the mind is analogous to management; One can lose one's ability to stand straight on one leg just by not paying attention to the big toe one is standing on. What is it analogous to? Regardless of how badly the mind wants the body to remain in the correct posture, the whole strategy of an organization can collapse if the last worker on the line (that is the big toe) does not cooperate. It is that worker who makes the strategy work.

They listen. They feel the pain in their bodies. They lose the posture. They cannot do that which they want to do. Thus, they develop humility, which is essential for enlightening the style of an (E).

Through yoga I try to enrich the style of an (E) experientially–to accept responsibility for the pain he gives others, accept mortality, keep breathing, and bring his mind back from the future to the here and now.

"Do not attempt to live your whole life in one day."

The statement above is a Jewish expression, related to the fear of death.

This fear of death has a high price. (**E**)s, perhaps subconsciously, fear that life is too short and that they will not accomplish everything they want to do before "the lights go out." So they try to do a lifetime of work every single day – by starting too many things at once.

The danger is that in doing so, you may end up with far less actually accomplished than you expected and wanted. As the Bible says *tafasta merube, lo tafasta* - the more you try to catch, the less you catch.

The rest of the above proverb reads: "…and it is not on you to finish what you started." In other words, have some humility. You cannot do it all. You can start. You can finish. But most probably you cannot start *and* finish everything you have started. It is not all up to you.

For an (**E**), in any case, there is no finish; there is no end. He is always raising the bar; his horizon keeps moving, so how can he finish? For an (**E**), to finish anything is analogous to death. So he is continually starting something new or changing something old. Everything is in flux.

You want "it," whatever "it" is – yesterday. You're haunted by the thought that every moment that passes is a lost opportunity. So when you ask for something, you do not just ask, you demand. When you request, you command.

It appears to me that because you *want* so much so soon, you also expect too much too soon.

Wanting and expecting are not the same. It is OK to want something; don't we all? When we get into trouble is when we expect it, which presumes that we control the outcome. When we expect what we want, we are taking it for granted that it *should* happen. But *should* it?

An (**E**) wants to build a monument; you are driven by your dream. It is great that you want it; that's what gives juice – meaning

– to your life. But if you *expect* everything that you *want* to actually happen and you want too much too soon, your behavior will be hasty, perhaps slapdash. And when your expectations are not fulfilled, your behavior becomes unbearable. You are like a spoiled child. You sulk, you look for villains and scapegoats, and you make a mess out of the organization.

Point at someone as if you are accusing him, but keep looking at your hand. When you accuse someone, your pointing finger is pointing at the one you accuse – but where does your thumb point? At God. Not everything is controllable by the person you are crucifying.

And the other three fingers? Whom are *they* pointing at? At yourself!! Have *you* done all that must be done to allow your scapegoat to succeed? Or did you just *want* something and therefore automatically *expect* it, while sending your subordinate into battle with a toy gun?

Slow down if you want to speed up.

"Make haste slowly," as Sophocles wrote in his classic play "Antigone."

Or, as a Yugoslav expression says, "Three times measure, one time cut." Speeding up can cause damage. Slow can be fast; fast can be slow. Why? Because the side effects of your hastiness could be disastrous. If you do not proceed slowly and carefully, the remedy could be worse than the disease you're trying to cure. And a solution that creates more problems is not, obviously, an ideal solution.

If you move too quickly, even if you understand an idea perfectly, there's no guarantee that you have fully understood its repercussions. Too many changes made too quickly create tremendous conflicts in an organization. This is also a risk with a (**P**), but a (**P**) is less dangerous because his actions are usually on a smaller magnitude.

You might be moving too fast, asking too much, because of your "bias multiple." That is the next point.

Check your "bias multiple."

An (**E**) is impatient. His vision is what drives him; once he sees this vision, he dismisses the implementation process as just a matter of details. In fact, once he envisions an action, for him it's already a done deal, already a reality. He's convinced that if other people were really committed to this vision, they would move faster.

Thus, he consistently underestimates how long it will take to complete any given task. Let's say you believe you will need to meet with someone for half an hour in order to solve a problem. The length of time that it actually takes is a measure of the magnitude of this (**E**)'s poor time-measuring skills. I call it his "bias multiple."

I've learned that my own bias multiple is six: if I expect something to be done in a week, it's more likely to take six weeks. So now, when I assign a task, I stop and think: I *expect* it to be done in a week, I *want* it to be done in a week, I *wish* they would do it in a week; but knowing my bias multiple, I understand it will probably take six weeks. Six weeks is the deadline I then give my staff.

Be aware of this disparity between what you expect and what the reality might require. Whatever it is, it is sure to take longer than you believe it should. In fact, the bigger your (**E**) – the higher off the ground you are, the wilder your dreams and the stronger your resolve – the more likely it is that your bias multiple will be very high.

Also remember that using unrealistic time pressure to make people work harder will only sow mistrust. Like the adage says: "Who sows mistrust, harvests lies."

To get the best sense of your own bias multiple, talk to the people you work with. If you trust a subordinate and believe he is working hard, then it follows that a task you give him *will* and *should* take as long as it *does* take.

Your tendency to expect something just because you want it, and your fear that nothing will happen unless you scream and pressure and threaten, have a negative impact on your ability to communicate with others. So it is crucial to figure out your bias multiple. Then, once you know how much you are likely to underestimate, you can correct your expectations upfront.

Communication

"Speak slowly, for me to understand you fast."

This is an Israeli expression, meaning, "It's better to feed people with a teaspoon than with a fire hose.

Because an (**E**) tries to fill his day with a week's worth of work, his mind works faster than his lips can move. He is constantly jumping from one subject to a second, which reminds him of a third. It's not so much his speed as his stream-of-consciousness speaking style that causes him to interrupt his sentences in mid-course or forget to complete his thoughts.

This bewilders his listeners. "What the heck does he want me to do?" they wonder. "What is really expected of me?"

In addition, an (**E**)'s excitement often stimulates other people's thinking. That's a good thing, except that while they're processing what you are saying, they cannot hear as well what you are telling them now — they can not listen to new inputs while they are processing old inputs. You can lose your audience very easily.

Each time you make a point, watch people carefully to determine whether they understand what you've said before you continue speaking. If their eyes "go out to lunch," stop talking and wait for their attention to return to you. It does no good to talk if no one is listening.

Find him an "interpreter."

The (**E**) communicates in a kind of hit-and-run, stream-of-consciousness style, changing course in mid-sentence, trying to solve numerous problems at once, changing his mind very often and very vocally. As a result, he easily confuses people.

When you sense that your audience can't follow your train of thought, stop. Their confusion might actually be a red flag, warning you that you don't quite understand what *you* are saying either.

To test yourself, find someone in the room who thinks he understands you, and ask him to restate what you said. If what he says is not what you meant, ask someone else to try. Keep asking until you feel comfortable with the interpretation of your ideas.

But be very careful how you do this. Some executives might try this exercise but edged with sarcasm or cynicism: "OK, you tell me now, what did I say?" This kind of subtle putdown demeans the other person, and he will lose his train of thought.

And be ready for surprises: What people understood might be very different from what you thought you said. This happens for a variety of reasons. Perhaps you were communicating a general idea, but your subordinates, who would have to implement it, are automatically adding a lot more detail. As a result, your idea will acquire some flesh and bones in the retelling, but may not appear to be exactly the same creature you dreamed about.

Nevertheless, there is a clear benefit from this exchange. You can hear and see upfront, before your idea is implemented, how it will play out. The angel of your imagination may be a Frankenstein's monster if implemented in reality.

To be understood, make (C) follow (B) in your alphabet.

An (**E**) will generalize, use analogies, examples, anecdotes, and quotations – *anything* to explain his ideas and their significance. But he rarely gives specific details, and he rarely is able to make his arguments in a linear, A-to-B-to-C form.

When you describe a problem, those around you might intuitively understand what you are talking about, but may not have a clear enough idea to be able to implement, or even articulate, it. There is a sense of a problem, but no specific task to pursue. Incredible misunderstandings can result.

Ideas are useless unless they can be implemented. The road to hell is paved with good intentions.

To make yourself understood, *substantiate* the problem, using specific, exact data.

Before speaking, prepare an outline of what you want to say, in a logical sequence, and then don't deviate from your outline.

Don't open your mouth too soon.

An (**E**) likes to think out loud, and this can be extremely dangerous. Without meaning to, he can send his subordinates in 15 different directions, chasing the rainbow and destroying the company – because what is merely an idea for the (**E**) sounds like an assignment to his staff. As a vice president of a Fortune 100 company once told me: "What just *interests* my boss, better fascinate me. That's how I advance in my career."

Because you're excited about it, your subordinates leap to the conclusion that your idea is an assignment for them. An order to be carried out And the moment it becomes an assignment, they go and chase it.

The danger is that since you have ten ideas a minute, you are soon going to run out of available subordinates – while they will end up running around in circles, working hard but getting nowhere.

This is a vicious circle, and the only way to stop it is to *keep your mouth closed* until you know what you want done.

The Slavs have an expression that puts the same thought another way: *Prvo ispeci pa posle reci*, which means, "First bake it. Then serve it." In other words, don't serve half-baked ideas – especially when you know your guests are paid to eat whatever you serve.

Instead, whenever you have an *idea*, write it down and file it in a folder called "Ideas," and periodically review them. After an interval, you might decide they were silly or not a high priority.

Tom Monaghan, the founder of Domino's Pizza, who used my methodologies extensively in building his company, once showed me a cabinet full of files called "Ideas." From time to time he would review them, but he only disclosed them one at a time, at a pace consistent with what his subordinates could absorb and implement.

If you're sure your idea is worth doing immediately, test it with a second-in-command, someone you trust who can also stand up to you if he disagrees with you. Make sure to get feedback *before* you start meeting people in the corridors and dropping assignments on them.

You believe that nobody understands you, but do you understand yourself?

It's possible that the disagreements and misunderstandings you think you're hearing from others are really coming from inside yourself.

Listen to yourself. You might be the first to disagree with what you just said.

You must know what you want before you can say what you *don't* want. To reach agreement with others, you must agree with yourself first.

Slow down. Make sure *you* understand what you just said. To make sure you understand it, write it down, then read what you wrote.

If you agree with what you've written, and it *is* inspect-able and implement-able, communicate it. You *do* understand it yourself.

If you need to change what you wrote, that means you did not understand yourself either. Your frustration and hostility toward others – "Why don't they understand?" – is misplaced. In reality, you are annoyed at yourself, for not knowing what you yourself want!

Always carry a pad and pen around with you so that you can write down your ideas and clarify them for yourself before you communicate them to others.

"A fish dies through its mouth" (Brazilian saying)

"In a closed mouth, a fly does not get in." (Spanish Sephardic saying)

"To speak up is silver, but to be silent is gold." (Hebrew saying)

"Life and death are in the power of the tongue." (Talmud)

There are aphorisms in many languages that all mean the same thing: *Be careful what you say.*

Think Yiddish. Act British.

An (**E**) usually speaks too much – the mouth is much bigger than the ears. It's the (**I**)s who are good listeners: (**P**)s *do*; (**A**)s *think*; (**I**)s *listen*; (**E**)s *talk*.

Yes, of course you get excited by your own ideas. Naturally you want to share your enthusiasm and convince others. But because you are so expressive, sometimes you say more than you should. And because in your excitement you tend to speak in an exaggerated style, people learn to take what you say with a grain of salt.

To be truly understood, you must de-escalate. Reduce the volume. Do not exaggerate to make a point. You can make a point calmly. It *will* be heard.

Furthermore, you *don't* need to tell everything you think. Be more reserved; give information only when it is needed. The more you over-express yourself, the more power you lose.

At the right time, silence is louder than the loudest noise. The less you say, the more others hear (and fear) you.

On the other hand, what people don't know can't hurt you. Nobody can hang you for what you *don't* say. And certain facts should never be spoken. Once you've said them aloud, you're left with nothing.

So please, bite your tongue. (I often claim that I can recognize a good (**E**) executive by the depth of the scars on his tongue.) Listen more, speak less. Control your emotions, or damn your destiny.

DECISION-MAKING

Best is the enemy of better. Good enough is good enough.

Sometimes an (**E**) will try to improve and improve and improve, until the cost of the improvement exceeds its value, making the situation worse, not better. At a certain point you have to say, "It's good enough. Stop!"

For example, fine art painters have a strong tendency to procrastinate. They keep working on a project and never finish it, because they're always trying to reach perfection. In the performing arts, artistic directors avoid finalizing a season's program until it's too late to meet the printer's deadline. Authors break their publishers' deadlines. Design engineers are always violating deadlines that the construction or production departments are relying on if they are to produce something on time at the expected cost. In other words, in the process of reaching for perfection, (**E**)s can ruin their chances of implementing a good-enough solution. Less happens, rather than more.

I learned this when I was doing my doctoral dissertation. I kept sending my advisor, Professor Newman, another chapter and another revision and yet another chapter. One day he sent me a letter: "Dear Ichak: You got your Ph.D. *Now stop!*"

When I talked to the professor about it later, he said, "Ichak, look at each book as if it were a progress report. Don't try to write your magnum opus or you will never finish anything. It's only a progress report." He must have known I was an (**E**) type; a (**P**), in contrast, would have asked how many pages a dissertation should be, then would have written exactly the number of pages expected and been done with it.

That letter saved my professional life. If not for that letter, which underscored for me my own style, I would still be rewriting my dissertation today.

Another example: For a while there was a big fad in American management called Total Quality Management: TQM. There was so much enthusiasm for it that organizations began to forget to monitor whether the costs of controlling quality were worth the value of that quality.

Better is not necessarily more. You might find out that what you're doing is beyond what's necessary and far too expensive.

As an (E), you tend to focus on the value of the alternatives you are exploring and not on the costs – such as the resources and time that's been dedicated to the exploration. But time is money. You have to learn to say, "Good enough is good enough; now onto the next thing."

How do you know when something is good enough? Well, does it do the job? Does it satisfy the need? Does it solve the problem? If so, then it is "good enough."

True, there are probably endless opportunities for improvement, but this is not an academic exercise. The goal is to get the job done. Period. Time and effort cost money. The cost has to reflect the value; otherwise you are a perfectionist, whom the organization can appreciate but cannot afford. Your solution doesn't have to be perfect, and it doesn't have to contain all of the wisdom in the world. It just has to work.

Set firm, absolute deadlines for yourself and others.

How do you learn to stop yourself from seeking that one "final" improvement?

First, set a deadline by which a finalization must be arrived at; do not procrastinate because you believe you *might* have or *will* have a better decision tomorrow. Use your bias multiple to set the deadline. At the deadline, if there is no finalization, the latest illumination must automatically become the finalization.

And, most important: Once you set up this rule, do not break it!

One of my past clients, the Franklin Mint, designs, produces, and sells gifts and collectibles that require lots of creativity from the designers. The designers were always late in delivering the final product. Linda

Resnick, one of the owners and the person in charge of design, had a theory that for artists, finalization is like death. Finalizing is admitting that you cannot do any better, which is very painful. So designers procrastinate. "They finish," Resnick told me, "when they are sick of it. When they want to throw it up. As long as they are in love with their creation, they hang on to it."

This is fine if you are an isolated, independent artist. You're allowed to choose your own misery. But if you work in an organization where others depend on your output, your procrastination can be prohibitively expensive.

So what did Resnick do? She set up a deadline. By that deadline, whatever had been created became the final product. You would be surprised how well these creative people produced once they knew there was a real deadline.

Clarity is achieved through attention to detail.

As an (**E**), you look at the big picture: The horizon, the excitement, the potential, the opportunities. You probably resent it when people ask about the details; you may feel they're nitpicking. It's as if you've given birth to a baby, and a neighbor says, "Hmm, yes, but it's got a birthmark on its nose."

(**E**)s typically enjoy dealing only with the first 20 percent of the decision-making process – the creative part. They'd prefer to skip the other 80 percent of detail work and drudgery.

A joke about a consultant makes the point: During the Second World War the Americans had significant problems with German submarines. So they hired a consultant, who told them the solution was to heat the ocean 150 degrees so that the German submarines will have to surface. "Then you can shoot them at will," he wrote in his report.

"How do we heat the ocean 150 degrees?" asked the Navy.

"That's your problem," said the consultant, a typical (**E**). "I'm a planner. I don't deal with implementation. I don't deal with the details."

Not good enough. Thomas Edison once said, "Genius is one percent inspiration, ninety-nine percent perspiration."

Talent isn't enough. Good ideas aren't enough. It's important to focus not only on a solution but also on the means necessary to implement that solution. The full process involves not only *what* and *why*, but *how* and *who*. Avoid the skimming process of decision-making that you're so prone to. Don't stop when the going gets boring.

It is said that "the road to Hell is paved with good intentions." In other words, it is not the goal itself but the small details that make or break a project.

The general concept is important – very important – but how it is translated into operative details is what really counts. You must go through the Hell of details to reach the Heaven of a workable solution.

Since a good decision is much more than a good idea, since the details must inevitably be worked out, never agree on a decision "pending details to be worked out." Postpone the finalization until the details are reviewed, approved and signed by you. If you can't work out the details, for whatever reason, then delegate the task.

Not all roads lead to Rome.

An (**E**) is excited by problems. In fact, he never sees them as problems – he sees them as challenges. He loves the process of debating the various potential solutions to a problem; like an academician, he likes to muse, "We could do it *this* way, and then again maybe we should do it *that* way."

If the (**E**)s of the world could adopt a slogan, it would be: "All roads lead to Rome"; in other words, no matter which road you take, you'll eventually end up there – or, to put it another way, all alternatives are legitimate. They love the exploration of the possible. Why not this? How about that? But by prolonging the exploration instead of taking the shortest route to the goal, they waste a lot of energy. Sometimes they never arrive at the destination. They become exhausted en route.

In Israel, a very (**E**) culture, I've consulted with companies that have taken simple problems and turned them into major projects – exploring one alternative, then another and another and another, and adding all the bells and whistles. They make the simple complicated. When the meeting is over, we have lots of options but no decision.

In America, an extremely (**P**) culture, the opposite happens. They take something complicated and try to make it simple. A (**P**) will say, "It works, leave it alone! Done! Next!"

An (**E**) might never get to Rome if he spends all his energies exploring every single road that might lead to Rome. Again, best is the enemy of better. If you want to get anything done, avoid altering it because you enjoy the process. Focus on a decision that works, instead of *all* the possible decisions that could work.

If it is similar, it is not identical, nor is it completely different. But it is similar.

(**E**)s paint with a wide brush. They tend to generalize and exaggerate what they know. They're hyperbolic: They love words like "never," "always," "everything." They find it difficult to interest themselves in small distinctions.

For an extreme (**E**), there are no nuances, no granularity. If we are discussing alternative A, and somebody suggests alternative B, an (**E**) will decide, "Both of them are no good."

"Why?"

"Because they are the same."

"But they are not the same," you might argue. "They're different. The difference is a small one, but they are different."

"No, they're the same," he will insist, because he is looking at the big picture and in the big picture small differences do not matter.

Often in my consultations I suggest a very small change, which will solve the problem. As a matter of fact, I work hard to make the smallest change necessary to solve a problem. I think of myself as a cosmetic surgeon. Can you imagine what would happen if clients came out of my treatment and people hardly recognized them? Ideally, people should not even realize there was a surgery; the person just looks better or younger, and people do not know why.

But when small changes are suggested, I am told – typically by an (E) – "No, we tried that and it didn't work." And it may be true that they tried something similar, but it was not the same.

They tell me, "It's more or less the same."

So I give them an analogy:

"Let's assume your car is not working properly. You take it to the garage, and the mechanic reconnects one wire – that's all. But now the car hums, it works. When you look at the car, it looks the same – except for one little wire that is now correctly connected. So it is a similar, but at the same time, it is a different car, because it works! One little variable can make all the difference."

In medical diagnoses, one symptom can make the difference between disease A and disease B.

Don't generalize unnecessarily. Pay attention to the details. Focus to see the differences *and* the similarities.

Not everything is equally crucial. Discriminate!

For an (E), the *newest* idea is the most exciting. Thus it's important to monitor who has access to him, because the last one to speak to the (E) very often wins the argument.

Of course, that doesn't necessarily mean the (E) will drop the old ideas. He just keeps adding to the mix, putting impossible pressure on the organization and diminishing the value (and likelihood of success) of *all* his ideas.

(E)s forget that not every decision or project has the same importance. Some are major; some are minor. Learn to discriminate between what is essential and what is optional. What is the driving force?

When I work with an (E), I say, "First, let's accumulate all the things we want.

"Good. Great. Now let's identify which are the things we *need* to have, and which are the things it's *nice* to have.

"Now, let's give each item on the 'need-to' list a priority."

There should never be more than ten "need-to" items; more than that is overwhelming. I usually try to pare the "need-to" list down to between three and five items and relegate the rest to the "nice-to" list.

Remember: You cannot have everything, and not everything is of equal importance. Or as the management guru, Peter Drucker, has said, "The essence of making priorities is choosing what not to do. What is left are the priorities. " And (**E**)s have lots of difficulties deciding what *not to do.* If you make priorities by deciding *only* what to do, you might end up with so many priorities that few if any get carried out.

Ask yourself: What are you committed to? What is really driving you? What are you trying to achieve?

An (**E**) sometimes becomes entangled in an ego trip, forgetting the overall mission of his organization: What is the long- and short-term need that his organization exists to satisfy?

I myself have fallen victim to this trap. Recently I almost made a decision to buy thirty-five acres next to my house. It was going to cost a lot of money – all of my retirement money, in fact.

My broker said, "Tell me why you are buying it so that I understand how to design the package." After I thought about it, I had to admit, "You know, Sandy, it's just an ego trip, so that I can look out to the horizon and see that it is all mine. It's a wonderful feeling, but the business rationale is just not there."

Sometimes an (**E**) is motivated by loneliness, the craving for a sense of belonging. Many (**E**)s, I have discovered, were somehow isolated in their childhoods. One of the ways they try to belong is by creating and building something. What they're really saying is, "Hey, watch me! I'm also here."

They try everything to design a business model that justifies their desires, but if they're really honest with themselves, they might recognize that there is no real logic to the business decision. It's just an ego trip.

I saw this problem with a client in Mexico. He was one of the richest men in Mexico already; he had an airplane, a yacht, many houses – and yet he was overextending himself financially to start up another business.

I asked him, "Why are you taking more loans, pushing the envelope, putting yourself into a place where you cannot sleep at night? What is the benefit of it?"

"I don't know," he admitted. "It's just, you know, bigger! More! It's like climbing a mountain. Why do you climb it? Because it is there!"

"So what are you going to do with the additional money you earn?"

"Maybe I'll buy a bigger plane."

A bigger plane is not a good business reason. Check your motivations. Ask yourself: Is this acumen, is it ego, or is it insecurity? More is not always better. Better is more.

Do not present a problem unless your goal is to arrive at a solution. Be constructive!

Because of their creative analytical ability, (E)s can spend an inordinate amount of time diagnosing the *why* and *who* of a problem instead of trying to solve it by focusing on the *what* and *how to do*. Actual problem-solving would mean leaving behind the intellectual excitement of analysis, on which they thrive, and focusing on the *what* and *how*, which they find boring. It also leads to an end, which (E)s perceive as a kind of death.

But diagnosing, discussing, and analyzing problems without focusing on potential solutions is like scratching and re-scratching a small scab. The mild pain gives some pleasure, but eventually the scab will bleed and the small cut can become a large wound.

In Israel, a very (E)-style culture, people will often debate a problem until you wonder whether they really want to *solve* it or they just enjoy *debating* it. It's called Talmudism: They start with a small problem and by the time they finish discussing it, a bigger, deeper problem has grown out of the discussion – but no solution.

A client who was on the board of directors of both an Israeli company and an English company once told me, "When I sit in the board of directors meeting in the English company, it's boring as hell. We go through the numbers, and everybody's falling asleep. And then a Jewish member of the board will say, "Why don't we...?" And everybody wakes up, says "Great idea!" and they finish on a high note.

But when he attends the Israeli board of directors meeting, he said, "One guy says, 'Why don't we...?' and another guy says, 'No! Forget it! Why don't we...?' Then a third guy says, 'No, no, no, why don't we...?' There are three hours of arguments and no decisions. Everybody goes home frustrated."

Try to set priorities and concentrate your resources and time on solving problems that can really be solved.

In solving a problem: Focus more on *what* should be done and *how* it should be done, instead of on *who* did it wrong and *why*.

Focus on the person who can solve the problem, instead of the person who is *causing* the problem – unless you are sure they are one and the same.

Present the problem *only* to the person who can implement your solution the best, instead of speaking to whoever is available to listen at that moment.

In other words, to solve a problem, focus more on the (**P**) and (**A**) aspects of it.

You don't have to untie the whole ball of string at once, which might take forever. Start doing something doable right now. Get some results soon. How do you eat an elephant? One piece at a time, and you should choose your first piece carefully.

This is especially important for (**E**)s in political leadership positions, where they have to watch the polls. Take President Vicente Fox of Mexico, whose cabinet I helped structure. I did a diagnosis of the political situation in Mexico. The long-term problem was lack of (**A**), or lack of law and order: Too much crime and corruption. But that problem could not be solved in a year or two. In the meantime, the president needed to (**P**)roduce results in order to maintain credibility. You need to focus on achievable short-term results to buy you time and political credit so you can deal with the long run.

Rudy Giuliani who was the mayor of New York City did it right. When Giuliani was elected mayor, New York was a crime-ridden city, businesses were leaving the city, and there were plenty of problems. What did he do? Did he go after big crime and the economic decline? No, he went after the jaywalkers. He went after the hotdog salesmen who were operating without a permit.

It sounds petty, but he created results that people noticed. He showed he could do things. Politically, that gave him more power to do the bigger things later on.

Mussolini is another example: He didn't try to clean up the whole messy Italian system; he made the trains run on time.

As an (**E**), you want to solve all the big problems now. But sometimes that's asking for too much. Look for some small, visible problems that you can crack right away. This will confer credibility. People will see that you're capable of getting things done, which amounts to political capital in your pocket. Then go for the next, bigger thing. And never outpace yourself: Do not take on that which you lack the political backing to achieve.

IMPLEMENTATION

Cool it! You must freeze a decision.

An (**E**) is always thinking of one more improvement, one tiny little change he wants to make. An (**E**) can't help himself, even though he knows that the more he stirs the pot, the slower it will boil. As a matter of fact, I advise construction contractors that if they have an (**E**) client, they should always underbid the job because they'll make the money back, and more, on changes.

The more changes you make, the slower the progress and the more expensive – and potentially disastrous – the change.

For example, if an (**E**) plants a tree and decides it isn't growing fast enough, what does he do? He digs it up and replants it somewhere else. As soon as he decides something isn't working right, he wants to try something else.

But relocating that tree won't make it grow any better or faster. On the contrary, without the opportunity to develop roots, it will die.

Sometimes, the solution to a problem is not to do something different but to do the same thing *a bit longer*. It takes longer to implement a solution than to identify it. It takes time to find out whether a solution really works. Be patient.

There is a joke about (**E**)s, that they will make love to nine women trying to make a baby in one month.

It just doesn't work; it takes nine months, no matter what. Certain things take time, and you must give them time.

Thus, once you have begun implementing, do not change a decision – *even* if you have a better idea. If you really want something implemented, you must stop making changes to it. Change a decision only if others – especially the (**A**)s – agree it should be done. (**A**)s are the last to believe that a change is needed; thus if they do, it is imperative to do it. But you, as an (**E**), should watch out. You are prone to changing direction too fast and too often.

What gets done is not what is expected but what is inspected.

There is an expression in the Talmud: "If the end is good, the whole thing is good." *(Sof tov, hakol tov).*

In other words, the proof is in the pudding. You know whether it's good by whether it works out well. In long races, the winners are known by how they run their last round, not the first round.

It's typical for an (**E**) to manage by expectations, although sometimes those expectations are not fully articulated or finalized. An (**E**) will say, "Here's what we should be doing, here's what I expect you to do. I rely on you. I trust you. Keep going." Then he gets frustrated and angry when the result is not what he expected, and fast enough.

To solve a problem, it is not enough to *want* to have a solution. Nor is it enough to find a solution. You have to invest the time and effort to implement it.

Expecting is not enough. You must also *inspect* the progress, because there are almost certainly going to be roadblocks and difficulties where your help and expertise will be needed.

It isn't about control. It's about communication: are they doing what you expected them to do? Is the result likely to be the result you expected?

In order to *inspect*, you must first define and articulate exactly what it is that you expect. There must be boundaries within which results are to be achieved. That means setting up policies and rules.

Then you start inspecting. How? You must have meetings, deadlines, and written instructions: Whose job it is to do what, what is supposed to happen by what date. On that date, you have a meeting: "OK, what happened with this? What happened with that?"

What an (**A**) will do automatically and naturally, an (**E**) must struggle to do. If he simply cannot do it, he should hire an (**A**) to do it for him.

Act only when you are calm.

(**E**)s are creative, exciting, expressive, vocal – emotional. That emotionalism is at once their greatest asset and greatest liability. When they are excited by someone or something, life is wonderful. When they get disappointed or upset, what was wonderful becomes ugly. They attack, despise, demean, and deflate egos.

(**E**)s are driven by emotion and nervous energy. They're hardly ever calm. But the truth is that they are far more powerful when they control their emotions, because their energy is focused. When they can't control their emotions, their energy becomes diffused and they can be destructive.

Excitement is good for generating ideas, but it's not good for acting on them. Ideas have to be washed, like a baby when it is newborn. They need careful monitoring and attention.

Hold back. Slow down. One way to slow down is to wait until you are calm; if you are still excited about something, then it's not yet time to act.

Team-building

Tell them, or better, do things that indicate you really care for people and need their approval and support.

An (**E**)'s behavior communicates just the opposite.

The way (**E**)s get attention is often by doing things that annoy those they want to attract. They search for a change they can instigate. The bigger the change, the more they believe they will be noticed. When the change causes a mess, they rejoice in the impact they've had and the fact that they've been noticed, neglecting to see that both the impact and the notice are negative. Naturally, the messes they make cause other people to resent them.

A love-hate relationship evolves: People love the (**E**) because he is exciting, alive, expressive, and charming; but they also hate him because of the way he upsets their lives. They resent him and perceive him to be inconsiderate and disrespectful.

The truth is that your attention-getting behavior is motivated by your need to be respected and loved. This disparity – between what you are trying to achieve with your behavior, and the response you get because of that behavior – may eventually turn you into a disengaged, lonely recluse.

It's easier than you think to satisfy your need to be noticed and loved. You don't have to do it with ideas, or by creating havoc. You can do it by just paying attention to people.

Being the only one to talk in a meeting does not mean they are the only ones who have to listen.

An (**E**) wants an audience and will create situations to make sure an audience is there to hear him. But he has great difficulty watching others perform. An (**E**) likes to lead the discussion; more often, he insists on *controlling* the discussion.

For example, you will call a meeting and insist that people attend, then practically ignore their contributions to the discussion. You seem to expect your audience to simply sit there, listen, observe, admire you, and approve what you say. They are certainly not expected to participate.

People are, justifiably, offended by this behavior. Why would someone invite them to a meeting, then not let them speak? They feel that despite your insistence on their presence, in spirit you are not with them. No wonder they just clap hands and wonder how to get you off your "high horse."

For goodness sake, increase the ratio of your ears to your mouth. Listen more, talk less. In fact, the higher your position, the more you should listen and the less you should talk. By the time you get to the top, your role is not to tell people what to do. Your job is only to tell them what *not* to do. Let *them* suggest what they should do.

Sitting quietly and listening is very painful for an (**E**), but it is a huge part of building mutual trust and respect. As a matter of fact, in my methodology there are rules of conduct that are mandatory in all discussions and deliberations. (See "Hard rules" in Chapter 9.) The first rule is that no one can interrupt when another is speaking.

There are penalties for breaking the rules. For an (**A**), paying some small amount of money for a transgression is an appropriate reminder that a rule was broken. For an (**E**), however, money is not a significant punishment. I have had cases in which an (**E**) comes to the meeting, plunks a hundred dollars on the table and says: "I am paying in advance. Now I'll talk whenever and however I want to talk!"

So I have changed the penalty for (**E**)s: Instead of paying a fine, they lose their turn to talk. That truly makes the point. Shutting an (**E**) up takes courage on my part if I am leading the discussion. It has to be discussed with the (**E**)s and agreed upon upfront, before the meeting starts. But this rule works. (**E**)s learn discipline and let others talk without interruption.

The less you interrupt the other person, the more you will hear what you yourself could have been saying.

In Mexico, they say that the first one who stops to breathe loses the argument. Mexicans are constantly interrupting each other. Italians and Israelis do it too; it's a Latin-Mediterranean characteristic.

I call this "the conversation of the deaf." *Both* participants are deaf. Neither hears the other, nor do they hear themselves, because they're too busy talking and interrupting.

When an (**E**) has a conversation, something the other person says often triggers a new thought in him. Excited, the (**E**) interrupts, talking and talking, just thinking out loud.

The danger is that because you've started talking even before the other person has finished, you haven't had time to listen to him or to yourself. So slow down. Stop talking and listen first. Stopping to take a breath does not mean you will lose the argument.

Why would it be difficult to hear yourself? Let me explain.

Imagine a computer. It has limited processing capability and memory. Now, if the task that needs to be dealt with requires more memory and processing capability than that computer has, you'll either need a bigger computer or a network of small computers that can work *together*.

How does the computer network divide the tasks? The most efficient way is for the first computer to keep those tasks that are most compatible with its programming capabilities, and spread the other tasks among the network.

Now, how does my analogy apply to people?

One person tries to solve the problem. The problem has many aspects to it, and his brain gets overloaded. One part of his brain is processing *why* there is a problem and what *should* be done with it. When he tries to think *how* to implement what he wants to do, he gets confused and very tired. There are too many alternatives, too many factors to consider.

So he approaches a person whose style differs from his, whom he nevertheless trusts and respects, and he asks for this person's opinion.

What is going to happen? If the *what* and *why* are clear, the second person is going to challenge the first by asking *how* and *when* questions.

Will the first person like it? Very often, no. He might even get annoyed and upset. But what the second person is doing is asking about elements that the first person was too overwhelmed to analyze himself.

Thus I suggest that when we do not listen to what others have to say, we are denying ourselves the chance to hear what *we* might have said – *if* we could have said it. When you refuse to listen, it is like a network of computers that cannot talk to each other. The task cannot be completed properly; the committee that was set up to design a horse ends up with a camel.

A question is not necessarily a disagreement, and good ideas can come from someone else too.

An (**E**) wants to control and win in any situation. He wants all the new ideas to be his own, and he is so sensitive that if someone so much as questions him, he takes that question as a challenge.

Try to remember that when a person disagrees with you, he is not necessarily disagreeing with *you*. He might just be disagreeing with your idea. Furthermore, if he has another idea, that does not necessarily mean he disagrees with yours. He just has another idea for consideration. That is all.

Always have a pad and pen in front of you when you are meeting with others. Let people talk, and as they talk, open your mind and let their ideas come in. They may be disagreeing, but just as easily they may be seeking further information, or they may be suggesting something that you can later change, improve upon, or store for future consideration.

Ideas don't all have to be yours. Don't jump down people's throats when they make a suggestion. Take notes instead. If you don't like their ideas, it's perfectly OK to write on the paper, "These people are idiots. I'm going to fire them." If it makes you feel better, write it down, but don't say a word. Later on you can consider them and decide how to handle them.

(**E**)s need to externalize ideas and feelings about others that bother them. But instead of externalizing through your mouth, do it with your pen, by writing what you would have said. Later, when you read what you have written, you might be very happy you did not say it.

This also applies to letters you write when you are emotional. After you've written it, wait 24 hours, then read it again before you send it. In many cases you will be glad you never sent it, and will toss it in the fire, never to be seen by anyone.

When you disagree, don't be disagreeable.

(**E**)s are frequently criticized for being insensitive. The truth is that they are extremely *sensitive* – but to how others treat *them, not* to how they treat others.

The (**E**) executive is as sensitive to disagreements as the princess in the famous fairy tale *The Princess and the Pea*, who is irritated by a pea placed beneath twenty mattresses.

But this princess of ours, the (**E**), does not just inform someone that there is a pea bothering her. Instead, heads start rolling. So people learn to keep quiet. They do not even dare to *agree*, much less disagree, for fear they will be misunderstood.

To really understand what someone is saying, you must be calm and receptive. You have to hear and listen to what is being said and to what is *not* being said. An (**E**) is not usually calm enough to do that, especially if the subject is close to his heart or stimulates his creativity.

Because you are so sensitive and easily hurt, you tend to attack precipitously – to the point that even when you agree, you seem to be disagreeing. Sometimes you behave so disagreeably that others feel offended and disrespected.

Louder is not clearer. You *are* powerful – you do not need to demonstrate it by raising your voice. A touch is usually enough; you don't need to hit. More aggressive is not more effective. People become confused and scared and, as a result, less productive.

Remember: Easy does it. The more strongly you feel about a subject – and you feel passionately about almost anything you do – the more peaceful you have to be in dealing with it. Slow down. Learn to breathe deeply. Relax. Bite your tongue. Hard.

Do you hear what is not being said?

In any group, there are certain things that everyone tacitly agrees not to talk about. It's as true of a company as of a marriage: There are certain subjects that are too dangerous to bring up, because discussing them might upset a delicate balance. Relationships may be ruined.

But the issues we don't want to talk about are often the most important ones – the issues we need to talk about. This, again, is the "dead moose in the living room" that I referred to in the last chapter.

When I was consulting with the coalition government of Macedonia, 1995 to 1997 for instance, I raised an issue and the minister of foreign affairs leaned over and actually whispered in my ear: "Don't discuss this subject. You're going to break down the coalition." In politics, sometimes to preserve a weak coalition, it is necessary to avoid discussing certain problems. But in a marriage or a company it is the kiss of death. Refusing to deal with the issues that you are afraid might break up your marriage is exactly what will ultimately break up the marriage. It is the stinking moose. And the same is true for a company. What you do not want to talk about is what is destroying you.

In a company, in a group context, are you aware of what is *not* being said? (**E**)s are usually so busy listening to themselves and their own ideas and deliberations that they have difficulty hearing what others have to *say*, much less to what they did *not* say but *should* have said.

You have to imagine what the group might have but hasn't said, and you have to try to figure out *why* they haven't said it. Then, you need to know the right time and way to bring it up.

If you cannot do that – if you have never done it and it is too late to learn now – then use your (**I**) team member to keep you informed.

Ask him what he thinks was said and what was not said. An (**I**) can smell an moose in a neighboring city; he has no trouble discerning what's right there in the room.

Managing Staff

Your attitude and preferences are to decentralize. Your decision style, however, leads to centralization. The result is a catch-22 for your subordinates.

The biggest Arsonist I ever worked with was an Australian (**E**)ntrepreneur. He was constantly complaining to me: "I'm *committed*, but my staff is only *participating*. They're not really committed. They don't take the bull by the horns. They're really not driving the business, you know?"

I replied: "Can you see that they *cannot* take the initiative because if they do, you'll be angry at them for not making decisions exactly the way you would have made them? But on the other hand, if they *don't* take initiative, they cannot be good executives or leaders.

"There is no way they can win. They cannot accomplish what you want of them. Can you see that?"

He couldn't. Why? Because he wanted to have it all: he wanted to control all the initiatives and at the same time have a creative and risk-taking organization.

There are certain trees that have such a dense top that no light or even raindrops can penetrate it. As a result, nothing grows under this tree. No other vegetation can survive.

That is the impact a big (**E**) executive has on an organization. My second-born son, Shoham, once told me after he had begun working with me at the Institute, "Dad, you are such a large umbrella. You don't realize how difficult it is to survive under it."

That really hurt. I want so much to have a creative, engaged organization, but my style, my dominance, my monopolization of creativity suffocates him and others who work for me.

So my advice to an (**E**), which I try to take myself, is: Give yourself some distance from the organization.

One huge (**E**) told me he lives an hour's drive away from the office to ensure that he doesn't show up too often. Give the organization space to breath.

Another client, Dion Friedland, one of South Africa's premier (**E**)ntrepreneurs who now lives in Florida and owns Magnum Funds, tells me that the more he traveled abroad the better the organization performed. Why? An (**E**) is like a mayonnaise salad dressing: Too much of it ruins the taste. In other words, you must monitor how much you intervene with the organization. You procreate at the rate of a rabbit, but one idea, one initiative, is probably all your staff can take at a time.

That is why I advised Bill Gross to start Idealab, one of the first Internet incubators in the United States. He was a client of mine when he ran Knowledge Adventure. After he sold it, he asked me what I thought he should do. I told him: "You are too much for any single company. Start a company that starts companies. Instead of owning one hundred percent of one company, own twenty percent of five companies, none of which you manage. You should only start companies. Once the company is established and capable of raising funds, let another CEO manage it. Visit once a month. Set direction, review progress, and each of your visits will give them enough work for at least a month. Too many visits means too many ideas. You will suffocate them." And that was how Idealab was born.

Too many ideas are as bad as no ideas. You must create space for your executives. Travel, go to spas, sail, live far from the office. … Do whatever it takes to allow your executives room to breathe.

Start managing by memos.

(**E**)s are constantly overflowing with ideas; they have many more ideas than they can afford to carry out. But it's hard for their subordinates to know which ideas are illuminations and which are finalizations to be implemented.

To avoid confusion, tell your subordinates that a "yes" is a real "yes" only when it is in writing and signed by you.

In my company I say, "A decision is not a decision unless it's in writing." To be sure that an idea does not become a premature decision, your subordinates must demand to have it in writing.

This is especially important in creative organizations, such as a movie or TV production company, a publishing house, a performing arts or visual arts organization.

In all these cases, there are parallel organizational structures – the creative structure and the business structure – whose decision-making authority and responsibilities overlap. Creative decisions have business repercussions and business decisions impact the available resources for creative endeavors.

This creates conflict and misunderstandings between the two structures. The business side might recommend something they believe will produce better financial results, while the creative side will feel its prerogative to make creative judgments has been threatened. By the same token, the business side could feel that the artistic side is out of control and risking the company's financial health.

Either side can dominate to the point that it destroys the other side. If business dominates, the creative side becomes mediocre at best. And if the creative side is too strong, the company might eventually go bankrupt.

What should they do? They should design a process that clarifies who decides in different situations. Which are merely suggestions that the other side has the right to ignore? Which subjects require joint discussion and unanimous agreement? If they cannot agree, who will have the authority to decide?

And put it in writing, because this forces people to think more carefully about their goals.

By the way, this would be just the opposite for an (**A**), who needs to write fewer memos.

If they are going to change, you have to change first.

During a company's early, "Go-Go" stage, when it is usually managed by its (**E**) founder, the (**E**) will often demand better rules and policies, more predictable behavior, and more efficient processes.

But who is the one who constantly breaks his own rules and interferes with the processes? Who is always tweaking decisions that were already finalized?

An (**E**) can be like a father who says, "Don't do what I do; do what I tell you to do." But the essence of leadership is behavior modeling. If you want to change people's behavior, you have to change first. And if you cannot change, why should you expect your staff to be able to?

If you cannot change your style on your own, you need coaching; otherwise the changes you want to introduce will not happen *with you.*

To win, you must take the risk of losing.

One way to continually win is to have weak opponents, and (**E**)s often arrange that. They surround themselves with weak people who can't stand up to them.

(**E**)s like to hire (**I**)s, who will always bend. (**E**)s will not hire (**P**)s, because (**P**)s are so busy doing that they have no time to listen to the (**E**). (**A**)s disagree with the (**E**), which is totally unacceptable to an (**E**). So the (**E**) surrounds himself with (**I**)s, or claques.

But hiring weak subordinates will eventually lead you to make bad decisions. Such subordinates won't dare to criticize or prevent you from instigating a bad course of action. They are scared, and rightly so: If they object, you will chew them to bits.

So for an (**E**), winning every battle may mean losing the war.

Here is an analogy: If I refuse to enter my racing horse in a race it might lose, then I can only enter it in mule races. What will happen? In the long run, I'm going to lose. Why? Because if my horse is never challenged, eventually it will run at the speed of a mule.

By surrounding yourself with people whose character is weak, you allow your racehorse ideas to be implemented by mules. If they never challenge your ideas, or their arguments are always weaker than yours, eventually your own ideas will lose strength. As the Zen Buddhist proverb says, "If all people think alike, none of them is thinking too hard."

The reason ideas stay strong is because of competition. To become a champion, you must enter races with top competitors. When your competitor is breathing next to your ear, you'll run faster. By enrolling in a race you might lose, you challenge and improve your performance, and eventually you win.

Any time you lose an argument, it means somebody has sharpened your mind. Losing in the short run is winning in the long run. Winning in the short run is losing in the long run. Surrounding yourself with people who are strong, not weak, is the way to win over the long-term. But in order to make this work, you must know how to disagree without being disagreeable.

If your staff really carried out all of your dreams, it would be your biggest nightmare.

Because (**E**)s have too many good ideas and try to implement them all, they often fumble, doing a partial or mediocre job on each of them.

If your subordinates took every one of your ideas seriously, as if each were a final decision to be implemented, there would be chaos. Luckily, they usually don't. They assume some of your ideas are *just* ideas – not to be acted upon. By making these assumptions, they risk your anger and their own careers, because they know they will pay dearly if they guess wrong. Although (**E**)s appear to have bad memories, they have an elephant's memory for those times they felt disrespected or disobeyed.

Your abundance of ideas is your strength; how can you avoid turning it into a liability? Whenever you have a new idea, ask your subordinates for a list of their priorities. Then ask yourself if this new project can reasonably be added to their basket of assignments. If not, what can you take out of the basket in order to put the new item into it?

Try to get feedback before handing out assignments, and put all final decisions in writing, so that your subordinates will know which of your ideas have priority. That will make life less stressful, both for your subordinates and for you.

Recognize that your subordinates have lives of their own.

When do the subordinates of a (**P**) come to work and leave work? They come after him and leave before him. With an (**A**), they come on time and leave on time.

With an (**E**), there's a big problem. When does an (**E**) come to work? Who knows? When does he leave? Who knows? But when does he expect his subordinates to come to work? He expects them to be there before him, and he expects them to leave after him.

If your subordinates don't know when you're going to show up and when you're going to leave, they have to be there all the time. They are on call twenty-four hours a day, seven days a week. A big (**E**) has no qualms about calling a subordinate to discuss business on Christmas Eve or his wedding anniversary.

(**E**)s call this "loyalty to the company," but in reality it's total subordination to him.

Remember that an employee with a stable home life is going to be a more productive team member. Everyone needs a personal life. Accepting certain boundaries will ensure more loyalty to you and the company in the long run.

When you hire, how you feel is important. But get some evidence. Confirm your gut feeling by getting other people's evaluations.

An (**E**) gets excited by people who are excited by him. This makes him easy to be manipulated. Prospective employees need only tell him how excited they are by his ideas and by the company, how committed they are, how they want to make his dream come true. An

(**E**) will invariably warm to someone who claps his hands and shouts "Bravo."

Before you hire, talk to your (**A**), (**P**), and (**I**). They can appraise a potential employee on elements of his personality that you will certainly have missed. An (**A**) can tell you about predictability of behavior: Is he going to follow the rules or not? A (**P**) can tell you whether he is going to work hard or not. An (**I**) is sensitive to how he will fit into the organizational culture and get along with others.

An (**E**) doesn't know any of this. He's excited by the fact that the job applicant is excited. He hires claques, who might easily turn into Deadwood.

The only solution is to surround yourself with a complementary team. Then, when you hire, you won't have to rely on your evaluation alone. Send your job candidate down the hall to someone whose opinion you trust and who isn't afraid to disagree with you. Make sure that another manager validates your judgment.

Hearing does not equal understanding, does not equal agreement, does not equal acceptance, does not equal commitment.

Because an (**E**) surrounds himself with claques – people who clap their hands and always agree with him – he assumes that their reaction equals commitment. If no one says "no," or even if everyone is silent, the (**E**) jumps to the conclusion that his decision will be implemented. Simple. Done!

But that applause may not be real, and those who seem to agree with your decision may not necessarily accept it.

Sometimes when people say "yes" to you, it is really a stalling maneuver, a way to catch their breath and gain time to think. People who like to think about the details of a problem need to disengage from the avalanche of ideas you pour forth, so they can think through and understand your reasoning. Once they understand, they might question, doubt, or disagree. They might even challenge your authority to make that decision.

Even after they understand and agree to accept your authority, they may not be fully committed to doing it. It may threaten their own interests. There is no guarantee that a decision reached unilaterally, without discussion, will be implemented.

When nothing happens, you feel your subordinates have let you down. You feel you are surrounded by people who lie to you, who agree and then do not deliver. You become frustrated and hostile. You do not trust them, and you fairly vibrate this lack of trust.

Remember that you are like an enormous engine, with 2000 watts of energy, while your staff people are working on 200 watts. If you aren't careful, you'll burn them.

The fact that your subordinates hear you doesn't mean they understand you. They may be afraid to ask questions.

Give them space to make a transition from hearing to understanding, and then from understanding to agreeing. Give them space to express their questions, doubts, and disagreements.

Keep in mind that even if they seem to agree with your decision, that doesn't mean they accept it; and even if they accept it, that doesn't mean they're committed yet. So slow down, and watch out. What gets done in a company is not what's expected but what's accepted.

Never put down a person in front of others.

One of the worst characteristics of an (**E**) is that he humiliates people, often in public. This is a pattern I've seen all over the world. (**E**)s don't control their emotions; they just go after their subordinates whenever it suits them – anywhere, anyplace, in front of anyone.

Nothing makes people more miserable than being criticized and demeaned in public. But an (**E**) expects them to simply accept it whenever it occurs, brush it off, and forget all about it. When these people later seem unmotivated and demoralized, the (**E**) cannot understand why.

I once consulted with a husband and wife, co-owners of a very large fast-food chain. He was a very big (**E**). He was the founder and chairman of the board; she was the president and a (**PAeI**) in style.

One day in a meeting, she said something he didn't like. In front of all the vice presidents, he exclaimed, "What a stupid thing to say! Go be managed by a woman!"

Hurting people's feelings is tantamount to firing them. They may not quit physically, but they do emotionally. An (**E**) cannot understand that either: "Oh, come on, what are you so upset about? It's a non-issue, I just said what I think. It was just feedback!" But most people aren't that thick-skinned. An (**A**), for example, will nourish his scars, nurture them, keep them, *index* them. An (**A**) never forgets.

The famous UCLA basketball coach John Wooden gave the right instructions on the subject. "Appreciate in public but criticize in private," he advised.

When an (**E**) wants someone to leave, he won't fire him; he'll just make his life a living hell: He'll criticize, attack his victim's self-respect and demean him publicly until he resigns.

Then, ironically, although he did everything he could to bring about that resignation, the (**E**) will feel abandoned and claim that the resignation proves this subordinate had no loyalty.

In the long run, this behavior is very destructive to an (**E**). If he speaks out too impulsively, he might easily say something that will shame or embarrass him later. In addition, this lack of discretion can be dangerous if the (**E**) happens to rant to the wrong person, someone who might use the information against him.

My advice is: Put your criticisms in writing to get them out of your system. File them in a secure place where no one else will see them. Having written them down, you'll be better able to let go of your anger, and that will limit the repercussions of your wrath. Later, when you calm down, let someone else fire them. You are not good at it.

MANAGING CHANGE

"Are you making it better or are you just making it different?"

(E)s want to improve things. For that, things need to change. Somehow they start to equate change with making things better, as if *different* were necessarily *better*. In other words, sometimes (E)s change things just for change's sake.

I, for example, have always written multiple drafts of each of my books. Each time I brought another rewrite, addition, or correction to my intelligent secretary, Rosemary, she would ask me: "Are you making it better, or are you just making it different?"

The bottom line can be suboptimalization: each incremental change makes the end result worse, not better. (E)s must know when to quit. How do you know it's time to quit? When you realize that your new change has made a difference, but not necessarily an improvement.

If you cannot make that distinction, write down your idea and put it aside. A week or a month later, read it again; this time you might find yourself questioning the wisdom of your idea.

Give time the time to do its job – to be the true evaluator of quality.

What you want is not always what is, or what should be.

(E)s are unreasonable. They don't take what is for granted. Frequently, they insist on changing something that cannot or should not be changed. Thus, an (E)'s solutions can create even larger problems than the ones they started out to fix.

(E)s are like children, no matter what their age. They can't take "no" for an answer unless it is their own "no." Like a spoiled child, they want what they want when they want it. They confuse *want, should,* and *is.*

Is, want, and *should* are very different perspectives that create a lot of conflict and frustration in human life, because we often confuse one for another.

Here's an example: An (**E**) comes into the (**A**)'s office and says, "We sold a million-dollar contract."

"Where is it?" the (**A**) asks.

"The client will meet next week to decide," says the (**E**).

"Then we really *don't* have the contract," says (**A**).

"But we will! They like it.There is no reason why they would not!" (**E**) is really upset because he feels mistrusted and his integrity attacked.

"But they might not. It is not sold till it is signed." says (**A**) frustrated with (**E**)'s managerial behavior which he believes is all hot air, as usual. He was burned before. This will not be the first time what the (**E**) said was, as far as the (**A**) is concerned, not even approximately right.

"But they *will*, because it makes perfect sense for them!" (**E**) raises his voice, believing that the (**A**) is belittling him, and nit-picking.

There are huge differences in these perspectives. Let's talk about how the *want, should,* and *is* perspectives differ.

Let me take an example form my work with Prime Ministers.

In the summer of 1991 I was invited to consult to the prime minister of Serbia, Professor Zalenovic, and the topic was the breakdown of the Yugoslav Federation. My diagnosis was that the problem was not Croatia nor Slovenia that were fighting for independence but Kosovo. The Serbian president, Slobodan Milosevic, was fighting for Kosovo because he was convinced that Kosovo *should* belong to the Serbs. Why? "Because 500 years ago, we lost our war with the Turks there. That is where the Serb nation was born. Kosovo is our Jerusalem. Kosovo *should* be ours," he told me.

His thinking was entirely based on I *want* what I *should* have: "Since I *want* it and it *should* be; therefore it is. Kosovo is Serbian. Period."

I made a presentation to the Serbian cabinet and Parliament and said something which in simplified form would be. "I understand that you believe Kosovo *should* be yours; you *want* it to be yours because that is where the Serb nation was born. You have people and monasteries there to which you are emotionally connected." (Notice the sequence in the argument: "Since you *want* it, you believe it *should* be and thus you claim it *is*.")

"But," I said, "let us look at reality. At what is. There are two million Albanians there now. How they got there and why, and whether Tito made a mistake in permitting the conditions in which they could multiply from 80,000 to two million people, is irrelevant *now*. What was was. It is sunk cost. What *is* relevant is that *today*, there are two million Albanians who hate the Serbs. And why they hate is again not that relevant. They do. And want independence from Serbia. Where will these Albanians go if Kosovo goes back to the Serbs? Do you and can you kill two million people? Can you expel them to Albania? Will you force them to go to Macedonia? Will Europe allow such a major population move without intervening? Will Greece allow such a development on its border? (As is now known, I was predicting what eventually happened. Nato did not allow any of that to happen.)

"Starting from the *is* analysis, then, what *should* you do? And in light of the realities, what *should* you want?" I asked.

"Given the reality (the *is*), what you should do is let Kosovo go. Emancipate it. Your strategy, what you want and should do must reflect reality."

As we know, Milosevic chose to do ethnic cleansing and expel millions of Kosovars. NATO, in response, bombarded Yugoslavia and brought the Kosovo people back. Politics and logical reasoning are not necessarily bedfellows but sooner or later, in my opinion, Kosovo will be emancipated; it is inevitable, because what is *is*.

In order to avoid a lot of wasted time and energy, you must accept that *what* you want is not always what *is*, or what *should* be. Sometimes, what is, is. Sometimes, the cost of changing a particular reality could be prohibitive compared with its value. Can you accept reality? Do you know when it's time to accept reality and when it isn't?

Sleep on a decision after deciding but before implementing.

(**E**)s are known for changing their minds and priorities faster than you can keep track of them. Because (**E**)s have a tendency to get excited by an idea, they prematurely finalize it and expect instant implementation; then they regret their decision and want to change it. This can have a destabilizing and destructive effect on an organization.

Thus, it is desirable to have a ritual, a system designed to prevent premature decisions. If a decision was made today, force yourself to wait a little while. You just might change your mind again. Even when you're sure you've finalized a decision, sleep on it. It's a safety measure, to ensure that you really are comfortable with the decision you made.

(**A**)s do this all the time – too often, in fact. With an (**A**) executive crucial decisions can be continually put on hold while years are passing by. Their faulty style is your medicine. Here is how I do it. When I tell my staff, "I made a decision and guess what? Two weeks have passed and I have not changed my mind," that's when they know they can proceed to implementation.

So write down your "final" decision, then sleep on it for at least one night. In the morning, read what you wrote. If you still agree with what you wrote, go for it!

Top Ten Prescriptions for the Predominantly (E) Type

1. Do not generalize the problem and solution. Substantiate your claims with facts. Don't exaggerate. Be specific. Give details.
2. Do not present a problem unless you are prepared to offer a solution.
3. Distinguish between finalizations and illuminations by presenting your finalized decisions in writing.
4. Present problems to the person who can do most about solving them.
5. Keep your emotions to yourself. Write them down and file them in a confidential file.
6. Finalize correctly; in other words, provide answers to the questions what, how, when, who, what not, and how not - and do it in writing.

7. Remember: An excellent idea is worthless unless it can be implemented.

8. Consider the interests of the parties involved in implementation.

9. When you disagree, don't be disagreeable.

10. You can't and don't comprehend everything. Use other people's judgment; learn from others who are different from you.

NOTES

1.   Becker, Ernest: *The Denial of Death* (The Free Press; NY, 1973, p. xvii).

2.   Ibid., p. 21.

3.   McClelland, D.: *The Achieving Society* (V. Nostrand: Princeton, N.J., 1961).

Chapter 7

(paeI) Prescriptions

BEHAVIOR

Stop worrying about what people will say. They will say something no matter what you do.

An (**I**)'s response to a problem is usually to ask, "What does Dan think?" "What does Jim think?" "What does Anne think?" "What does Bill think?" He will make up his mind on most issues based on what the consensus seems to be.

But sometimes worrying about a consensus is dysfunctional. There will be situations where the circumsatances dictate that you jump into the fray and take immediate action without waiting for agreement. *You* have to decide, on your own, what the organization needs. It's good to seek out others' opinions, but you also need to think independently. When there is time pressure, pay attention to your own logic and your own intuition, and don't worry quite so much about others.

Going with the flow does not make you a leader.

There is a story about a political candidate who saw there was a parade going by and told his campaign manager, "I'd better go find out where they're going; after all, I am their leader."

An (**I**) manager will often approach a problem by saying, "Let's wait. I don't think we (or the people) are ready yet."

The (**I**) wants to find an organic solution. He does not want to act unless a majority of the staff already supports the action. It is as if he believes that with time, people will eventually reach the right solution. "Time will tell," an (**I**) will often respond to the question of what to do.

Just yesterday I had this conversation with an (**I**)-type executive of a Fortune 500 company. I asked him if he supported a certain action I was suggesting to his vice presidents – an intervention that I tried to convince him was essential for the company's survival.

"Do you support the suggestion I am making?" I asked him.

"Do they?" he asked.

"What do you think?" I pressed on.

"Let me think about it," he wiggled out again.

"But the company must act!" I pleaded.

"I hear you," he said, and that was it.

If the company is relatively healthy and the market is growing – i.e., the wind is blowing in your sails – then going with the flow could be the right strategy. There is no need to trouble yourself or others; let's act only when the wind changes.

But if the company is in trouble, that strategy can be disastrous. Standing at the intersection and not moving won't take you anywhere. You're just standing there. If you have to wait for total agreement before you can act, it could easily be too late. One of the essential roles of management is to *act*, to take the *lead*, when necessary, instead of waiting for people to tell you what they've agreed to. So stop jumping on the bandwagon while pretending to lead the parade.

In real estate, I am told, there are three conditions for success: Location, location, and location.

In leadership, may I suggest there are also three: timing, timing, and timing.

Your style might do too little too late.

Take a stand.

Because organizational change is constant, the focus of an organization must and should change over time. An (**I**) manager might be the perfect leader for a young, high-tech company, because he generally gives lots of space to the engineers, doesn't get involved in ego trips, and creates an atmosphere in which creative people can express themselves.

However, when the driving force of the company changes – perhaps from technology to distribution, or marketing, or customer service – the (**I**) style may become detrimental to the organization. Why? At that point the organization needs to be firmly guided in a new direction, and an (**I**) is not comfortable taking the initiative or opposing the prevailing culture.

What you may not realize is that not taking a stand is taking a stand. What is the stand you are taking? It is that by not deciding to act you have actually voted quite forcefully and by default for the status quo. But is that what the company needs?

Because you dislike conflict, hurt feelings, anger, and resentment, you avoid taking the bull by the horns. But ultimately, this can be very destructive to the organization. A company that really needs more attention paid to reliability, cost, and quality will not prosper if it remains stuck on its original path, working toward better technology, when that is no longer what the market wants.

And there could be other consequences. When forceful action is called for but you avoid making a decision, your staff will begin to regard you as unable to function competently in your job. Increasingly, you'll be ignored and disrespected.

So when in doubt, try to heed the (**P**)'s slogan: "Lead, follow – or get out of the way."

Visualize the organization as a power boat. In order to change direction, you must increase the power of one engine and decrease the power of another. In other words, you must manage the power structure, rather than be managed by it.

No pain. No gain.

It's interesting to note how different styles react to different kinds of pain. The (**P**) can take lots of physical pain. The (**E**) takes in stride the pain of ambiguity, while the (**A**) and the (**P**) can't tolerate it.

An (**I**) can take the pain of political uncertainty, which would cause a (**P**) great suffering. But this, which seems to be a virtue, can also cause an organization to suffer needlessly from political infighting. The company is falling apart, everyone is begging for relief – but because the (**I**) has a high threshold for such infighting, the situation continues to deteriorate while he waits on the sidelines for a solution to emerge.

I repeat, if the company is to succeed: "Lead, follow, or get out of the way."

COMMUNICATION

Noisy discussion is not necessarily a disagreement.

An (**I**)'s role resembles that of a sheepdog who runs around the flock incessantly, corralling the sheep together. An (**I**) likes harmony and easy-flowing discussion. If there is a disagreement, especially a noisy one, he might interpret it as uncontrolled disagreement and try to stop it. His main fear is that the disagreement will spiral out of control, to the point where his ability to achieve harmony – where he feels comfortable– will be overwhelmed.

But a noisy disagreement just means that there's a lot of emotion and many different opinions. It doesn't necessarily mean the group is heading out of control.

No matter how heated the discussion is, don't forbid it. That will only push the disagreement under the rug. Don't be afraid of emotional discussion. To quote President Franklin D. Roosevelt: "There is nothing to fear but fear itself."

Mean what you say.

An (**I**) makes it a rule never to get into the crossfire. How does he accomplish that? He hedges: "It appears to me that…." "Perhaps under the circumstances, we might consider…." "On the other hand, however…." "I have an idea but I'm not so sure I agree with it."

It sounds moronic, but the (**I**) often finds great success with this style, which essentially floats trial balloons to see which way the wind is blowing – who will agree with what. Then he adjusts his views based on the reaction he senses. In this way he never exposes himself to serious conflict. When someone begins to disagree with an (**I**), he immediately backtracks: "Yeah, good point, I agree with you. Ahmm. Ahmm."

The downside of this behavior is that because you hardly ever stick your neck out, you are perceived as wishy-washy. People get disgusted: "What the heck is he trying to say, anyway?"

That's why, especially in times of crisis, (**I**)s are shunned, pushed away, ignored. Why? Because you won't take the bull by the horns. You are not clear. No one knows which side you're on when factions are warring. You are on everyone's side and thus on no one's side. In time of crisis, action is called for, and you do not take action because you do not take sides. Your inaction will cause great resentment, and will eventually transform you from being everyone's ally to become everyone's enemy.

It is essential to take a position; otherwise you will lose credibility and your leadership will be compromised. Go for what you believe is right even if it is not popular. Go for what *you* believe in, not just what other powerful people in the organization believe in.

If you keep all your cards close to the vest, you may lose some. Not knowing what you have, people might conclude that you have nothing.

The (**I**) doesn't tell you what he thinks; instead he asks you what you think. He's always trying to find out which way the wind is blowing, where the point of weakest resistance is, in order to tease out the political common ground. In that process, disclosing his own thoughts would be counterproductive.

This reluctance to disclose gives the (**I**) executive, just like the (**A**) executive, a lot of power, because people are always wondering, "What is he thinking?" If people don't know where you stand, they also don't know what you're going to do. And at the same time, because you have accumulated so much information, people won't dare to challenge you because they do not know what you actually know. But, particularly at the lower levels of the organizational hierarchy, this behavior can be dysfunctional. Eventually people will conclude that you have nothing to say, no thoughts of your own, and nothing to contribute. After that, you will be ignored.

So depending on your position in the hierarchy, by withholding information you could be accumulating power or losing it.

Another big problem with remaining silent is that by doing so you are not helping the organization to make good decisions. If the organization makes the wrong choices, your leadership will be challenged and no one will accept your explanation that "the group decided." Your power will decline, and you will eventually be eased out.

If you do not say it, how will they know it?

An (**I**) can wait forever for a consensus to emerge, and while he's waiting he will avoid voicing any opinion. He doesn't say what he thinks; he doesn't indicate in which direction he thinks the organization should go. Instead, he utters vagaries like, "Let me think about it," "Let's wait for a while," or "I don't think we're ready yet." He's waiting for the dynamics of the system to express themselves.

But the problem is: Unless you take some position, unless you say *something*, how will anyone know what you think? If you don't express yourself, people have to shoot in the dark until they hit something. Are you leading or following? Are you (**I**)ntegrating or is your inaction triggering further disintegration? Any bad situation, not acted on, becomes worse over time. Since you are not taking action although you are the leader, your leadership will be justifiably questioned, and you'll find yourself being pushed aside.

DECISION-MAKING

How people feel is important but it is not always the most important.

An (**I**) pays less attention to *what* people say than to how they feel about what they say. Many people think of this as a predominantly female characteristic – that females worry more about feelings than about practical strategies to improve whatever situation is causing the feelings.

Feelings are important, but what is more important is what is causing those feelings: *The problem itself.* For a little while at least, in the interests of getting what you want, you need to be able to hear what is being said and simultaneously ignore the subtext. Can you, temporarily at least, raise function above form in order to better focus on the actual message?

Bad decisions can be made by consensus.

Because an (**I**) focuses on people and feelings, rather than on what the problem is in itself, he can easily arrive at a very dangerous situation that I call "management by committee."

What is "management by committee"? Let me give you an analogy: A camel is a horse designed by committee. In other words, when we are more concerned with compromising with each other than with ending up with the best result, we may set out to design a horse and come up with a camel.

To prevent that, you need to focus on *what* is being said rather than exclusively on *who* is speaking. *What* is agreed upon is just as important as *who* agrees on it. The quality of a decision is not a function of how many people agree with it; rather, it is a function of how successfully it moves the organization forward.

Conflict resolution is not the goal. Comfortable relationships are not the goal. What is the goal? The goal is to make effective decisions that (**P**)roduce results. Don't lose sight of the result in your effort to reach an accommodation. You want to be sure that the decision is good, even if not everyone agrees with it.

Stop the endless meetings. Not all decisions need to be made by holding meetings.

An (**I**) likes to hold a lot of meetings, always trying to "cover all the bases" before making a decision.

This is also true for an (**A**), although an (**A**) likes meetings for a different reason: He wants to be absolutely sure that all the details are worked out and everybody understands them.

An (**I**)'s motivations have more to do with arriving at an agreement that everyone can live with. But often such meetings just waste time.

First of all, the only people who should be in a meeting are: those whose expertise is needed to make the right decision, and those who are critical for implementing the decision.

If you already have the right answer and you're sure of it, then why have a meeting? Why waste time? I've seen too many meetings where the decision has already been made and yet people are still sitting around discussing it, going around and around until everybody feels as if he or she has been heard.

This is usually unnecessary and can even be counterproductive. The longer you hold out for a consensus to develop, the worse a bad situation can get.

When time is of the essence, a good manager will make a painful and difficult decision alone. Sometimes there simply isn't time to wait for a consensus. The right timing for a solution must be dictated by the problem and not by how expedient it is to make it acceptable.

When you finalize, keep your doubts to yourself. Don't apologize. Just announce your decision.

Even when an (**I**) finalizes a decision, he continues to have doubts. Bothered by the need to reach agreement, he will spend a lot of time listening and sharing his doubts, although the decision was already made and communicated for implementation. This undermines people's commitment to carry out the decision.

This trait to accommodate endlessly usually drives the (**P**) up the wall. He wants to move. He wanted to move a long time ago. And you are still acting like a "doubting Thomas," causing dissention and uncertainty about the validity of the decision. This is why (**P**)s usually avoid (**I**)s and actually dislike them.

Your endless accommodating can cause you to lose power. Why? It is asking permission to make the decision that's already been made. So while you continue trying to reach absolute agreement, you are causing dissention in the ranks.

Express all your doubts and accommodations *before* a decision is finalized. From then on take a stand and stick to it. Remember that no decision is perfect. All decisions have points of weakness that may cause doubts. Keep those doubts to yourself. You have to make a choice about what counts – what is the driving force? – and then decide. And then stick to your decision. If you reveal your doubts after the decision was made and finalized, you may weaken your staff's resolve to implement your decision.

Your job is to inspire them, not to cater to them or make them accept all decisions. That is not what they need. They need a decision and a direction they can believe in, to which they will be willing to commit their time and efforts. Give them that inspiration or they will hide behind your doubts, and little if anything will happen.

I honestly believe that one of the functions of management is to endure rejection, even to the point of being disliked. When there is a problem and it needs to be solved and there are many doubts about whether the proposed solution is going to work, someone has to "absorb" the uncertainty, to take the risk and take the heat that such a decision entails, and accept the fact that some people will be upset. It is like being a parent. If you try to please your children all the time, your children will not know any boundaries and will grow up unbalanced and miserable. So if you make a decision that you believe is right, and your child nevertheless starts to cry and complain, you just have to let him cry. Assume that when he grows up he will understand the validity of your judgment and thank you for it.

Implementing

Agreeing is not enough. It is better to have a mediocre decision implemented than an outstanding decision never implemented.

Some people make outstanding decisions that they never implement. This is, obviously, ultimately ineffective. It is much, much better to make the best decision you can make, even if it isn't perfect, and then go and implement it.

You tend to postpone and postpone a decision until there's a consensus. You need to make the distinction between a *total consensus* and a *workable consensus*, which is an agreement that the critical people have bought into and that can safely be implemented.

There is a price to procrastination, and value in a decision made in a timely manner. Remember that a decision is rendered successful by its results, not by how many people agree with it.

A perfect consensus is a rare and wonderful thing, but it is not necessary in order to make a decision and implement it. If one or two people continue to disagree, are they critical for the implementation? If yes, you have to convince them or accommodate them. If not, then tough luck for them: You've heard them out, you've made your decision; now let's move on.

The fact that people agree does not mean they are going to implement the decision; you are responsible for implementation.

For some reason, an **(I)**, like an **(E)**, often assumes that once the work of arriving at a decision has been done, the job is over.

Not so. It is not a given that if people agree on a decision, they are automatically going to implement it.

As a manager, you are responsible for implementation, just as you are responsible for making the decision.

Because the people who work with you know your strengths and weaknesses quite well, they may try to give you the impression that they agree with your decision – either to stay out of trouble or to shorten what, with an **(I)**, can become a very long, drawn-out process of decision-making.

You need to be aware of that pitfall – that people may be telling you one thing and thinking quite another. To prevent problems, you must still oversee the implementation of any big decision – even if you believe you have a consensus.

TEAM-BUILDING

Conflict is not a personal rejection.

(I)s, like **(E)**s, do not like conflict; both feel that conflict will undermine their power. Actually, it's more complicated than that: an **(I)** doesn't really mind conflict as long as it doesn't threaten him. If there is a conflict in which his intervention is necessary and if he can be instrumental in resolving it, he will welcome it, because it increases his power. So it's more accurate to say that an **(I)** hates only the kinds of conflicts that he feels he cannot resolve. If conflict creates a situation in which the **(I)** is being ignored, then he will resist it.

But conflicts can be extremely helpful in filling out a picture and seeing all the dimensions of a problem. Remember that a conflict can be an opportunity to learn as well as an opportunity to consolidate your power. It is not a personal rejection of you. Often, in fact, the conflict has little or nothing to do with a difference of interests. It is merely a difference of personalities.

The appearance of consensus may be just that: the appearance, not the reality.

Naturally, the people who work with an (**I**) are aware of his need for harmony and agreement. So they are very careful about when they provide him with information about conflicts and when they don't disclose that there is conflict.

In other words, you might think you have a consensus, simply because the people around you know that the current conflict would upset you if you knew about it. The conflict, in that case, will go underground. And whenever you ask somebody, "How are things going?" they'll tell you, "Oh, everything's fine."

This is also true for an (**A**): Nobody wants to upset him, either. Therefore, "No problem; everything is OK." might be a *fata morgana*. In reality, it ain't so.

Being "against" can be "for," and being "for" can be "against."

(**A**)s and (**I**)s are focused on form, not function, whereas (**E**)s and (**P**)s are focused on function.

What does this mean for an (**I**)? An (**I**) values agreement and an organic sense of harmony above all else. Function is secondary. This can be destructive, because often the appearance of consensus is just that: The appearance, not the reality. When that consensus is inevitably tested by some kind of crisis, the shallow agreement swiftly falls apart.

This is why being against a decision can often be helpful in arriving at a better decision. When someone objects to a decision, he is challenging it, testing its validity and spurring more creativity from others on the team. While a desire to resolve conflicts is useful, it is also true that healthy confrontations can be extremely valuable. So do not fight dissenters. The organization needs their input.

If all people think alike, none of them is thinking too hard. When we think differently and oppose each other's arguments, we're sharpening our own thoughts.

Short-term unity may have long-term costs. If you are reluctant to disagree or encourage disagreement from others, you are in effect refusing to challenge or be challenged. Be careful. That refusal to challenge cripples the decision-making process.

The best decisions are not reached by people who insist on avoiding conflict. When two people agree on everything, one of them is dispensable. What you need – what every manager needs – is a complementary team, which enables you to hear differing perspectives and potential solutions.

Managing Staff

Constantly making people feel up may end up making them feel down.

In recent years, self-esteem has been the byword in education. According to this theory, children need to feel good about themselves before they can be motivated to learn. It's become the norm to constantly tell kids how great they are and to give them good grades in order to boost their self-esteem.

My belief is that by giving people unearned admiration, you're ruining them. You're confusing them. You're neglecting to give them boundaries – what's good, what's bad, what's right, what's wrong. When you continually send the message that everything is good, that they are worthy of admiration without having to earn it, eventually you will cause them to lose sight of what's good and what's bad.

Be honest. Use tough love. Be supportive and complimentary, but only when your staff's actions truly deserve praise.

Do not hire and promote people because of their personality in spite of their performance.

An (**I**), like an (**E**), likes to surround himself with supportive people who agree with him, who do not create conflict and don't make waves.

The (**E**) surrounds himself with claques – people who clap their hands and call, "Bravo!" but don't mean a word of it.

An (**I**) hires people like himself – people who will always bend when pressured, and whose job, as they see it, is to support and agree.

I recently had the experience of trying to hire someone for a company whose style was to challenge management and to constantly try to improve and change the system. A typical big (**E**), in other words. Now, the president of this company is a big (**I**), and I could see that he was fearful of hiring this person. It is not in his nature to want to encourage conflict and turbulence, even though he knows, at least intellectually, that a complementary team is necessary.

People naturally resist others whose styles conflict with their own; it's something you have to work at accepting and managing.

This is most important when you are hiring staff. Yes, it's important to pay attention to personality; you don't want a person who will create gratuitous conflicts. But pay attention also to the performance, because the performance may justify the behavior. You need subordinates who are going to counterbalance your tendency to seek consensus too soon.

A manager's job is not necessarily to be popular. His job is to be effective.

Ironically, although an (**I**) desperately wants peace, his wishy-washy behavior often causes his staff to dislike and disrespect him.

Tough love is a necessary component of being a good parent, and being a good parent is much the same thing as being a good manager or a good government. In the simplest terms, you have to do what needs to be done. Doing so will eventually and in time earn you the respect and admiration of your staff, even if they don't always agree with you right now.

If you don't care what we do, or how or why we do it, just as long as we agree, that's not motivating; that's surrendering.

There can be situations in which a minority will convince the majority. When there is a strong single voice, articulate enough and convinced enough, that voice can speak up and actually change the decision of the majority.

An (**I**) will habitually surrender a decision to the power structure of the moment. But the fact that a group of people agree on something doesn't mean it's the right decision. It could be that they agree on a short-term, self-serving common interest that will not serve the organization well in the long run. Thus you must pay attention to what you believe are the needs of the organization, its present and future customers. Are we doing what we need to do, the way we need to do it, and for the right reasons? Do you yourself believe in the decision? If you put in one room all your current and potential future customers, all your employees, and your investors, would they agree with your decision? Or would they want something altogether different from what the group now in power wants?

Not all those who say they support you, actually do.

Subordinates know that an (**I**) wants to be supported and agreed with, and that an (**I**) always wants to be kept informed of office gossip that might prove useful politically.

So that's what they do. They'll happily provide the information you want so that you will trust them. But because they want to appear supportive of you, they will never tell you bad news about yourself. Nor will they criticize you to your face – but they might be undermining you behind the scenes.

Why?

Because if the changing situation in an organization calls for a (**P**) style that you are not providing, somebody will always step up and do it instead – except he'll have to do it behind your back. And once your subordinates have been persuaded – or forced by a leadership vacuum at the top – to participate in covert strategies to move the organization forward, you have been rendered irrelevant and your days are truly numbered.

Your natural tendency is to be suspicious of people and analyze their interests and motivations. But you also easily fall prey to people who put on a show of agreement and subordination and thus put you at ease. They are probably bigger (**I**)s than you. So be careful. Silence could be misleading. It could be suppressed noise.

MANAGING CHANGE

What they want is not necessarily what needs to change.

The people in a company don't necessarily think of the best interests of the company first. Every person associated with a company has his own interests, which may deviate quite a bit from the company's interests.

The stockholder may want one thing, the management something else, and the labor unions' agenda might be totally alien to either of the others'. None of them may know or even care what the company needs to do to preserve its health and continue to grow. Each faction protects its own interests, which may conflict radically with what the company as a whole needs.

As a parent, you pay attention to what your kids want, but you cannot always give them what they want; sometimes tough love is appropriate. You love them, you care for them, but at the same time you tell them what needs to be done.

Like a parent, a manager's role is to represent future interests, balancing them with the interests of his immediate constituency.

You have a strong tendency to give people what they want, because, at least on the surface, the result is a satisfied staff with good morale.

But keep in mind that your real mission is to identify for the organization the direction that would be best in light of all the conditions the organization faces. Remember that the company is itself an entity, with interests of its own that are not only the most important interests, but are also the ones that will most benefit the employees in the long run.

By playing to the immediate constituency in the short run, you might be helping to create difficulties for the organization in the long run.

There is no change without conflict, and if you try to stop conflict, change will stop as well.

An (**I**) shuns conflict. He hates to rock the boat. He will go to great lengths to avoid discussing a subject that might create a lot of heat.

I'm working with a company right now where changes need to be made in accountability and budgeting systems. But the CEO, who is a big (**I**), is pressuring me very hard not to make any changes. "It is the wrong time," he insists. "We have other, bigger fish to fry." He is giving me a (**P**) reason for resisting change, but I know what is hiding behind it: The organization does not want to change – or it wants to change without changing, which is a typical, if irrational, expectation – and he does not want to swim against the political stream.

That's flawed thinking. "Do not worry if the people are upset," I tell him, "because in the long run, if the company is not functioning properly, they are going to be even more upset."

But he will not do it. He will not initiate change, although the company needs to change, because he does not want to take the heat.

Remember: A politician worries about the next election, whereas a statesman worries about the next generation.

What are *you* worried about? The next election or the next generation?

"Lead, follow, or get out of the way."

Top Prescriptions for an (I) Style

- How people feel is important but it is not always the most important factor.
- Going with the flow does not make you a leader.
- If you keep all your cards close to the vest, you may lose some. Not knowing what you have, people might conclude that you have nothing.-
- Mean what you say.
- Take a stand.
- Stop the endless meetings. Not all decisions need to be made by holding meetings.
- Bad decisions *can* be made by consensus.
- Noisy discussion is not necessarily a disagreement.
- The appearance of consensus may be just that: The appearance, not the reality.
- Being "against" can be "for" (reaching a better decision) and being "for" can be "against" (reaching a better decision).
- A manager's job is not necessarily to be popular. His job is to be effective.
- Do not hire and promote people because of their personality in spite of their performance.
- If you don't care what we do, or how or why we do it, just as long as we agree, that's not motivating; that's surrendering.
- Constantly making people feel up may end up making them feel down.
- What they want is not necessarily what needs to change.
- There is no change without conflict, and if you try to stop conflict, change will stop as well.
- No pain, no gain.

Chapter 8

Management Style Comparisons

In this chapter, the prescriptions for the four styles are repeated but in a comparative format. This highlights the differences among them and may make it easier to guide you in coaching a manager or in coaching yourself to be a better one. As Miguel de Cervantes once said, "Make it thy business to know thyself, which is the most difficult lesson in the world."

BEHAVIOR COMPARISONS

Wilkerson's law: The anatomy of any community or organiza-
tion includes four kinds of bones [The (PAEI) styles or roles
added by me]:
"Backbones," who get behind the wheel and do the work – (P)
"Knucklebones," who knock everything everyone else does – (E)
"Wishbones," who will go along with an idea but want some-
one else to do the work – (Deadwood)
"Jawbones," who do a lot of talking but not much else – (I)?

THOMAS L. MARTIN, JR., *MALICE IN BLUNDERLAND*

IS, WANT, AND SHOULD PRESCRIPTIONS

For a (P):   What is, is not necessarily what should be.

For an (A):   What is, is what it does, not what it should do.

For an (E):   What you want is not always what is, or what should be. Sometimes what is, is.

For an (I):   What they want is not necessarily what should happen.

Success

For a (P): People who work too hard have no time to make serious money. Your success depends on working smarter instead of harder.

For an (A): Your success depends on how much you can let go.

For an (E): Your success depends on how much self-control (discipline) you are able to exercise.

For an (I): Your success depends on taking a stand.

Rewards

For a (P): He expects pay per performance (commission and bonus for predetermined, short-range results).

For an (A): He wants fixed, predetermined periodic raises when predetermined expectations are met.

For an (E): He wants stock options, equity, ownership, a voice in the company's direction and goals.

For an (I): He expects a good working environment, where everyone gets along and feels that they fit in.

Self-realization

For a (P): Self-realization is not just more of the same.

For an (A): Self-realization is not just more control.

For an (E): Self-realization is not only immortality.

For an (I): Self-realization is not just peace of mind.

Managerial Pitfalls

For a (P): Unless you change your style, you will burn out.

For an (A): Controls mushroom. Unless you change your style, you will become an obstructionist.

For an (E): If you do not change your style, you will lose credibility and eventually become ineffective.

For an (I): Unless you change your style, there will be a coup d'etat against you by your subordinates.

WORRYING

For a (P):   Stop worrying that "it" will not get done. Maybe it should not be done.

For an (A):   Stop worrying about what should be done and pay more attention to what is.

For an (E):   Stop worrying about immortality. Just do your thing and let the work determine whether you qualify for immortality or not.

For an (I):   Stop worrying about what people say. They will say something no matter what you do.

VISION

For a (P):   Can you see the forest for the trees?

For an (E):   Can you separate the trees from the forest?

RIGHT AND WRONG, TYPICAL MISTAKES:

For a (P):   You don't care if it's right or wrong: "Let's just do whatever works and do it more and faster."

For an (E):   You do not care if we do it right. You just want to do it differently.

Prescriptions for Good Managerial Behavior (PAEI)

Self-actualized managers are self-reliant and make their own judgments. They are autonomous and independent in thought and action. Their decisions are guided by internal standards and values rather than by what others are doing.

Self-actualized people are willing to learn from anyone. They enter into fruitful exchanges with anyone they meet. They are also willing to ask questions that others hesitate to ask. They do not fear blunders. They know their weaknesses and have learned to be humble.

What counts in life is not who you are, but where you are coming from and where you are going.

If you want to know who you are, watch the impact you have on others. Be sensitive to how people react to you.

In other words: We are how we behave with others.

Remember: You can be your own worst enemy.

The person who is undermining your career progress might be you. Do not seek the culprit elsewhere until you have examined yourself.

Communication Comparisons

Sign in a factory supervisor's office: "Caution – be sure brain is engaged before putting mouth in gear."

Bits and Pieces, volume C no. 12

The Value of Speech (1)

For a (P):   Think before you speak.
For an (A):   Speak first. Think more later.
For an (E):   Think more – speak less.
For an (I):   Speak so they know what you think.

The Value of Speech (2)

For a (P):   If you stay in one place long enough, they might be able to tell you something you should hear – although you might not want to hear it.

For an (A):   Say what you think. If you don't say it, how will they know it?

For an (E):   You do not have to say everything you think. What people don't know can't hurt you.

For an (I):   Not taking a stand is taking a stand, and it might be the wrong stand.

THE MEANING OF SILENCE

For a (P):   Can you hear what people are not saying?
For an (A):   Silence does not necessarily mean disagreement.
For an (E):   Silence does not necessarily mean agreement.
For an (I):   If there is silence, how do you know what is going on?

THE VALUE OF SILENCE

For a (P):   Silence speaks.
For an (A):   Silence is not necessarily a good thing.
For an (E):   At the right time, silence is louder than the loudest noise. The less you say, the more others hear (and fear) you.
For an (I):   If you keep all your cards close to the vest, you may lose some. Not knowing what you have, people might conclude that you have nothing.

CLARITY (1)

For a (P):   Harsher is not clearer.
For an (A):   Slower is not clearer.
For an (E):   Louder is not clearer. Faster is not clearer.
For an (I):   Saying nothing definitely does not make it clearer.

CLARITY (2)

For a (P):   To make this discussion short you might have to take the long route.
For an (A):   (C) does not necessarily follow (B). It depends on what one wants to say.

For an (E): To be understood, make (C) follow (B) in your alphabet, and if you still are not understood, let someone else try to explain what you meant.

For an (I): Stop hedging. You are confusing people.

CLARITY (3)

For a (P): Wait before you act. Are you sure you've heard it all?

For an (A): Being precise can be very imprecise.

For an (E): Being imprecise can be very confusing. Tell your subordinates that when you say "yes" to them, it really means "maybe," and when you say "maybe," it means "no." Are you confused? Just imagine how *they* feel.

For an (I): Don't be a soapy fish. Take a stand.

INTERPRETING OTHERS

For a (P): Focus on *who* is speaking and *why* he is saying what he's saying, rather than exclusively focusing on *what* is being said.

For an (A): Accepting does not necessarily mean agreeing.

For an (E): Hearing does not equal understanding, does not equal agreement, does not equal acceptance, does not equal commitment.

For an (I): The appearance of consensus may be just that: the appearance, not the reality.

LISTENING CAREFULLY

For a (P): Don't just say, "Call me when you finish." Listen to what is being said.

For an (A): Ambiguity is not the worst evil.

For an (E): It takes at least two people to understand one.

For an (I): Noisy discussion is not necessarily a disagreement.

Prescriptions for Good Communication (PAEI)

For a (P): If you can't communicate and convince, you cannot manage.

For an (A): What they are telling you might be what you *want* to hear, not what you *need* to hear.

For an (E): The more emotional you feel about the subject, the more relaxed you should feel and act.

For an (I): Use soft words and hard arguments.

For (P)s and (E)s: Make eye contact with the person you are talking to. When that person's eyes wander, or "go out to lunch," that means he is listening to himself, not to you. If your eyes go out to lunch, you are listening to yourself, not to him. By keeping eye contact, you know you are listening to each other. When eye contact stops, stop talking until eye contact is reestablished.

DECISION-MAKING COMPARISONS

"Once you make a decision, the universe conspires to make it happen."

RALPH WALDO EMERSON

DEFINE YOUR GOALS

For a (P): Not everything that needs fixing is your responsibility.

For an (A): Problem-solving is not a mechanism for firmly establishing a book of rules.

For an (E): Do not answer the question you were not asked, or solve the problem that doesn't exist yet.

For an (I): Resolving conflicts may not be the most important issue.

Typical Technique

For a (P):   First aim, then fire.

For an (A):   Aim… aim… but eventually you should fire, too.

For an (E):   Fire but with focus, not in all directions, because you might shoot your own foot.

For an (I):   Don't just stand on the sidelines and watch those on the firing range and give them advice. Get involved.

Setting Priorities (1)

For a (P):   Not everything that squeaks needs to be oiled.

For an (A):   Not everything that is broken needs to be fixed.

For an (E):   Not everything is equally crucial. Discriminate!

For an (I):   Timing is essential for success.

Setting Priorities (2)

For a (P):   The squeakiest wheel is not always the most important one.

For an (A):   You might know the cost of everything but the value of nothing.

For an (E):   You might know the value of everything but the cost of nothing.

For an (E):   How you feel is important but it is not always the most important.

Speed of Decision-making

For a (P):   Slow it down, if you want to get anything done. Sometimes it takes time to get a quality decision.

For an (A):   Speed it up. Slower is not clearer.

For an (E):   Slow it down if you want to speed up implementation. Fast can be slow. Slow can be fast.

For an (I):   Speed it up. Endless meetings slow down the process unnecessarily.

To Fix or Not to Fix

For a (P): If it ain't broke, that doesn't mean it isn't *going* to break; it might need repair or maintenance right now, *before* it breaks. Take the time to check.

For an (A): Not everything that's broken needs to be fixed.

For an (E): If it ain't broke, don't fix it. (*American expression*)

For an (I): What they want is not necessarily what needs to change.

Timing (1)

For a (P): Problems can wait.

For an (A): Time is of the essence.

For an (E): Why is there always time to do it wrong three times and never enough time to do it right once?

For an (I): Missed opportunities will not come back.

Timing (2)

For a (P): Take your time to decide. You do not have to solve a problem the moment you realize you have it. There are back burners, too.

For an (A): The fact that a problem has a long history does not necessarily mean that the solution must have a long implementation.

For an (E): The fact that you realize there is a problem does not mean there should have been a solution *already*.

For an (I): The right timing for a solution is dictated by the problem and not by how expedient it is.

Timing (3)

For a (P): Treat a problem before it becomes a crisis.

For an (A): The time lag between when you cut costs and when you see sales decline can make your company look profitable while it is actually going bankrupt.

For an (E): Not all priorities should have been set and achieved *already*.

For an (I): Sometimes there isn't time to wait for a consensus.

Timing (4)

For (P)s and (E)s: Don't go for a temporary solution to a permanent problem.

For an (A): You don't need to find a permanent solution for a temporary problem.

Process

For a (P): Do not focus only on the solution. Focus on the *process* of arriving at a solution. The right solution with the wrong process, in the long run, is worse than the wrong solution with the right process.

For an (A): You always know the cost of doing something, but did you estimate the cost of *not* doing something?

For an (E): Do not present a problem or problems unless you believe there could be a solution – in other words, stop complaining! Be constructive!

For an (I): Short-term unity may have long-term costs.

Focus

For a (P): Stop looking exclusively at the *what*, and pay attention to the *how*, too.

For an (A): Pay more attention to the *what* and *when*, and less to the *how*.

For an (E): It's not enough to say *why* you want something; you must also decide exactly *what* should be done, *how* it will be done, and *who* will do it.

For an (I): *What* is agreed upon is as important as *who* agrees on it.

Yes, No, and Maybe

For a (P): Not everything is black and white, and not everything needs to be decided now. Learn to say "maybe."

For an (A): You must learn to say "yes."

For an (E): You must learn to say "no."

For an (I): You must learn to say "yes" or "no" instead of "maybe."

Knowing and Not Knowing

For a (P): Not to know is to know something very important.

For an (A): The fact that you don't know about something does not mean it isn't happening.

For an (E): If you stay on one subject long enough, they might be able to tell you something you should know – although you might not want to know it.

For an (I): Sometimes the more meetings you have, the less you know what it is all about.

Solutions

For a (P): "Leave it on my desk" is not a solution.

For an (A): A solution does not have to have precedents.

For an (E): The side effects of your solutions might be more dangerous than the problem you are trying to solve.

For an (I): The appearance of an agreed-upon solution is not a guarantee that the solution will work.

Deciding (1)

For a (P): Stop shooting from the hip; think before you act.

For an (A): Stop thinking everything is forbidden unless expressly permitted.

For an (E): Stop thinking everything is permitted unless expressly forbidden.

For an (I):   If you wait to see where your partner is going to hit the ball in the court, it'll be too late to return it.

DECIDING (2)

For a (P):   To get it right, you do not have to be tense.

For an (A): When there's a choice, do the right things instead of doing things right.

For an (E): You must do things right too, as well as doing the right things.

For an (I):   Take a stand.

EVALUATING DECISIONS (1)

For a (P):   You do not have to wait to see the results to know if you were right. If the process was right, you were right, even if the results are not right. Not everything is under your personal control.

For an (A): It could be the right thing to do although it is not yet *proven* to be right.

For an (E): It is not the right thing to do unless an attempt is made to *prove* that it is workable and valid.

For an (I):   Whether a decision is correct is not a function of how many people agree on it.

EVALUATING DECISIONS (2)

For a (P):   Not everyone who works hard is necessarily doing the right thing.

For an (A): It is better to be approximately right than precisely wrong.

For an (E): Are you making it better or are you just making it different?

For an (I):   Wrong decisions *can* be made by consensus.

COMPARING OPTIONS

For a (P):   Harder is not necessarily more.

For an (A):   If it is similar, it is not different. But it is similar.

For an (E):   If it is similar, it is not identical. It is *only* similar.

For an (I):   Compromise is the *appearance* of agreement. Consensus is the *support* of an agreement.

HEDGING

For a (P):   Not to hedge is expensive.

For an (I):   Hedging is expensive.

REACHING A DECISION

For a (P):   The solution may not be more of the same but may be less and different.

For an (A):   Stop worrying that it will not be done the way it *should* be done. What will be done will be done the way it *can* be done. What else can you expect?

For an (E):   Cool it! You must freeze a decision. Set a deadline by which a finalization will be arrived at. At the deadline, if there is no finalization, the latest illumination will automatically become the finalization.

For an (I):   Not to decide *is* a decision, whether you like it or not.

FINALIZING

For a (P):   Not every idea is necessarily a final one.

For an (A):   No decision should be permanent.

For an (E):   Never finalize a decision pending details to be worked out. Postpone finalization until details are reviewed. Then sleep on it for at least one night before approving and signing off on it for implementation.

For an (I):   When you finalize, apologize less, and communicate your decision firmly.

Success

For a (P):   More might be less; don't confuse quantity with quality.

For an (A):   Better is not necessarily more.

For an (E):   Best is the enemy of better: It is better to have a mediocre decision implemented than an outstanding decision never implemented.

Prescriptions for Good Decision-making (PAEI)

To understand the totality of a system, you must view it from many angles.

A person who truly never makes mistakes does not exist. Even God admits to making a mistake by bringing the Flood.

The purpose of decision-making:

Who are the clients? Why do we exist? (**I**)

What are their needs; i.e., why do we do this? (**E**)

What can we do to satisfy the present needs? (**P**)

How do we satisfy those needs repetitively with a minimum of energy? (**A**)

There is really no such thing as a good decision; it's only a good decision for the *time being*. The higher the rate of change, the shorter the time span for the validity of the decision.

Expected problems that we can deal with are not problems. They are the necessary by-products of our past decisions.

Preventive medicine seems expensive (because the necessity has not imposed itself), but it is comparatively the cheaper option.

It is the curative medicine (which seems cheap because there is a crisis) that is expensive. By that time, the problem is bigger and deeper, and you need to solve it under time pressure.

You do not know *what* to do until you know what *not* to do.

You do not know *how* to do something until you know how *not* to do it.

You do not know *when* to do it until you know when *not* to do it.

You do not know *who* should do it until you know who should *not* do it.

Good decisions are based on good judgment.

Good judgments are based on bad decisions from which you learn.

You can't have good judgment unless you made bad decisions yourself or learn from other people's bad decisions.

First why,
>then *what*,
>then *how*,
>then *when*,
>then *who*.

Change the *why* if needed by the *what* decision.

Change the *why* and *what* because of the *how*.

Change the *how*, *what*, and *why* because of the *when*.

Change the *when*, *how*, *what*, and *why* because of the *who*.

You have a decision only when the *why, what, how, when,* and *who* all make sense.

IMPLEMENTATION COMPARISONS

"Men do not stumble over mountains,
but over molehills."

CONFUCIUS

PROCESS

For a (P): The road to Rome will not necessarily take you there. They might have diverted the road since the last sign was erected. Periodically, check and recheck the purpose of your actions.

For an (A): There *is* more than one way.

For an (E): Not *all* roads lead to Rome. You might never arrive in Rome if you spend all your energies exploring all the possible roads that might lead to Rome.

For an (I): Standing at the intersection won't take you anywhere.

Form and Function

For a (P): For a long-term solution, function *does* need form.

For an (A): Form does not necessarily produce the desired function.

For an (E): If the decision is ambiguous, it's not going to be implemented the way you want it to be.

For an (I): Any decision is not necessarily the best decision.

Rules

For a (P): There are guidelines, rules, and policies. Do you know the difference?

For an (A): Not every guideline is a policy.

For an (E): Not every policy is a guideline.

For an (I): Not all decisions need to be made by holding meetings. Establish guidelines, rules, and policies.

Details

For an (A): For you, the devil is in the details.

For an (E): For you, God is in the details. Details are not irrelevant. Clarity is achieved through attention to detail. Lay down your shotgun. Use your microscope. Focus to see the differences.

Control and Supervision

For a (P): To get overcommitted to any task can be expensive.

For an (A): Holding tight won't make it better.

For an (E): What gets done is not what is expected but what is inspected. "If the end is good, the whole thing is good." (*Sof tov hakol tov* – expression from the Talmud)

For an (I): Not taking a stand is taking a stand.

FLEXIBILITY

For a (P): Beating a dead horse won't revive it. Be flexible in implementation.

For an (A): Do not react in a programmed way to altered situations that call for a new approach.

For an (E): If you keep changing horses in mid-race you might end up on your butt, with no horses at all.

For an (I): If you don't care what we do, or how or why we do it, just as long as we agree, that's not motivating; that's surrendering.

EFFECTIVENESS

For a (P): You might be running a very efficient railroad, but in the wrong direction. The harder you go forward, the more behind you'll get.

For an (A): To be more effective, you might have to be less efficient.

For an (E): To be more efficient, you might have to be less proactive.

For an (I): The effectiveness of a decision is not a function of how many people agree on it.

GETTING IT DONE

For a (P): In the long run, it is better to do one hundred percent of eighty percent than eighty percent of one hundred percent.

For an (A): To rephrase Pareto's law: A hundred percent of a hundred percent is sometimes less than eighty percent of a hundred percent.

For an (E): It is not enough to want something to happen; you have to actually do it.

For an (I): After you sit in the meeting and agree on what should be done, someone still needs to go out and get it done.

GETTING IT DONE, PITFALLS (1)

For a (P): Taking on more tasks than you can do might result in doing less than you can do.

For an (A): The fact that you took copious notes does not increase the probability that it will get done as written.

For an (E): The more you stir the pot (change your mind), the longer it will take to implement your decision (if it gets implemented at all).

For an (I): The fact that people agree on a decision does not mean they are going to implement it; *you* are still responsible for implementation.

GETTING IT DONE, PITFALLS (2)

For a (P): You do not know which is the right thing to do. You just do – even though it might be the *wrong* thing to do.

For an (A): You often do the wrong things right.

For an (E): You might do the right things wrong.

For an (I): You do not know which is the right thing to do. So you don't do anything until they tell you what to do. And they might be wrong.

Prescriptions for Good Implementation (PAEI)

Good management is democracy in decision-making and dictatorship in implementation – what I call "democratship." It is a difficult process.

The quality of management is a function of:

1) effective decisions, plus

2) efficient implementation.

Wanting a decision is not enough. Deciding that it should be done is not enough. You must also accept the decision you have made if you are going to implement it.

Tell me which way you face during decision-making and implementation, and I will tell you how well-managed your organization is. If you face the team when making a decision and turn your back to them when implementing it, that signifies that there is trust and respect among you; you are doing well. If it is the opposite, your organization lacks trust and respect, and you are doing badly.

TEAM-BUILDING COMPARISONS

"Getting together is a beginning. Staying together is progress. Working together is success."

HENRY FORD I

TEAMWORK

For a (P):   Telling people what to do does not mean you have a team.

For an (A):   Teamwork does not mean that everyone else should surrender to you.

For an (E): In a discussion, if the other person stops to breathe, it does not necessarily mean that he should lose the argument.

For an (I): Stop jumping on the bandwagon while pretending to lead the parade.

MEETINGS

For a (P): Not having meetings forces people to have meetings in the corridors.

For an (A): Fewer meetings will mean more things get done.

For an (E): In a meeting, stay with the subject being discussed. Avoid mercurial decision-making – constantly moving to the next subject.

For an (I): Stop the endless meetings.

LISTENING

For a (P): Don't tell them, "Call me when you finish." To have a team, you have to listen.

For an (A): The worst is when you hear no complaints. It seems good because you hear nothing, but apathy is one step away from death.

For an (E): You can't listen to others until you have finished listening to yourself.

For an (I): What appears to you to be an agreement may not be real.

GATHERING SUPPORT

For a (P): Don't make unilateral decisions. Try to build consensus.

For an (A): Stop being naive. Not everybody agrees with you.

For an (E): Stop that paranoia. Not everybody is against you.

For an (I): Stop that Pollyanna thinking. Not all those who say they support you, actually do.

Seeking Agreement (1)

For a (P): There is much to learn from people who discuss problems rather than just jump to fix them the quickest way they can.

For an (A): A disagreement is not a derailment.

For an (E): A question is not a disagreement.

For an (I): When two people agree on everything, one of them is dispensable.

Seeking Agreement (2)

For a (P): "Yes" does not always mean yes; "no" does not always mean no.

For an (A): To have a team, you must allow discussions.

For an (E): To agree with others, you must agree with yourself first.

For an (I): Being "against" can be "for," and being "for" can be "against."

Conflict

For a (P): Easy does it. You do not need a two-by-four to make change happen.

For an (A): Interpersonal conflict will not necessarily "rock the boat."

For an (E): If you continually insist on winning, the other parties will continually lose. This is a game most people will sooner or later refuse to play, and you will wind up arguing with yourself while your opponents watch, confused.

For an (I): Confrontations *should* be allowed.

Getting Along

If you are in pain with the decision-making process, the way to relieve it is to get involved in the process. The more disengaged you are, the more painful it will be.

For an (A): Teams must have flexibility.

For an (E): Tell them, or better, *do* things that indicate that you really appreciate people and need their approval and support. Your behavior, and especially the way you exhibit frustration, communicate just the opposite.

For an (I): There is no change without conflict. If you try to stop conflict, change will stop too.

Controlling Emotions

For a (P): When the gut is engaged, the mouth should stay closed.

For an (A): No pain, no gain.

For an (E): Do not chair meetings on subjects you are emotionally involved in. The moment your stomach starts getting into a "squeeze," ask someone else to moderate the meeting. Then listen, take notes, and act only when you are calm.

For an (I): There is a limit to how long most people can, and should have to, tolerate conflict.

Prescriptions for Good Team-building (PAEI)

The success of any system can be predicted by one and only one factor: The ratio between external and internal marketing.

A person should not be part of the solution if he isn't part of the problem; but if he is part of the problem, he had *better* be part of the solution.

For good management, conflict is inevitable – and a certain degree of conflict is even desirable.

When self-interest equals common interest, you have succeeded in (**I**)ntegrating.

When no one is indispensable, the organization is efficient in the long run.

A friend is someone who agrees with you. A colleague is someone whose disagreements you are grateful for and appreciate.

Unless everyone who shares the problem feels responsible, no one can be responsible.

Given synergy, management will occur. To put it another way, if there is no synergy, there is no management. The role of management is to create a friendly environment for synergy.

There is no respect without tolerance;

there is no tolerance without patience;

there is no patience without pain.

To practice mutual respect is painful.

Thus, management development is experiential training in taking ever-higher doses of pain.

The longer our perspective is, the more of a win-win climate we will have.

There must be a consciousness of interdependence, whether the organization is a nation, a business, a marriage, or an individual. The Old Testament says the perfect spouse is *ezer keneged*, or "helpful against." In other words, we always need a complementary person.

The more people disagree respectfully, the higher will be the value of the truth they will achieve when they agree.

No one has a monopoly over objective truth. Objective truth is a vector between equal, contentious, subjective truths that are freely discussed and understood with mutual trust and respect.

The people who need to be managed are all those whose help or services you need to carry out your responsibilities, whether those people report to you or not – or, for that matter, whether they are paid by the organization at all.

MANAGING STAFF COMPARISONS

"Leadership: the art of getting someone else to do something you want done because he wants to do it."

DWIGHT D. EISENHOWER

HIRING (1)

For a (P): Do not hire and promote people because of their performance – in spite of their personality.

For an (A): Do not hire and promote people because of their obedience – in spite of their performance.

For an (E): Do not hire and promote people because they seem enthusiastic about your ideas, in spite of their past performance.

For an (I): Do not hire and promote people because of their personality – in spite of their performance.

HIRING (2)

For a (P): Surrounding yourself with errand boys and gofers is never going to free you.

For an (A): "Yes, yes" men do "no, no" behind your back.

For an (E): Surrounding yourself with people who do not threaten you is not the way to leave a legacy behind.

For an (I):   Surrounding yourself with people who always agree with each other is not the way to make good decisions.

HIRING (3)

For a (P):   Hire someone who will also train for you.

For an (A):   When you hire, put those tests aside. Ask yourself also: Does it *feel* right?

For an (E):   When you hire, how you feel is important. But get some tests done. Get evaluations from others to confirm your gut feeling.

For an (I):   You usually read people well. But you must be willing to hire people who might cause conflict with their strong opinions – if that is what the organization needs.

SUBORDINATES ARRIVING AND LEAVING WORK

For a (P):   Coming to work first and leaving work last does not mean they are getting a lot accomplished.

For an (A):   Coming and leaving right on time does not mean that people are doing the right things in between.

For an (E):   If no one knows (including you) when you will come to work and when you will leave, but you expect people to be at work ahead of you and leave after you, how do you expect people to have lives of their own?

For an (I):   Going with the flow does not make you a leader. Ask them to do what needs to be done, even if it is not popular.

MEETINGS VS. MEMOS

For a (P):   Meetings *do* have a purpose.

For an (A):   Stop managing by memos.

For an (E): Start managing by memos.
For an (I): Stop the endless meetings.

Staff Relations (1)

For a (P):   Easy does it. You do not need a two-by-four to get subordinates to do something.

For an (A): People can't be programmed.

For an (E): Stop complaining. Skip the witch hunts. Be constructive! Do not only criticize. When warranted, be supportive. And by the way, killing the messenger who brings the bad news won't kill the news.

For an (I): Being nice to your staff does not necessarily make them more productive.

Staff Relations (2)

For a (P):   It helps no one, and especially you, to say: "I love to manage. It's people I can't stand!" People come with the territory of managing.

For an (A): The fact that you don't know about something does not mean it isn't happening.

For an (E): Putting people down does not make them feel up. Never put someone down in public unless you intend to fire him immediately afterward.

For an (I): Constantly making people feel up may end up making them feel down.

Popularity

For a (P):   Being popular can improve your effectiveness later on.

For an (A): A question is not necessarily a personal challenge.

For an (E): You do not like to fire. But humiliating a person so that he will eventually resign is not the cheapest way to discontinue a relationship.

For an (I):   A manager's job is not necessarily to be popular. His job is to be effective.

DELEGATING

For a (P):   Delegating is a sign of a good manager. Do those things that only you can do – not all the things that you can do.

For an (A):   Delegation is not synonymous with decentralization. In order to decentralize, freedom to make non-programmed decisions must be granted.

For an (E):   Your attitude and preferences are to decentralize. Your decision style, however, leads to centralization. The result is a catch-22 for your subordinates.

For an (I):   Make yourself dispensable, but don't *start out* dispensable.

TRAINING

For a (P):   "Do as I do" is not an effective training strategy.

For an (A):   Everything does not have to be written into manuals and codified.

For an (E):   People can't follow when they don't understand what is wanted.

For an (I):   Training only in human relations is not enough.

Prescriptions for Managing Staff Wisely (PAEI)

It is better and a lot easier to hire someone who is and teach him to *know* than to hire someone who *knows* and teach him to be.

For the best team performance, subordinates should be superior to the manager in some respects.

Unless inhibited, people rise to meet challenges. The environment in which we operate makes our latent capabilities either grow or disappear.

Authority is defined as the right to say yes *and* no. If managers you report to cannot say yes, neither should they be able to say no.

The day you have to remind people of your authority when it should be obvious is the day you are in managerial overdraft.

In order to manage well, you have to manage the people who will work on the problem, not the problem itself.

CHANGE COMPARISONS

The prayer with the prescriptions to the (PAEI) styles provided by me:

"God grant me the courage to change the
things I can ... [Good for (A)s and (I)s],
The serenity to accept those I can't ... [(E)s,
can you take it?],
And the wisdom to know the difference."
[This is for you, (P)]

THE SERENITY PRAYER

PROBLEMS AND OPPORTUNITIES

For a (P):   Manage your problems; don't be managed *by* them.

For an (A):   Not every opportunity is a problem.

For an (E):   Not every problem is an opportunity.

For an (I):   There is a price to procrastination in the face of problems and opportunities.

COST VS. VALUE OF CHANGE

For a (P):   Not to do, frequently requires doing a lot. Not to act is an active act. Do only when necessary.

For an (A): The cost of change is not always higher than the value of change.

For an (E): The value of change is not always higher than the cost of change.

For an (I): Going with the flow can be expensive.

PLANNING (1)

For a (P): There is enough time, if you plan and delegate properly.

For an (A): Forecasting is not planning.

For an (E): Planning involves commitment.

For an (I): A politician worries about the next election, whereas a statesman worries about the next generation. Which are you?

PLANNING (2)

For a (P): *Proact*, don't just react.

For an (A): Does the organization have to achieve its goals in spite of you?

For an (E): Wanting is not planning.

For an (I): An agreed-upon plan can still be a bad plan.

PLANNING (3)

For an (A): You think that since you don't have the funds, you don't have to plan.

For an (E): You assume that anything you want is automatically worth having, and you assume you can figure out how to pay for it later. *Don't assume!*

DIRECTION

For a (P): There might be an easier highway next to the arduous road you are walking on; can you stop walking and look for it?

For an (A): Where you are coming from is not where you should be going.

For an (E): If you try to get everywhere, you will get nowhere(I) asking for directions when you do not know where you want to go will get you nowhere.

JUGGLING CHANGES

For a (P): Take it easy; slow down! Those are eggs, not balls, you're juggling with....

For an (A): You can add balls to the hands you have.

For an (E): Do you have the hands you need for the balls you keep throwing in the air?

For an (I): When juggling, look at the balls, not at the hands.

TIME AND CHANGE

For a (P): If you have no time to attend training, that's the best reason to get training.

For an (A): We will stop encountering problems only when there is no more change, and that will happen only when we are dead.

For an (E): Do not attempt to live your whole life in one day.

For an (I): Consensus might be short-lived.

THINKING ABOUT THE FUTURE

For a (P): Now is not the future. Not all the problems are evident now.

For an (A): Remember the future.

For an (E): The future is not now.

For an (I): An important role of the manager is to represent future interests, rather than the interests of his immediate constituency.

Prescriptions for Managing Change Wisely (**PAEI**)

Change is constant. And change creates problems. And problems require solutions. And solutions create more changes. Thus, since change is forever, we will have problems forever too – "Life's a bitch and then you die." But if you can accept that, you might start to enjoy yourself.

There is no growth without change. There is no change without conflict. For conflict to spur growth, it should be based on mutual trust and respect; otherwise conflict will be destructive.

The typical path of resistance to change:

First they say, "It is not true," or "It is not valuable."

When the truth or value cannot be denied, they say,

"It can't be done," or "It's too expensive."

When the fact that it *can* be done and it is *not* too expensive cannot be denied, they say,

"Why did it take you so long? It was so simple."

What is the desirable sequence for deciding on change? Start by accepting what is, then realize what you want (and note the contrast between what is and what you want). Then decide what you should do: can you afford what you want? Now accommodate until what you want is what you should do and it is different from what you have. Then go and make it be!

Chapter 9

Dealing with Other People

Imagine that four people are looking through a window, but they see totally different things. One person sees a big picture through the window – of trees and mountains and birds and sailboats and clouds – the whole world through that window.

Another person looks through the same window and sees no birds, no trees, no clouds, no sailboats – nothing. What he sees is that the frame is dirty.

The third person looks through the window but doesn't see what either of the others are seeing, because he's busy wondering: How do you open this window? How do you wash this window? Why is this window positioned here? Are we getting enough light through this window?

The fourth guy isn't looking at the window at all. Instead, he's looking at the other three guys and wondering, "What are you guys looking at?"

These, of course, are the four (**PAEI**) styles. The person who sees the big picture is an (**E**). The one who only notices that the frame is dirty is an (**A**). The person looking at the functionality of the window is a (**P**). And the one who's looking at the other three is an (**I**).

Sometimes I joke about how the different styles might handle the sexual act. A (**P**) might say, "Start without me. When you're ready for an orgasm, call me."

An (**A**) would say, "Did you take a shower? Did you wash yourself thoroughly?" By the time you'd made all the necessary preparations, the window of desire might have closed.

An (**E**), while he's making love, would be imagining all the other partners he could be making love to instead.

And the (**I**) probably loves to talk about it more than to do it: "It's not the sex but the feeling that counts. I am not ready yet. Let's talk about it first."

Different people motivate, organize, and discipline differently, and it is crucial to pay attention to those differences. Everyone has a unique way of looking at the world, and each wants to be treated differently. This has implications for designing reward systems, hiring and promoting staff, evaluating performances, even how we treat our children and how one should treat one's spouse. It affects how we should treat each other.

Let's look at advertising, for instance. One way to look at market segmentation is through demographics – people's income, education, gender, or geographical location. Another way is through personality traits – marketing to different types of people differently. My methodology has been used now by quite a few advertising agencies.

(**P**) types look for the functionality of the product. Let's take the example of a car. Advertising directed toward (**P**)s should include the amount of leg room, how much baggage space there is, how many people can fit comfortably, how much head room there is. Does it have four-wheel drive? Practicality is key.

If you're talking to an (**A**) type, you'll want to stress the car's great warranty, its resale value, its ease of repair, its repair record.

An (**E**) is probably not especially interested in the resale value or the functionality. It's the creativity, the general idea behind it that fascinates him. Sometimes you wonder why people pay $100,000 or more for a Ferrari Testarosa, when it's very uncomfortable to sit in and it's illegal to drive 150 miles an hour anyway. What is the appeal? It's the idea, the image it communicates to others. It's not about what it can do but what it could mean. Thus, if you're selling a car to an (**E**), it had better have a sexy lady or man posed suggestively on the hood. If it's a house you're trying to sell to an (**E**), drape a negligee artfully across the bed in the master bedroom of the model house. You must stimulate his imagination if you want to sell him anything. He is not buying the product; he is buying what the product can do as he imagines it. (**E**)s respond to the colors, the music, and the image an ad creates. Sometimes, when you look at advertising targeted at (**E**)s, it's hard to know exactly what the product is, because the ad is selling a total image rather than any particular feature of that image.

For an (**I**), you're selling affiliation. A good example of that would be the Rolex watch advertising. Rolex ads feature celebrities who wear a Rolex, implying that if you want to belong to that class of people you should be wearing the same watch. The watch becomes a symbol of affinity and belonging.

A good advertising campaign should hit all four market segments; each type might require a separate ad. But this is tricky, because what attracts one type might repel another if the messages are incompatible.

Another familiar conflict in advertising stems from the fact that the ad director is probably an (**E**) type, and the client is probably a (**P**), if he is in sales, or an (**A**), if he works for a large company. Can you see the conflict these people will encounter? The ad manager is likely to create an (**E**) ad, which will have to be approved by an (**A**) or (**P**) executive. No chance! That ad manager could easily find himself without an account.

COMMUNICATING

We all know how easy it is to get off on the wrong foot when we're explaining something, and how the other person can seem to hear something entirely different from what we thought we said. In order to manage well, you need to sell your ideas. You must convince others to cooperate.

Miscommunication is a major source of organizational conflict. However, you can avoid the most damaging kinds of miscommunication by matching your style to the needs of the person you're talking to. Too often, we expect others to adapt to us. But if you genuinely want to be understood, you have to be the one who adapts. Do not be product-oriented in your communication. Be market-oriented. Focus on the communication needs of the person with whom you are communicating.

If you are new in the organization, or you are trying to communicate to a new client whose typical style you don't know, what should you do? Ask what job he performs. Look at the organizational chart. That can tell you a lot. If the person is in marketing, you can expect him to be (**E**)-oriented, or (**E**)ntrepreneurial. If he is in sales, he should be (**P**)-oriented, a (**P**)roducer. If he is a VP for sales and marketing, his (**P**) will probably overshadow his (**E**) tendencies, so take the (**P**) orientation. An accountant will very likely have an (**A**) orientation.

You can also find clues by looking at his office, his desk, how he dresses, his posture, his energy. In other words, be sensitive to the other person. Observe whether he understands you or not, and adapt your style to him so that you can communicate to him clearly.

You'll remember that (**E**)ntrepreneurs are global in their views, result-oriented, fast-moving, and unstructured. (**P**)roducers are also result-oriented and fast-moving, but they are local, or task-oriented, in their views, structured, and detailed. (**A**)dministrators share the (**P**)roducer's interest in detail and immediate results, but they tend to be slow and process-oriented, very organized. Finally, (**I**)ntegrators, like (**E**)ntrepreneurs, take a global view and are unstructured. But like (**A**)s, they are process-oriented and slow. They wait for others to blaze the trails. (For more tips on how to identify a style without giving a psychological test, see: Ichak Adizes: *The Ideal Executive*, chapter 9.) Now let's discuss in a sequence: How to deal with a (**P**)roducer, then how to deal with an (**A**)dministrator, then how to deal with an (**E**)ntrepreneur, and finally how to deal with an (**I**)ntegrator.

Bear in mind that to accomplish the complex tasks of management, you need to be able to persuade, convince, and even lead, not just your subordinates, but also your colleagues and even your boss. If you can successfully handle all three, you are potentially a leader.

What is leadership? A leader is to a complementary team what a thumb is to a hand: It is the one essential part, which (**I**)ntegrates all the other parts together to make a single entity: A hand, a team. To be a true thumb – to know how to lead your subordinates, your colleagues, and even your boss – you must know how to handle all four styles.

A note of warning: Surprisingly, it is hardest to communicate appropriately with subordinates. Why? Because we tend to take them for granted and are less careful about how we communicate. And thus we miscommunicate.

To communicate well, you must be conscious at all times. Try to think about all the people in your organization as if they were your bosses, whether they are or not. Start from the premise that you have to sell them your idea. In other words, instead of falling back on your authority and power, try to use your influence.

Dealing with a (P) – a (P)roducer or Lone Ranger

A (**P**)roducer is fast, doesn't have a lot of time, and is usually under pressure to deal with a crisis. He is generally highly structured, detail-oriented and result-oriented.

What does this mean? How should you communicate?

Getting His Attention

Well, think about what would happen if you called a (**P**) type and said, "Boss, I need you for three hours to discuss a problem." Will that work? Obviously, he's going to say, "Three hours? Fine. How about in October 2012; maybe then I can find three hours. Where the heck am I going to find three hours to talk with you? I have so many crises I can't even tell you where I'm going to be tomorrow!"

How much time can you realistically ask for? Five minutes. Ten minutes. Fifteen minutes. Try to be short.

But first, how do you get his attention? You have to figure out: "How can I make this problem look like a crisis?"

Why? Because he is so busy! Since he has more problems than he can solve, he deals only with crises. If your problem is not a crisis, it's going to have to wait. He will tell you, "Put it on my desk," and you will never hear about it again; it will just sit there with the 350 other problems he has sitting on his desk, and it won't get attended to.

On the other hand, if it's a crisis, to him it's legitimate cause for concern and he will give you time.

Making a Presentation

Next: when you get into his office, do not start with Adam and Eve. Start from the end; give him the bottom line. Tell him what your conclusions are.

Then give him any supporting material he asks for. Answer questions. But it's important to start from the end – with the decision you have already come up with.

Next, you must tell him that you're already working on it and all you need from him is approval: "Boss, we have a crisis and we have very little time to deal with it, and because of that I've already come up with a solution. All I need is your approval."

Enabling a Solution

Why must you phrase it like that? Because if there isn't any time pressure, or if you are not already in the midst of implementing the solution, what will he say? "Put it on my desk."

If this (**P**) is a Lone Ranger, you really have to take the initiative, because he's not going to delegate to you; you have to delegate to yourself. But you don't want to take unnecessary risks either, so you want him to approve what you're doing. Thus: "Jim, we have a crisis, I need fifteen minutes of your time, here is the problem, here is what I am already doing, I just need your approval so I can finish it." Done. There you go.

Imagine doing this with an (**A**). You call him and say the same thing: "There is a crisis, and I am already midway into implementing the solution." What's going to happen? You'll be fired on the spot: "Who gave you the right to start implementing the solution? How dare you take initiative without getting approval?"

With an (**A**), you can't do anything without asking permission first. With an (**E**), too, you'd be fired – because what you did was not his idea. With each of them, you have to take a different approach.

If you are a (**P**) type working for an (**A**), you've probably made this mistake. You probably saw a problem and figured out how to solve it. Then you went to your boss to tell him how you solved it, and you couldn't understand why he got apoplectic and jumped down your throat. Well, the answer is, you used a (**P**) solution for an (**A**), and an (**A**) cannot tolerate that style. You have to do it his way.

KILLING A BAD PLAN

What should you do if your (**P**) boss assigns you to do something that you think would be a giant mistake?

You can't just tell him you don't have time. He doesn't understand that. "Just work harder," he'll tell you.

Instead, tell him that you have a much bigger crisis to attend to and you will turn to the new assignment as soon as you can. Whenever he asks you for an update, just describe the latest crisis you are attending to and assure him again that you will get to it as soon as you can. Eventually, the task will become obsolete and you can safely ignore it.

If that strategy doesn't work, however, you'll have no choice but to be blunt: "I will not do it. It is going to be a disaster." A (**P**) will accept your strong position as long as it is honest and sensible. As should be obvious from my recomendatin here, I do not support anyone carrying out a decision which they honestly believe is an absolute disaster. I recommend try stopping it or resign, but you should not give a hand to a decision you are sure will bring a disaster. If you are in doubt if it is a disaster, try dissuading the decision maker, but if you fail to do so, you have to carry it out.

DEALING WITH AN (A) – AN (A)DMINISTRATOR OR BUREAUCRAT

The (**A**) type is more interested in the how than in the what. What does this mean? He confuses form with function, so you have to pay enormous attention to the form. He doesn't care if something is a crisis or not. He cares about whether you are following correct procedure.

GETTING HIS ATTENTION

You should never talk about crises with an (**A**); they hate crises with a vengeance. If you want to grab an (**A**)'s attention, you must show him that your problem is actually a violation of some longtime, preexisting policy, rule, or decision – even of common-sense principles: "A rule has been broken. We decided, but guess what? They are not doing it as it was agreed they would do it. It's not working right." The word "right" is important.

ENABLING A SOLUTION

Next, present a solution – one and only one. Do not confuse him by giving him choices. Then, to prove the validity of your proposed solution, bring as many examples as you can find of cases where your solution was successfully implemented – the more pages, the better, with lots of details and footnotes. In other words, you must prove that this solution has been supported by all the luminaries and the gurus; that it's been tried before, and that there is no risk.

Finally, you have to add a sentence at the end of your proposal that states: "This is my recommendation, and I take full responsibility for it, and if it does not work I will be accountable."

Basically, an (**A**) wants no risk. When a problem arises, you have to find a way in which the problem can be interpreted as a deviation, thus a legitimate problem to work on. Ideally the solution should also have no risk. Then the (**A**) is going to say, "Fine, go ahead and do it."

MAKING A PRESENTATION

How do you handle an (**A**) under ordinary circumstances, in your day-to-day meetings and communications when there is no urgent matter to be dealt with? You must follow a protocol.

First, no surprises. When you need to meet with an (**A**), you must ask for an appointment. If you catch him unawares, you'll lose the first half hour of the meeting because he won't be listening; he'll be obsessing about how you came and interrupted him, and angry that you did not give him time to prepare for the meeting. He will feel exposed and thus resentful. Remember, he has his day planned. His week planned. His year planned. Most probably his life planned. So your unannounced interruption is disrupting his entire life.

Instead, you must make an appointment and tell him what the agenda is going to be, so that he has time to prepare himself.

Next: You have to use what I call your bias multiple. What does this mean? Each management style has a different view of time; (**E**)s and (**P**)s move fast, while (**A**)s and (**I**)s take their time.

I have found that as an (**E**), my own bias multiple is six, which means that if I tell my subordinates, "We can do this in one hour," how long does it really take? Six hours. If I tell them, "Ah, we can do that in a week," how long does it take? Six weeks. An (**E**), an eagle, up there in the sky, can cover half a mile down on the ground with one beat of his (my) wings. The higher I am, the smaller my movements have to be to cover the same amount of ground.

But the people on the ground who have to cover the same territory are climbing up and down canyons, mountains, rocks; and for them it might take many hours. An (**E**) tends to forget this, which is why it's important to keep in mind your bias multiple.

If you are a (**P**) or an (**E**), and you need to meet with an (**A**)dministrator for what you estimate will be half an hour, you'd better call and say, "I need a meeting with you for three hours." Why? Because of your bias multiple. What the (**A**) cannot tolerate is if you ask for half an hour and stay for three hours. You must ask for a specific amount of time, and you must keep to that schedule.

The next step, before the meeting, is to prepare yourself. How? By breathing. Deep, slow, breathing. (**E**)ntrepreneurs and (**P**)roducers are not very good at breathing; they're always running out of breath. Why? Because they're running full speed ahead, all the time. In countries like Mexico, which is very (**P**)-oriented, it is said that in an argument, the first one who stops to take a breath loses the argument. What (**P**)roducers and (**E**)ntrepreneurs have to learn, especially when dealing with (**A**)dministrators and (**I**)ntegrators, is to slow down. That means breathing.

The more relaxed you are, the more slowly you'll make your presentation and the more chance you'll have of being understood by the (**A**).

When you slow down, you can also be more observant of the person you are talking to. Watch his eyes, eyebrows, and hand movements. Watch his body and synchronize what he says with how he says it. You can't do that if you are rushing.

So before you enter the (**A**)'s office, slow down – physically slow down. Take deep breaths. Do it in the corridor as you're going there, because your tendency will be to speed up. He will be moving at his usual speed of one mile an hour, and if you don't slow down you will be hitting him at 150 miles an hour. It's crucial to slow down to his speed, because for every one of your ideas, he's going to think of ten or even a hundred repercussions of that idea. He needs time to process that information. So slow down.

You begin the meeting. You tell him what you want to talk about; confirm your agenda. Again, no surprises.

Now start with item No. 1. As you present it to him, it's very important to watch his eyes. The moment his eyes wander, or go "out to lunch," it means he's not listening anymore. He's thinking. What is he thinking about? The repercussions of your idea. Who is he listening to when his eyes are out to lunch? To himself. Is he listening to you? No.

What should you do while he's listening to himself? Stop talking. Stop talking! This is very difficult for an (**E**)ntrepreneur, I know. But it's crucial to wait until the (**A**) has finished processing the information before you continue.

What should you do while you're waiting? If you are an (**E**), you will probably will have 300 other ideas crowd into your mind while you are waiting, and you will want to say them before you forget them. Don't. Write them on a piece of paper. You can get to them later. If you write them down, you will immediately feel calmer because you'll know you can get back to them whenever you want. You will not have to overburden the (**A**) person you're talking to. (**A**)s drink with a tea spoon. (**E**)s download with a firehose. Slow down. Do not drown the poor guy.

When the (**A**)dministrator comes back from "lunch," he will usually have a question. And what will that question be? It will be about some detail of implementation, which, especially if you are an (**E**)ntrepreneur, will probably upset you: Here you are trying to deal with the big picture, and this (**A**) type is asking you about some totally irrelevant little details.

Don't get upset. Take another deep breath and acknowledge the question: "Good question, let me write it down." Even better, write it on a flip chart, so the (**A**) can see that you did not ignore it or disrespect it. Write it down and say, "Thank you. Great question. I would like to address it later, when I finish my presentation, if you don't mind, so it can be discussed in the full context of what I am presenting." And continue with your presentation. The (**A**) will feel that you've acknowledged his concerns, and you will not be sidetracked.

Continue with your presentation until the next time his eyes go out to lunch. Then stop again. Take a deep breath. Wait. Acknowledge his question when it comes up. Write it down. Continue again with the big picture.

What you are doing, in effect, is presenting the what and why before you address the how, or the problems of implementation.

When you finish explaining the big picture, summarize it for the (**A**), making sure he understands it, and conclude, "Now let me address your questions." Then it's time to deal with the details, one by one by one. This way the (**A**) cannot veto your idea, or even argue against it, until he has heard the whole thing and knows what it is. You must not be drawn into discussing the how until you've communicated the what and the why. I have seen situations where a presentation was given to an (**A**), who interrupted with a question that was discussed in so much detail that the presentation was never completed. That is called going into a rat hole and ending up in China, when you were only trying to propose a road to the local shopping mall.

If you know the answers to the (**A**)'s questions, then go ahead and answer them. But beware: If you are not absolutely sure of your answer, it would be much better to ask for time to look into it, and make another appointment to come back with the answers.

Honestly addressing the (**A**)'s concerns might mean that you will have to change your original recommendation. So be it. The important thing is that by giving yourself extra time, you were saved from making some major mistake. Be thankful.

How long should you stay in a meeting with an (**A**)? Only the length of the time that was allocated to you. Don't say, "Ten more minutes, just ten more minutes and we'll be finished." The worst mistakes are usually made in the last ten minutes of an extended meeting, because that's when you start rushing.

If you're an (**E**) type, this will be very difficult for you. But remember: management is about selling ideas. And you're not selling them to yourself, you're selling them to somebody else. You must talk to him in a language he understands if you want him to buy.

Killing a Bad Plan

What should you do if your (**A**) boss gives you a plan to implement that you know would be disastrous? How do you stop it from going forward without risking your job?

Again, you can present it to your boss as a violation. Find a way in which this plan violates a policy or precedent. Is it too costly? Might it have too many unpredictable repercussions? An (**A**) cannot bear too many broken or bent rules, and he also secretly believes that anything unpredictable is out of control. Eventually, if you keep piling up the "violations," he himself will reject the plan.

There is one more important point to remember when communicating with an (**A**), especially if you yourself are an (**E**).

For an (**E**), numbers tend not to be meant literally. They're really only a magnitude. Thus, an (**E**) might say, "We sold a million." What he really means is a million more or less – somewhere between half a million and a million and a half.

Now for an (**A**), a million is exactly a million. If it is 999,999, then it's not a million.

This is a huge issue between (**E**)s and (**A**)s, and contributes to the (**A**)'s mistrust of the (**E**). The (**A**) thinks, "That guy – you really don't know what he's saying. His word is not his word. He says, 'I need to talk to you for half an hour.' Then he comes half an hour late and stays for three hours. To him, numbers, time, words have no meaning. This guy is full of hot air and I don't trust him!"

(**A**)s are very literal-minded. If you are an (**E**) talking to an (**A**), you have to honor that. You have to be very careful not to confuse ideas with facts, because if you say something as if it is fact and the (**A**) catches you in a mistake, you're dead. He won't trust you anymore and he will dismiss everything else you've said, whether it's true or not.

Dealing with an (E) –
an (E)ntrepreneur or Arsonist

With an (**E**) type, it would be a waste of time to approach him the way you would an (**A**) – with a thirty-page report detailing a problem and the solution. An (**E**) will not read the thirty-page report. He will put it on his desk and forget about it.

Furthermore, we know that an (**E**)ntrepreneur resists any idea unless it is his own. If you walk into a meeting with an (**E**) and say, "Boss, here is the problem and this is the solution, and I just want your approval," there is a good chance he's going to say, "Wrong problem, wrong solution." He's going to try to change it, he's going to attack it, he's going to look for a loophole, he's going to try to find out what's wrong with it. Why? Because he wants to put his stamp on it. He does not like finalized ideas, where there is nothing for him to add. For an (**E**), this signifies that you are taking charge, you're charging ahead and leaving him behind, forgetting him, ignoring him. He feels disrespected. Sooner or later, he's going to find a way to put you in your place.

Getting His Attention

So how do you approach an (**E**) with a problem? First of all, you don't call it a problem. An (**E**) is not interested in problems; he gets annoyed when you talk about problems, because problems are something he doesn't have time for.

Instead, you must figure out how to make your problem into an opportunity. When you get to his office, instead of saying, "We have a problem," you say, "We have an opportunity to do something better," or "We have an opportunity to change something. What do you think?"

So making the problem into an opportunity is the first thing you think about. The second is: "How do I make the solution his idea?" Use the phrase, "I suggest …," or "May I suggest …," or "I've been thinking …," or "It appears that …," or "What do you think?" Let him put his stamp on it.

Again, I'm not talking just about your boss; I'm talking about your subordinates too. If you treat an (**E**)-type subordinate as a subordinate – telling him what to do, how to do it, when you want it, now go do it! – he's going to hate it, because you aren't giving him a chance to use his brain. (**E**)s are creative: They like to design the train, they like to design the route the train is going to follow.

So you have to talk to them – boss, peer, or subordinate – in that language: "What do you think?" "What would you suggest?" "How would you improve this?" Eventually they will get excited and say, "Yes, that's good, but what if we also …?" and begin to add their thoughts to the mix. Then you have to incorporate their ideas so that they can own the solution.

MAKING A PRESENTATION

An (**E**) is the worst listener of all the types, because he's so creative that anything you say will stimulate his thinking, and he will stop listening to you while he processes his own ideas. Fortunately, you know when he stops listening, because you see his eyes wander. So, just as you would do when making a presentation to an (**A**), you must watch an (**E**)'s eyes and observe when they go "out to lunch." The moment his eyes wander, you know he isn't hearing a word you say. And if you continue talking he will get annoyed because you are interfering with his capability to listen to his own ideas he is formatting right than and there.

Once you understand why the (**E**) is not listening, the best approach is to give him the time and space to debate himself. Ask him to give you five minutes to tell him what you want to say, and suggest that he write down his comments for discussion after you have finished speaking. Then start talking. Whenever he starts writing or his eyes wander, stop talking and wait. Let him finish thinking. Begin speaking again only when he stops writing or re-establishes eye contact with you.

Do not ask for more than five, or at the most, fifteen minutes. (**E**)s have so many new ideas and questions about what you are saying that they cannot keep quiet for longer than five or fifteen minutes. When you're listening to them, it's like having to drink from a firehose; but when you talk to them, you need to feed them with a teaspoon.

Often the (**E**) will come back from "lunch" with questions and disagreements. Just as you said to the (**A**), you tell him, "Good question, let's address it later," and write it down in a notebook, or even better, on a flip chart. This is important; you must write all the questions down, and you really must address them after you've finished making your presentation.

Now that he knows that his questions will eventually be addressed, his eyes clear up and he's ready to accept more information. Then you continue, and then wait while he processes the new information. Write down his questions and continue your presentation.

At the end of the five or fifteen minutes, let the (**E**) react to what you've said; then ask for five more minutes to respond and repeat the exercise. Don't worry about time. He will give you as much time as you want, as long as you give him time to add to what you say and *change* what you say.

Finally, when you have finished the presentation and are answering his questions, make sure that the solution ends up having his "fingerprints" on them – that either it is his idea or it would not have worked without his corrections.

PRESERVING YOUR SOLUTION

What should you do if you already have a solution and you are afraid the (**E**) might change it? How do you make sure it will be left intact? Here is a tactic that I admit is manipulative; if you were caught doing it, the consequences would likely be unpleasant.

Present your solution – but with an intentional mistake, a very obvious mistake, right at the beginning. An (**E**) will see it immediately and correct it, and in correcting it he will feel ownership of the solution because he's put his stamp on it. From there on you might be free to do as you suggest.

In the advertising business, this is called "the hairy arm" strategy: When artists draw a storyboard for a TV ad for a difficult client, they often give the figure in the ad excessively hairy arms. When the (**E**) client sees the storyboard, he immediately says, "That's wrong, fix it," and thus feels he owns or has created the whole art piece. But beware, if it is an (**A**) client, can you imagine what would happen? You would be hearing about the hairy arms for a long, long time.

But for dealing with (**E**)s, it really works. One of my clients, an architect, once told me, "I listened to your crazy idea and I did it. Now when I design something, I put an intentional error up front – it must be up in the beginning, otherwise I'm dead. I insert an error that's very easy to identify, so that the client doesn't get distracted by something else and start to make changes that I don't want him to make. What happens is they pick up the problem and they correct it, which you know they're going to do because you planted it yourself, and then you're home free.

"But watch out. It can't be too stupid, or they'll fire you."

KILLING A BAD PLAN

If you work for an (**E**) and you strenuously object to one of his plans, don't ignore him. Don't assume he's going to forget about it. And don't talk to other people behind his back about how terrible this idea is. It will get back to him.

Instead, figure out how to confront him without threatening him. There are a number of ways to do that.

1. *Try to discourage him:* "Look, you're the boss, your decision is final and I will follow it, but before you make up your mind please give me fifteen minutes to tell you why I'm worried about what you want me to do." When I do this, I sometimes actually put my watch on the table, so that he won't interrupt me.

Never say, "Here is why I disagree with you," because the moment you say the word "disagree" he will stop listening. "Here's why it's a bad idea" is not good either. Try something like: "Here's why I'm afraid it's not going to work and produce the results you want." Feed his narcissistic need for adulation: "I will do whatever you want, it's not that I'm fighting you, I'm just afraid it won't produce the result you want. I'm afraid there may be serious side effects, so I need to discuss it with you to be sure that what you want will actually happen."

Basically, you're reassuring him that you're on his side. Usually, an (**E**) will respond helpfully: "What is it that bothers you?" "What are you afraid of?"

The important thing is not to let him interrupt you. Make sure he has a piece of paper so he can write down his thoughts while you're talking. And don't make it too long. Fifteen minutes is about all he can take.

2. *Ask for more time to implement:* "Can we wait a little while, let me think this through?" He may forget all about it, or he may not. Or, if you give him time, he might come back and say, "I have

another idea." That's how he kills his own bad ideas: he replaces it with another idea.

3. *Say "yes":* Because the moment you say "yes," he will relax. Then go back to your office and make a long list, the longer the better, of all the details of implementation, phrased in such a way that choices must be made – "Should we do this or that?"

Then go back and say, "I have some questions to ask you. What do you want me to do about this? And this? And this?"

An (E) hates to finalize anything and doesn't like dealing with details and choices. He wants to have his cake, eat it, lease it, and give it. So it's likely that after being forced to make a couple of difficult choices, he will say, "You know, it's a good idea, but let's put it on the back burner for now. We can get back to it later." And that usually does not happen.

4. *Put it in writing:* If your (E) boss is adamant and still wants the job done, but you don't want to take the responsibility, request that he put the assignment in writing and sign it. He does not like to put anything in writing if he can help it, so it won't happen.

5. *Quit:* Finally, if the situation is dire – you believe his plan is morally wrong and should not be implemented – you have no choice but to say, "Sorry, I cannot do that. It would be a disaster for the company and I won't be party to it. I resign."

RELAYING BAD NEWS

Finally, how do you give an (E) bad news? If there is any hint in your presentation that the (E) himself is somehow to blame, he will immediately attack you: "I don't know what the heck you're talking about!" "You have completely messed this up!" "You are creating political upheaval!" "You're totally dysfunctional!" He will accuse you of trying to create turmoil in the organization.

So the key is that the bad news must not reflect badly on him. An (E) easily becomes emotional and paranoid, so you must be extremely careful in your choice of words: "It appears that we have an opportunity to do something better here; what do you think we should do?" Always "it appears." If he denies what you're telling him, you have no choice but to retreat. If he replies, "That's interesting, but don't worry about it," you can press a little harder: "Well, but it appears that...." But be very careful, because if he interprets the bad news as making him look bad, he will look for a scapegoat, and you will be the most convenient target.

DEALING WITH AN (I) - AN (I)NTEGRATOR OR SUPERFOLLOWER

What is an (I)ntegrator, or an extreme (I), a SuperFollower, looking for? He wants everyone to agree: Is there a political consensus?

GETTING HIS ATTENTION

If you go to an (I) and say, "Joe, here is the problem and here is the solution and we want your authorization," what is he going to say? "It's not time yet, we are not ready, have you talked to Rudy, have you talked to Paul, have you talked to Denise?" He's going to want to assess the political climate.

Thus, before you go to the (I) with a problem, you must cover all your bases. You have to talk to Rudy and Paul and Denise and Nancy and find out where they stand. Then you can go to the (I) and say, "Joe, we have a problem, we have discussed it, we all agree, we think this is the solution and we want your approval." An (I) will immediately want to know: "Who are the people who agree or don't agree with this solution? And what about Dan? And did you talk to Bill?"

If Dan is very important to him, and you haven't talked to Dan, he's going to say, "Well, I think we're not ready yet."

But if you say, "Yes, we talked to Dan and he's going to resign unless we implement this solution," he's going to say, "Okay, what about Bill?"

"He's totally behind it."

At that point, an (**I**) will say, "Then what are we waiting for? Let's do it."

Now imagine using an (**I**) approach with an (**E**).

Imagine that you are an (**I**)ntegrator with an (**E**)ntrepreneur boss. You believe you know how to solve problems, so when a problem comes up, what do you do? You go and talk to all the relevant people, you resolve all the conflicts, and then you go to your (**E**) boss and say, "Boss, we had a problem, we all met, we all agreed what the problem is and we all agreed what the solution should be. Now we want you to approve it."

How is the (**E**) boss feeling? He's probably sweating. He's thinking, "My god, this guy has done a coup d'etat behind my back. He's building a revolution. My staff never told me about the problem, they just went into a back room, they all talked about it, they have a solution, now they're cornering me to force me to approve it!"

An (**E**) will never forgive you, and he will never forget. At the first opportunity, he will fire you. This is a frequent problem for (**I**) types: they try to build a consensus, encourage participatory management – and the (**E**) ends up firing them.

Summing It Up

Different people understand different words differently. They look for different needs to be satisfied, and their style of decision-making is different. To successfully communicate and sell your ideas to them, you need to adapt yourself to their style. This is complicated, because nobody is really a perfect, exclusive (**P**) or an exclusive (**A**); we are usually an amalgam. So how do we figure out which style to use?

Making the Presentation

The answer is that a manager must be sensitive. If he tries one approach and sees it's not being understood, he tries another approach. He's constantly watching the person he's selling his ideas to, and adapting his style of communicating until the other person fully understands.

Knowing whom you are talking to and how to talk to them is essential for succeeding in management and, I believe, life in general. A well-rounded person must be able to communicate with all styles. It is like knowing several languages: You can probably get away with knowing only English, but you gain priceless respect, admiration, and good will when you are able to speak with other people in their own languages.

In the next chapter there are some specific prescriptions for dealing with each type.

Chapter 10

Prescriptions for Dealing with Others

DEALING WITH A (P)

BEHAVIOR

Ignore his complaints, and set priorities.

(P)s constantly complain that they don't have enough time for all the work they need to do. But it isn't really a complaint; it's actually bragging.

(P)s want something to do all the time. They are very passionate about whatever they do, they go full blast at it; and by going full blast at it they remain very busy.

As a joke, I sometimes say that a (P) worries if he's not worrying. He's always working, and if he's not working on something he becomes anxious. That's why his desk is always piled with work and papers and telephone messages; this makes him feel needed. If the desk is empty and clean, he feels unneeded, dispensable, and he gets worried.

So the first principle for dealing with a (P) is: Don't get overly upset when he complains about being overworked. He has designed it that way. Don't lessen his load, or you will make him even more unhappy.

The second thing is to carefully set priorities for him. A (P) is not very good at setting priorities for himself. Assign him one priority at a time, telling him exactly which problems need to be handled first and which can wait. A (**P**) cannot juggle too many balls at the same time. If you set and assign his priorities, he can stay as harried as he likes, and you will still get your problems solved.

Communication

You have to use a two-by-four.

(**P**)s get on a certain track and stay there. To move them away from that track, you have to use a two-by-four.

What do I mean? A (**P**) is thick-headed and forceful. To stop him or change his direction requires hitting him with equal force. In other words, before you even try to change a (**P**)'s direction, you'd better accumulate a huge amount of evidence of potential trouble, so that you can come to him with lots of support. Don't do it one step at a time. No hints, no Chinese torture for (**P**)s; it doesn't work. You cannot be gentle with a (**P**). You *can* hint to an (**E**) or an (**I**); they will get the message. With a (**P**), you have to tell it like it is – no sugar coating, no diplomacy. Then he'll understand what you meant to say.

Decision-making

Point out the gray areas.

(**P**)s think everything is black or white; they get very frustrated with gray. They want a "yes" or a "no": "Just give me an answer; I want to know where I stand." They think discussion is a waste of time.

You have to remind them that not everything is black or white; there are gray areas in between, and sometimes you have to grope your way around until you find a solution. All of this is alien to a (**P**), which is why you will have to repeat it continually.

For a (P), not to act is an active act.

In a meeting, a (**P**) is very eager to get moving. He sees any movement as positive, even if it's moving in the wrong direction.

So (**P**)s fidget a lot. They expend a lot of energy just on restraining themselves from taking action. Imagine a car with a tremendous engine. To keep this car with its big engine from rolling forward requires a lot of energy to hold the brakes down.

In my work with (**P**)s I have to relentlessly be aware of their eagerness for action. My prescription is simply: Watch out, don't give in to their intense pressure to start doing something, *anything*. Make sure you have the right solution before you allow a (**P**) to act.

If you cannot hold them back from acting, find something for them to do that you want done; otherwise they are likely to busy themselves with something you did *not* want done.

Not to know is to know something very important.

(**P**)s feel very uncomfortable when they don't know something. When I coach them, they often say to me, "Dr. Adizes, where in the world are you taking us?" They're very upset when I tell them, "I don't know, I'm still exploring, I'm taking it one step at a time."

Problem-solving is like entering a maze: We have to choose each step that we take forward, and sometimes we have to go back and re-find our way. This exploration is very painful for (**P**)s. They want to handle a problem right away, bingo, and move on.

So I tell them, "The fact that we don't know – we *know* that we don't know. That's important. So slow down; we don't need to know everything right away. We have to find out."

IMPLEMENTATION

Set policies, rules, and guidelines.

(**P**)s operate best in conditions of certainty, where everything is black and white. The moment there is any ambiguity, they lose track and start to lose their effectiveness.

To help a (**P**) become more effective, establish strict policies and rules, then set priorities for him. "Go do this. Then come back." "Now go do that." In that kind of environment, he will flourish.

TEAM-BUILDING

Help him delegate.

A typical (**P**) feels responsible for the whole world. He believes everything is on his shoulders. So if you come into his office to tell him about a problem, he will immediately say, "Put it on my desk." He wants to fix everything. He's like a dog in front of a steak: every time he smells it, he goes for it.

How can you explain to a (**P**) which tasks are his responsibility and which are not? You have to define his role very clearly – what to do and also what *not* to do, because if you don't tell him what *not* to do he'll inevitably take on tasks you didn't want him to do. You must set strict boundaries.

MANAGING CHANGE

The future is now.

(**P**)s are reactive instead of proactive; they wait for a crisis to develop before they deal with it. They're very short-range-oriented. So when I work with a (**P**), I try to create a scenario that illustrates how terrible things are going to be any minute, unless he does something *right now*. I try to make this problem as close to the present as possible, because if I tell him something terrible is going to happen ten years from now, he'll simply ignore me.

For example, one company I consulted with needed to reinvent itself. Their competition had not only copied their product very successfully but were doing better marketing. So far, the competition had only entered the United States market, but sooner or later they were going to enter Europe and then England, where my client's home office was.

So I said, "All right, it's three years from now, and this is what it looks like: You have your competitor from the United States here in England, and they have 300 stores with much better merchandising, a better product line, better advertising, and better marketing. What have we done to prevent that? What's going to happen to us? Where are we?" I present the picture as if it's happening now. Then, instead of reacting, they will proact.

Dealing with an (A)

Communication

Encourage (A)s to speak up.

(A)s keep their mouths shut; they don't disclose their thoughts easily and willingly. An (A) prefers to say nothing until he's thought an idea all the way through.

So you just have to wait until he is ready.

But you can also encourage him to speak: "Say what you think even if you're not sure. Just tell us what you *think*, not what you have *decided*. It's OK to be inconsistent. If you tell us what you think, maybe we can join you, we can understand you, we can give you information you can use."

DECISION-MAKING

Being nonlinear is not a crime.

(**A**)s are very linear thinkers; they don't understand that sometimes item (C) can precede item (B) in the discussion. It depends what one wants to say.

(**A**)s get very upset when they perceive a discussion as getting out of order. It's too complicated for them: "Stop! What are you talking about? Where are the repercussions, and how are we going to deal with them, and how much does it cost?" This will drive an (**E**) absolutely crazy; he'll scream, "I don't know, I am just thinking aloud!"

Discussions need to be open to lots of different options, but an (**A**) can't see that. So you have to strongly reassure him: "Relax, we don't have a final decision. We're just exploring different alternatives.

"Stay calm. Like they say, happiness is not a destination but a journey.–Join the journey. We are exploring the different alternatives and possibilities. We are not deciding yet. We are just kissing; we are not getting married yet."

TEAM-BUILDING

A question is not necessarily a disagreement.

This applies to both (**A**)s and (**E**)s. In both cases, when you ask them a question, they often take that question as a challenge or disagreement with their ideas.

Here is how I handle it: In a meeting, when we finally have an idea (illumination), I say, "All right. I want everyone to take a piece of paper and divide it into three by drawing two horizontal lines across it. The upper part is called 'questions'; the middle part is called 'doubts'; and the lower part is called 'disagreements.'"

Let me define each.

"Questions" means you're asking for more information. "What is this?" "What is that?" "What happened to this?" "What happened to that?" "How will this work?" "How will that work?" You don't have an opinion; you're simply asking for more details.

"Doubts" means you have all the information you need but you're in doubt about whether it's going to work. Here you list your concerns.

"Disagreements" means you're not in any doubt; it's not going to work, and you know why.

Next, I spell out the proposed solution in detail, and everybody writes down their questions, doubts, and disagreements in the appropriate space.

Then we accumulate *only* the questions – not the doubts and not the disagreements – and try to answer the questions. Nobody feels threatened or gets upset, because we've already established that a question is not a disagreement and they expect the doubts and disagreements to be dealt when they turn comes, so they are relaxed. We take the questions one by one and we try to answer them together until they are all answered.

By separating the questions from doubts and disagreements, I make everyone understand, "Oh, it's just a question. Nobody's decided. I can relax." And as we deal with the questions – and the questions are often very legitimate – we change and adapt the proposed solution, so that it is constantly evolving, growing, changing, right in front of our eyes.

When all the questions have been answered, we again accumulate questions, doubts, and disagreements (the QDD list). The doubts from the previous list move up to become questions in the new list, and the disagreements move up to become doubts. And we start the process again. Again we deal only with the questions, until they are all answered.

Next we do another QDD list, and now the disagreements move up to become questions. Repeat the process until, when you ask, "OK, any new questions?" there are none. "Any doubts?" There will be none because they were all dealt with. "Any disagreements?" None as well.

Sometimes we hit a question that people cannot resolve by using this process. When that happens, we use a methodology called dialectical convergence: We start looking for the assumptions behind the disagreements. We're dealing with the *why*, and we go deeper and deeper and deeper, looking into the *whys*, until we find the source of the disagreement. Then we attack the source of the disagreement.

If even this doesn't work, I postpone the discussion until the next meeting. Usually, what happens after people sleep on it is they come back much more relaxed and willing to change. Time is a good healer. What people cannot agree about today, they've already gotten used to by the time we meet next week or next month.

Managing Change

Not doing something also has a cost.

An (**A**) will usually tell you, no matter what you want to do, that it's too expensive. But the cost of *not doing* may be higher than the cost of *doing*. Consider the American expression, "If you think education is expensive, think of the alternative."

So when an (**A**) tells you how expensive something would be to implement, the way to respond is, "All right, I understand it's very expensive. Now, how expensive would it be not to do it?" Then compare the two costs.

Dealing with an (E)

Communication

It takes at least two people to understand one.

Often it's very difficult to understand an (**E**). They're way ahead of everyone else: They see the contours of the problem, the direction they want to go, but they have difficulty explaining it. Then they get upset when people don't understand them.

This happened to me recently in Mexico. The executive I was consulting with already knew where he wanted to go, but he couldn't explain it, and when I tried to help him he nearly bit my head off. He could not articulate it well but *my* attempt to articulate it made him even more upset – as if he had always suspected he was surrounded by imbeciles who could not understand his genius, and now I had confirmed it.

The way to deal with this is to say upfront: "I am not disagreeing with you. I just want to understand you. (Do *not* say: "I *don't* understand you" – that will simply confirm his long-held suspicion that you are an idiot.)

To show your admiration for the (**E**) and your desire to understand him, you should say: "I want to understand you better; is it OK if I ask you a question?" Then ask – and be sure to present it as a question.

If he gets upset – and he can easily lose his temper – just keep repeating: "I'm sorry, I want to understand *what it is you want* so I can carry it out faithfully."

If after a number of questions you still don't understand, ask if there is anyone in the room who understands and can explain. Often you will find an "interpreter," someone who knows the (**E**) very well and can translate his ideas for you and everyone else. If that person's attempt fails, try someone else, and keep trying, until the (**E**) says, "Yes, that's what I meant to say." But be sure that it is always in the spirit of trying to understand, not disagree.

Before he can hear what you're saying, he has to listen to himself.

After an (**E**) speaks, you often see his eyes wander. What is he doing? He's actually listening with his inner ear to what he just said, and checking whether it was in fact what he wanted to say.

Don't interrupt. If you do, you're interfering with his ability to listen to himself. Be very quiet and wait. Watch his eyes. What's going to happen is very interesting. Very often he comes back and immediately contradicts himself: "Well, but what I *really* wanted to say...." He's listened to what he said and it wasn't exactly what he wanted to say. What came out was too raw. So he starts the circle of thinking and communicating and thinking all over again; his eyes go to lunch, and when he comes back he says, "And also what we should do...."

This is the creative process at work. It's just like writing a book: the final product is never the first draft. A good book is rewritten numerous times.

If you're an (**A**), you will want to say, "You just contradicted yourself; it doesn't make sense." Don't do that; let the (**E**) create. They create on the run, and they need a sympathetic audience.

You know he's finished when his eyes clear up and he looks directly at you; and if you have been patient and waited for him to finish thinking, he'll ask you, "What do you think?" If you tried to rush him, however, he's going to be annoyed with you. So always wait.

It is important to have a pad with you at every meeting, no matter what your typical style is. Here is a good example of why. While the (**E**)'s eyes are out to lunch, you can organize your thoughts and write down what you want to say next. In my sessions with clients, everybody is required to bring a pad, because that's what enables you to record what you want to say without having to say it immediately. That's what gives discipline to the meeting.

Ask him to repeat back to you what you just said.

When you ask an (**E**) to repeat what you've just said, be ready for a surprise. It will not be what you said. Why? Because what you said stimulated new thoughts in his mind, and already he has a different idea about what you said or what you *should* have said.

If you want to be sure that an (**E**) will do what *you* want and not what *he* wants, you must ask him to repeat what was said and be sure he understands it in (**PAEI**) terms, i.e., *what* is to be accomplished; *how, when,* and *who* will do it.

DECISION-MAKING

Try not to go to an (E) with a problem.

If you go to an (E) with one problem and ask him to help you solve it, you're going to have twenty more problems to solve by the time you leave his office.

(E)s love to solve problems, but they usually solve them by using a stream-of-consciousness style that produces lots of questions and complications, while the (E) grows more and more excited by his own ideas and more eager to try them out. Any problem you bring to him will remind him of a hundred other potential problems that need to be addressed, and he will try to address them all and start handing out assignments.

As a result, most of the staff learn not to go to him with problems. If he asks, "How is it going?" they tell him, "Fine."

If you must go to him, however, don't present him with a finished product – a solution that's been finalized – before he's had a chance to add to it, alter it, approve it, *own* it – in other words, to figure out some way to make it his.

Stay with the agenda.

How can you prevent an (E) from making decisions in his typical mercurial style, constantly moving from one subject to another? I have a set of strict rules for dealing with an (E) in a meeting:

An agenda must be prepared and distributed at least twenty-four hours before the meeting. No new items may be added to the agenda after it is distributed.

All material in support of an item on the agenda must be submitted at least twenty-four hours before the meeting, so that people have a chance to read it *prior* to the meeting. It is forbidden to read material during the meeting; otherwise, people will be reading during the discussion; thus they won't know what's going on and will not be able to participate. No material can be distributed during the meeting.

The (**E**) should not be the facilitator or moderator, because he will violate every rule that's been agreed on. I usually ask an (**A**) or an (**I**) type to manage the meeting. That does not mean the (**E**) loses his right to decide; if it is his responsibility to make the final decision, then that won't change. But in the meeting, he should listen and participate when his turn comes.

When I work with a company, I usually form an executive committee composed of people who fit the four essential roles. Each person has a different task to perform in the meeting. There's someone who's called the (**I**)ntegrator, and I usually choose an (**I**)-type person to run the meeting – *not* to make the final decision, only to run the meeting.

I choose an (**A**) to prepare the agenda and to distribute the material. The top person performs the (**P**) role; in other words, he or she will make the final decision. No decisions will be made without their approval.

If it's not in writing, it's not a decision.

(**E**)s are very creative and very expressive about it, but they also tend to forget, in the throes of today's new and exciting idea, what it was they said yesterday.

If an (**E**) gets caught with somebody in an elevator, and the other person says, "What do you think about doing such and such?" the (**E**) might say, "Oh, good idea," and forget all about it by the time he's off the elevator. And anyway, when an (**E**) says "yes," he often only means "why not?" or "maybe." But he says it with such conviction that it really appears as if he is finalizing. It feels like a true "yes." The person he's speaking to thinks, "Great! We have a decision," and that's when trouble starts brewing.

I have a rule in my organization that I recommend to all my clients who are (**E**)s and all my clients who *deal with* (**E**)s – particularly in companies managed by (**E**)s. The rule is: "If it's not in writing, and signed and dated, then it's not a decision." In other words, without that crucial signature, it's just another idea. The opposite rule is for companies run by an (**A**) where you do not want *everything* in writing. It will paralyze the company. Unfortunately, (**E**)s hate to put anything in writing. The details, the long pages, frustrate them. They also hate to read. This isn't just a question of availability or efficient use of time. It is their preferred method of communicating. "Talk to me," they say. They rarely say, "Write me a memo about it."

One reason might be that speaking instead of writing gives them the flexibility to change their minds, to continue illuminating. The danger is that without a paper trail, it's harder to keep track of who is accountable for what gets done. It is also difficult to carry out a decision if it is subject to constant change.

So, after a successful meeting with an (**E**) – even if it is in an elevator – always ask whether an apparent decision is a *finalization* or an *illumination*. *Finalization:* A decision communicated for action and implementation. *Illumination:* An idea that *could* be the solution but needs further evaluation.

If the (**E**) tells you it's a finalization, write it down and get him to sign it: "In the meeting we had on such and such a date, we agreed on this, this, and that." Then send it to him. Don't wait for the (**E**) himself to put it in writing; you'd be waiting forever. Write it yourself and send it to him as a record: "For the record, it is agreed that...." (By the way, sometimes he'll sign it, and years later when you bring it up he'll say, "I don't remember signing that," and when you put the page with his signature in front of him, he still won't believe it.)

Even after you send him the agreement you wrote up yourself, he probably won't return it to you or respond. You'll have to corner him again and say, "Here's what we discussed, here's what I think we agreed on, and unless I hear from you within two weeks, I will assume you are in agreement with what's written." That way you're forcing him to agree by default: if he doesn't respond, that means he agrees.

Don't be surprised if, after you write down the agreement and give it to him, he changes it. His mind has already moved on to another improvement, another iteration.

It is exciting to work for an (**E**), but it's also exhausting.

Set a deadline for finalization.

Creative people hate to let go of their projects; they invariably believe they can still be improved upon. Letting go feels like death.

Of course it isn't death. It's a birth of another progress report. But the (E) has trouble seeing it that way. That's why you must set a deadline.

At Franklin Mint, there were a lot of artists designing the products, and when I consulted with them we made a rule: "Your design is finished at midnight, April 15th. That means whatever you have at midnight on April 15th, that's the product. Sorry, no more. I know you can improve it, but time has run out."

That is also how editors work with authors; if you don't give a deadline to an author, he will never finish. Give him an early deadline because he's going to violate it. But give him a deadline, otherwise he will never give birth.

With (E)s you actually need two deadlines, because they will always violate the first one. You must have the deadline you give them and the deadline you're going to enforce. And you have to live up to it, because the (E) is going to push the envelope, he's going to cry and shout and scream for more time. But if you allow him to violate the deadline you meant to enforce, he will violate your deadlines forever.

So set a reasonable deadline by which a finalization should be arrived at. At the deadline, if there is no finalization, the latest illumination will automatically become the finalization.

Work out the details before finalizing.

(E)s like to finalize by saying, "We can work out the details later." Don't let them do that. Do not finalize until the details are reviewed.

In Israel, whenever they tell me, "Come on, let's get going, we're not going to the rabbi" – in other words, we're not going to have to go to court about it – that's when I know for sure we're going to end up going to a rabbi.

One way to prevent this is to make a rule that every finalization must be written down and must contain all the elements of implementation: *What* is to be done, *who* will do it, *how*, and *when*.

TEAM-BUILDING

Don't disagree prematurely.

An (**E**) often changes his mind as he listens to himself. He might say three different things one after another. If you prematurely start to disagree with him, he will announce, "It's too late for you to disagree with me; I've already changed my mind."

So wait until he finishes. Let him settle down before you start dealing with his suggestion. If you sit quietly long enough, you might find that there is nothing for you to do, because the (**E**) has done all the discussing, arguing, and disagreeing by himself.

Don't use the word "disagree."

When you disagree with an (**E**), find some other way to express it. The word "disagree" is worse than a red flag in front of a bull.

You can say, "I have different information," "I have a question," "I have a difference of opinion." It's even safer to say, "OK, let me think about it," and then wait, because he's going to change his mind anyway. So wait. Don't oppose; don't stand against him. Let him feel he is winning.

As long as the solution makes sense, you don't have to beat him in order to convince him. That's just an ego trip. It's much wiser to let him think he won. But ironically, you need to be very strong for that; it's painful to let someone else have all the ego gratification.

My other methodology for dealing with disagreements, which I describe in the (**A**) section of this chapter, is to have the group divide their feedback into three categories: Questions, doubts, and disagreements. We only deal with the questions, never the disagreements. As we answer the questions, the doubts move up to become questions, and eventually the disagreements also become questions. That way the (E) never feels threatened. And when an (E) feels in control and knows that you know he is in control, he can relax and let *you* speak.

The very *worst* thing you can do is to say: "Jim, I disagree with you. What you should do, Jim, is....." If you start off like that, you're dead meat and your idea will be DOA.

It's true that the (E) himself usually speaks like that. But do not imitate him, even if you too are an (E). If you are an (E) working for an (E) boss, let him be the (E). You should find some other role to perform that he is weak at.

Once an (E) has made a final decision (something he does not do easily), he can become very hostile if anyone disagrees with him. Under these circumstances it can be disastrous to call a meeting where people will object to the (E)'s decision. Instead, whenever you feel that there will be disagreement, try to have a private conversation first. Four eyes only. No audience. Ever.

Separate the idea from the person.

An (E) personalizes his ideas, so when you disagree with his idea he feels you're criticizing him. He takes it very personally.

Before I disagree with an (E)'s idea, I try to reassure him: "You know, Mike, you've proven to be right in the past, so I might be totally wrong, but I have a question to ask you about this idea."

Or, "I'm uncomfortable about something, and I wonder if you could help me out on this so I can implement this plan better. What do you mean by this word? What do you mean by that word?"

Or, "You know, I think your solution is correct, but there are several things I'm worried about. If we do *this* and *this* and *this*, *that* could happen, and if *that* happens, how do you think we could overcome it?"

The idea is to separate the idea from the person. Be sure that in attacking the idea you aren't inadvertently attacking the person.

For example, at one of my client companies, we were doing some succession planning, and I said, "We need to announce who the successor is."

Now, the danger was that the successor's competitor might decide to leave, and he was extremely important to the company. So the big (E) said to me, "I don't think we should announce anything yet." Now – how could I disagree with him?

I did not say a word – in public. But during a break, I took him in the corridor and said, "You know what, you're right – but here's what worries me. If we do not announce it now, over time this competitor will become stronger and stronger and gain power. How will we deal with that? Maybe we should nip it in the bud."

Instead of saying he was wrong, I showed him my fears: "I'm afraid if you do that, look what might happen."

He reacted very well and said, "You're right, I think we should do something now."

He might agree while seeming to disagree.

No matter what you say, an (E) will typically respond, "I disagree with you. What we really should do is...."

But if you ignore the first four words and pay attention to the rest of what he's saying, it's often pretty much what you said, rephrased and with a small variation.

That's because an (E) has to put his stamp on everything. And he does it by disagreeing – although in reality he is agreeing to the concept in its entirety.

Give him a chance to put his stamp on the decision, and try not to get ruffled that he is doing it in such a disagreeable way. The fact that he's saying something differently does not mean he's saying something different.

Don't confront him about it; don't say, "But actually you're agreeing with me." Let him win: "Hmmm. Very good. I agree with you. Fine. Let's go and do it."

Make it his idea.

Do not give a solution to an (**E**). He will change it. Instead, you might say, "Would it make sense to…," "It appears…," or "What do you think?" That way, he can own the idea.

I even try to avoid saying something is a good idea. If I say it's a good idea, then I own it. The (**E**) will immediately jump on it and say it's not a good idea. The principle is never to come on too strong.

Another way of dealing with an (**E**) is simply to give him the problem, the expected results, and the boundaries of what *not* to do. Then let *him* figure out what to do.

Don't take it personally.

(**E**)s can get very personal and turn a discussion into an ugly exchange of accusations and put-downs. When someone has an idea they don't like, they don't just criticize the idea, they demolish the messenger.

When confronted by an (**E**)'s wrath, don't take it personally, even though it certainly sounds personal. It is just his way of disagreeing with an idea that threatens his own. He doesn't really mean to be personal at all, and as soon as the argument is over he forgets all about it. The more you try to defend yourself and prove him wrong, the deeper and deeper you dig yourself in. Remember: (**E**)s are seldom right but never in doubt. So who are you to *prove* them wrong? Just let them download and go on your way. They will forget about it anyway, so if you can control your pride, in the long run you will end up winning.

Stay out of the penalty box.

Many (**E**)s have a scapegoat, somebody they vent their frustrations on all the time.

This is a miserable position to be in. I recently saw it in a company managed by an (**E**). First the scapegoat was the chief financial officer. When the CFO quit, the (**E**) immediately switched to the human resources chief. There was always somebody in the penalty box. It's even possible to predict who it will be: usually an (**A**) type, somebody who is in an (**A**) job. If there are not enough (**A**)s, then it will be a (**P**): "He's too busy, he doesn't know what the heck he's doing, he's going in circles, he's wasting time." (**E**)s have to hit on somebody, and if there are not enough (**P**)s, they'll choose an (**I**). That's the sequence.

If you *do* become the scapegoat, what should you do?

First of all, yield: Lift your hands in the air, raise the white flag, say you're sorry, say whatever is necessary. Don't fight it.

Next, try to get out of his stream of energy. The way you become a scapegoat is by interfering with the (**E**). He perceives you as being critical of him or disagreeing with him. So whatever you're doing, stop doing it.

Force him to set a bias multiple.

(**E**)s are impatient and unrealistic about how long it takes to get some- thing accomplished. If an (**E**) tells you, "I want this done in a week," and you know it's going to take six weeks, what should you say?

You have to bring the eagle down to the ground. How do you do that? Don't argue with him. Write down the assignment. Then go back to your office and make a list of all the other things you have to do. Return later and say, "You gave me ten assignments, and this one makes eleven. Please show me how to do all of them, or tell me in which sequence of priorities to do them."

Since (**E**)s hate to choose among options, they will usually put off the discussion. That's how they give up an unreasonable demand without having to admitting defeat.

DEALING WITH AN (I)

This section of the book is shorter than the others. That is a reflec- tion of my experience, or lack of experience, with (**I**)-type managers. I have worked mostly with (**E**) and (**A**) executives: (**E**)s lead grow- ing companies while (**A**)s manage aging companies. (**P**)s are usually found in the lower levels of an organization, with which I have less contact. And I rarely deal with (**I**)s at all: They tend to be clustered in human resources departments, a place where I am never welcomed because I am perceived as causing too much change. If an (**I**) does happen to be the leader of a company, I am unlikely to be hired there for the same reason.

So I apologize for my relative lack of information and advice on this style of manager, but what is, is.

Perhaps some of my readers can contribute. If so, I am all ears. Write to me at Ichak@adizes.com. I thank you in advance.

COMMUNICATION

Ask an (I) to interpret himself.

(**I**)s don't like to get into the crossfire. So they hedge and double- and triple-hedge. "It appears that under certain circumstances, we might say...." "On the other hand, I'm not so sure I agree...."

What the (**I**) is doing is floating trial balloons, to see which way the wind is blowing, so that he can come out on the winning side. But his unwillingness to express an opinion often renders him incomprehensible.

If I am dealing with an (**I**), and I don't know what he means to say, then I look around for somebody who is known to be very outspoken. Then I ask the (**I**): "What do you think Joe would say on this subject?" The (**I**) will then tell me what he thinks but state it as Joe's opinion. That way, he's not exposed.

TEAM-BUILDING

Beware of manipulators.

An (**I**) is much more aware of what people are feeling than an (**E**) or (**P**) or (**A**), but the danger is that he may become a Rasputin, enjoying his power position and abusing it. An (**I**) needs to feel essential to the resolution of a conflict. If he cannot be the (**I**)ntegrator, the source of the resolution, either he will not allow conflict to emerge or he will try to undermine a resolution that took place without him.

Human resources executives are usually (**I**)s, and they almost never have any power – so if they get it they have a tendency to become little manipulators. People soon start to fear and distrust them, and ultimately they lose their ability to manage.

When dealing with an (**I**), the key is to make him feel essential to the group effort. This will smooth the way for a resolution that the (**I**) will not attempt to undermine.

MANAGING CHANGE

We have already discussed this item. Just to repeat: Get consensus of the key people he wants agreement from upfront, before you approach him with a solution.

REWARDING

How to be appreciated.

(**I**)s surround themselves with informers. They want to know who said what and why he said it. And how Jim feels about David, and David about Sam and Sam about XYZ.

And they want to know what will be the reaction of Jim to situation A or situation B.

If you want to be appreciated by an (**I**), you better have good answers to those questions. As a (**P**) you will probably be dumbfounded and fail the test.

BEHAVIOR

Do not push.

(**I**)s have their own tempo. It is usually dictated by the political realities as they see them. They hate to be pushed. If you are a (**P**) and you want to impose your tempo on them, you are out of luck and probably out of favor with the boss.

Can I disagree?

You can disagree with an (I) and even with others in the team as long as you are not causing disintegration and hard feelings. So with an (I) watch more *how* you say things than *what* you say.

What does he want?

If you tell an (E) you love him he feels awkward. He even wonders what is your hidden agenda. An (E) wants to be admired, not loved. At least do not talk about it. They have problems with intimacy. The opposite is true for an (I). They thrive on love. They want to know if they are loved and they will go to courses and workshops that teach love, relationships, intimacy. So when you relate to an (I), take it slowly. Relationships do not develop in a haste. Eagerness, which is music to an (E), is a disturbing noise to an (I).

Summary

When working with a (P) boss, peer, or subordinate

1. No small talk: Get right down to business. Do not bother him with problems unless they are crises.
2. Start "from the end"! Go for the bottom line from the beginning.
3. Present goals and priorities (the deliverables) so that he understands the point of any exercise.
4. Move, speak, and act as rapidly as you can.
5. Be precise and literal in your language.
6. When delegating, be specific about who, what, when, where, and how.

7. Praise his efforts; make sure he knows that you know how hard he works.
8. Tell him exactly what results you expect.
9. Reward for performance, short-term performance, deliverable results that can be measured. Reward at short intervals.
10. Be good to your word: "Yes " means yes and "No" means no.

When working with an (A) boss, peer or subordinate

1. You should take the risk for change.
2. Give him plenty of time to make decisions.
3. Make systematic, linear presentations, using as many supporting documents as possible.
4. Persuade him with facts, not opinions.
5. Gather and present successful precedents for your plan.
6. Listen carefully to his objections, write them down, return later with detailed responses.
7. Don't use gimmicks. Plain, factual language – especially numbers – are best.
8. Maintain your credibility by doing exactly what you said you'd do.
9. Focus for him on the "How."
10. Reward him with security of employment and expected raises.

When working with an (E) boss, peer or subordinate

1. Give him the "big picture" first. You deal with the details later.
2. Be sure you give him space to make corrections and contribute ideas. Do not ever give him something that cannot be changed.
3. Never take what he says literally; an (E) exaggerates when making a point.
4. Once he agrees to a general idea, work out the details before the plan is signed off on.

5. You write what was decided and let him sign on it. Do not expect him to write it. You have to submit it for signing as soon as the decision was made or he will not sign it; he will change his mind.

6. Remember that underneath the arrogant veneer is a lot of insecurity. Thus, never disagree with him in public. Never show that you disagree, period. Show your disagreements as questions that need answers if you are to implement his idea well.

7. Remember he wants to be admired, not necessarily loved.

8. Be willing to appreciate him nonstop, but don't expect any appreciation back.

9. Never criticize his ideas. Let them be. Give time for them to become obsolete.

10. Be loyal. Do not talk about him behind his back. Learn how to disagree without being disagreeable. Do not mimic him.

11. Learn to be available to him constantly; if you can't handle it, find another job.

When working with an (I) boss, peer, or subordinate

1. Act warm and interested in him.

2. Be a source of his information.

3. Do not force him to make rapid decisions. Be open for discussion.

4. Spend time helping him identify his goals and tasks.

5. Listen actively.

6. Take the time necessary to ensure that communication is working.

7. Be open to his feelings and opinions when he is involved in the decision-making process, even if you disagree with him.

8. Be supportive of him as he implements his tasks.

9. Before approaching him about a plan, make sure you have already established support for your plan among other team members who he believes have a political power base.

Afterword

We are all different. Thanks God. Life would be so boring otherwise. And from whom would we learn ? Who will disagree with us and thus force us to open our minds and learn something new?

In this book I tried to communicate what I have learned from working with thousands of executives all over the world. Forty-eight countries to be exact. Thirty years of note taking. Thirty years with many sleepless nights trying to understand what is going wrong. Where did I go wrong and why.

I hope that my experiences will help you make less mistakes than I did. That you will learn from my mistakes – they were many. As a matter of fact, each prescription I give in this book is based on some mistake I have seen or personally experienced.

I hope that my pain is your gain.

Thank you for taking the time to get to this page. It was a long "trip" to read this book; just imagine how long it was to write it.

Bibliography

Abravanel, E. and King, E.: *Dr. Abravanel's Body Type Program for Health, Fitness and Nutrition* (New York: Bantam Books, Inc., 1985).

Adizes, Ichak: *How to Solve the Mismanagement Crisis* (Santa Monica, Calif.: Adizes Institute, Inc., 1979).

Adizes, Ichak: *Industrial Democracy, Yugoslav Style: The Effect of Decentralization on Organizational Behavior* (New York: Free Press, 1971; reprinted by MDOR Institute, 1977, paper).

Adizes, Ichak: *Managing Corporate Lifecycles* (Paramus, N.J.: Prentice Hall Press, 1999).

Adizes, Ichak, with Griffin, Patrick H.: *Managing the Performing Arts Organization: Founding Principles in the Management of the Arts* (Santa Monica, Calif.: The Adizes Institute, 1999).

Adizes, Ichak: *Mastering Change: the Power of Mutual Trust and Respect* (Santa Barbara, Calif.: Adizes Institute Publications, 1992).

Alessandra, A. and Wexler, P.: *Non-Manipulative Selling* (San Diego: Courseware, Inc., 1979).

Bell, Gerald: *The Achievers* (Chapel Hill, N.C.: Preston Hill, 1973).

Bennett, E.: *What Jung Really Said* (New York: Schocken Books, 1967).

Bennett, J.: *Enneagram Studies* (York Beach: Samuel Weiser, Inc., 1983).

Berliner, Joseph S.: *Factory and Manager in the USSR* (Cambridge, Mass.: Harvard University Press, 1957).

Berne, Eric: *Games People Play* (New York: Ballantine, 1996, revised edition).

Blake, Robert, and Mouton, Jane: *The Managerial Grid* (Houston: Gulf Publishing, 1964).

Blau, Peter M.: *The Dynamics of Bureaucracy* (Chicago: University of Chicago Press, 1956).

Bolton, R. and Bolton, D.: *People Styles at Work* (New York: American Management Association, 1996).

Bolton, R. and Bolton, D.: *Social Style/Management Style* (New York: American Management Association, 1984).

Choiniere, R., and Keirsey, D.: *Presidential Temperament* (Del Mar: Prometheus Nemesis Book Company, 1992).

Drucker, Peter F.: *Management: Tasks, Responsibilities, Practices* (New York: Harper & Row, 1973).

Fieve, Ronald R.: *Moodswing: Dr. Fieve on Depression* (New York: William Morrow and Co., 1989).

Francis, Roy G., and Stone, Robert C.: *Service and Procedure in Bureaucracy: A Case Study* (Minneapolis: University of Minnesota Press, 1956).

Fraser, J.: *The Chinese Portrait of a People* (Glasgow: William Collins Sons & Co. Ltd., 1981).

Gordon, Dr. T.: *L.E.T. Leadership Effectiveness Training* (Wyden Books, 1977).

Halberstam, D.: *The Best and the Brightest* (London: Pan Books Ltd., 1972).

Hartman, T.: *The Color Code* (Taylor Don Hartman, 1987).

Herrmann, N.: *The Creative Brain* (Lake Lure: Brain Books, 1990).

Keirsey, D. and Bates, M.: *Please Understand Me* (Del Mar: Prometheus Nemesis Book Company, 1984).

Lear, F.: *The Second Seduction* (New York: Alfred A. Knopf, 1992).

Lowen, A.: *Depression and the Body* (New York: Penguin Books, 1981).

Lowen, A.: *The Language of the Body* (New York: Macmillan Publishing Co., Inc., 1979).

March, James G., and Herbert Simon: *Organizations* (New York, London: John Wiley & Sons, 1958).

Mottram, V.: *The Physical Basis of Personality* (Baltimore: Penguin Books, 1960).

Parkinson, C. Northcote: *Parkinson's Law: The Pursuit of Progress* (London: John Murray, 1958).

Peter, Laurence J., and Hull, Raymond Hull: *The Peter Principle: Why Things Always Go Wrong* (New York: William Morrow & Co., 1969).

Rothchild, J.: *Going for Broke: How Robert Campeau Bankrupted the Retail Industry, Jolted the Junk Bond Market and Brought the Booming Eighties to a Crashing Halt* (New York: Simon & Schuster, 1991).

Schumpeter, Joseph: *Business Cycles* (New York: McGraw Hill, 1939).

Soros, George, Wien, Byron, and Koenen, Krisztina: *Soros on Soros: Staying Ahead of the Curve* (New York: John Wiley & Sons, 1995).

George Albert Steiner: *Top Management Planning* (New York: Macmillan, 1969).

Storm, H.: *Seven Arrows* (New York: Harper & Row, 1972).

Sundberg, N.: *Assessment of Persons* (New Jersey: Prentice-Hall, 1977).

Waldo, Dwight, ed.: *Ideas and Issues in Public Administration* (New York: McGraw Hill, 1963).

Woodward, Joan: *Industrial Organization: Theory and Practice* (New York: Oxford University Press, 1965).

Additional Works by the Author

(All available from the Adizes Institute at www.adizes.com)

Books

Adizes, I. *Industrial Democracy Yugoslav Style*. New York: Free Press, 1971.

Adizes, I. and Mann-Borgese, Elisabeth, eds. *Self-Management: New Dimensions to Democracy*, Santa Barbara, CA: ABC/CLIO, 1975.

Adizes, I. *How to Solve the Mismanagement Crisis*. 2nd printing. Santa Barbara: Adizes Institute Publications, 1980. (First printing, New York: Dow Jones Irwin, 1979.)

Adizes, I. *Corporate Lifecycles: How and Why Corporations Grow and Die and What to Do about It*. Englewood Cliffs, NJ: Prentice Hall, 1988.

Adizes, I. *Mastering Change: The Power of Mutual Trust and Respect in Personal Life, Family, Business and Society*. Santa Barbara: Adizes Institute Publications, 1993.

Adizes, I. *The Pursuit of Prime*. First printing, Santa Monica, CA: Knowledge Exchange, 1996.

Adizes, I. *Managing the Performing Arts Organization*. Santa Barbara: Adizes Institute Publications, 1999.

Adizes, I. *Managing Corporate Lifecycles: An Updated and Expanded Look at the Corporate Lifecycles*. First printing, Paramus, NJ: Prentice Hall Press, 1999.

Adizes, I. *Management/Mismanagement Styles: How to Identyfy a Style and What to Do about It*. Adizes Institute Publications, Santa Barbara, CA, 2004.

Adizes, I. *The Ideal Executive: Why You Cannot be One and What to Do About It*. Adizes Institute Publications, Santa Barbara, CA, 2004.

Articles

Adizes, I. "The Role of Management in Democratic (Communal) Organizational Structures." *Annals of Public and Cooperative Economy.* Quarterly review of CIRIEC. Brussels: CIRIEC, No. 424 (1971): 399–420.

Adizes, I. "Administering for the Arts: Introduction and Overview." *California Management Review* 15,2 (1972): 99–103.

Adizes, I. "Boards of Directors in the Performing Arts: A Managerial Analysis." *California Management Review* 15, 2 (1972): 109 117.

Adizes, I. "Economic Changes in Yugoslavia." *East Europe* 21, 10 (1972): 8–16.

Adizes, I. "Management in Der Demokratischen Organisationen." *Annalen der Gemeinwirtschaft* 41 (Januar-Marz, 1972).

Adizes, I. "Samoupravljanje Kao Drustveni Cilj i Organizacijski Proces - [Self-Management as a Social Goal and an Organizational Process."] *Socijalizam* 11, 12 (1972): 1324–1333.

Adizes, I. "Uloga Rukovodjenja u Demokratskim Organizacionim Strukturama." [Serbo-Croatian translation of "The Role of Management in Democratic Organizational Structures"]. *Moderna Organizacija* 6 (1972): 937–951.

Adizes, I. "Uloga Vodstva v Demokraticnih (Skupnostnih) Organizacijskih Strukturah." ["The Role of Management in Democratic Organization"] *Moderna Organizacija* 6 (1972): 437–451.

Adizes, I. and Weston, F. "Comparative Models of Social Responsibility." *Journal of the Academy of Management* 16, 1 (1973): 112–129. Reprinted in F. Luthans and R.M. Hodgetts, *Social Issues in Business.* 2nd ed. New York: Macmillan, 1974.

Adizes, I. "Gerencia y Estructuras Comunales (I)." "The Role of Management in Democratic Organization" *Gerencia.* Instituto Peruano de Administracion de Empresas (IPAE) Lima, Peru, (Noviembre/Diciembre, 1976): 23–76. Adizes, I. "On Conflict Resolution and an Organizational Definition of Self-Management" in *Participation and Self-Management*, Volume 5 "Social

System and Participation," 1–73. First International Sociological Conference on Participation and Self-Management. Zagreb, Yugoslavia (1973).

Adizes, I. "Le Role de la Direction Dans une Communante Organisée Sûr une Base Democratique." "The Role of Management in Democratic Organization" *Les Annales De L'Economie Collective* 1 (Jan.-Mars, 1973): 83–109.

Adizes, I. and McWhinney, W. "Arts, Society and Administration: The Role and Training of Arts Administrators, Arts and Society." *Arts and Society*, 10, 3 (1974): 40–50.

Adizes, I. "Gerencia y Estructuras Comunales (II) Management and Communal Structures" *Gerencia*, IPAE (January/February, 1974): 36–43.

Adizes, I. "Relaciones Organizativas en la Empresa Autogestionaria [The Self-Managed Enterprise]." *Apuntes* 1, 2 (1974): 21–30.

Blame, M. and Adizes, I. "Parkview Symphony." In *Business Policy: Strategy Formation and Management Action*, ed. W. Glueck, 366–374. 2nd ed. New York: McGraw-Hill, 1974.

Adizes, I. "Autogestion y Naciones en Dsarollo [Self-Management in Developing Nations]." *Apuntes* 4 (1975): 106–122.

Adizes, I. "The Cost of Being an Artist: An Argument for the Public Support of the Arts." *California Management Review* 17 (Summer, 1975): 80–84.

Adizes, I. "Mas Alla del 'Principio de Peter': una Tipologia de Estilos de Incompetencis Gerencial." *Instituto de Administracion Cientifica de las Empresas* (IACE). Monterrey, Mexico (1975).

Adizes, I. "Mismanagement Styles." *California Management Review* 19, 2 (1976): 5–20.

Adizes, I. "Seattle Opera Association." *Business Policy: Strategy Formation and Management Action*, ed. W. Glueck, 610–634. 2nd ed. New York: McGraw-Hill, 1976.

Adizes, I. and Zukin, P. "A Management Approach to Health Planning in Developing Countries." *Health Care Management Review* 2, 1 (1977): 19–37.

Adizes, I. "Industrial Democracy and Codetermination." *Encyclopedia of Professional Management*. New York: McGraw-Hill, 1978.

Zupanov, J. and Adizes, I., "Labor Relations in Yugoslavia." Handbook of Contemporary Developments in *World Industrial Relations*, ed. A. Blum. Westwood, CT: Greenwood Press, 1978.

Adizes, I. "Mismanagement." *Affarsekonomi Management. Stockholm*, Sweden, 1978.

Adizes, I. "Organizational Passages: Tools for Diagnosis and Therapy of Organizational Behavior." *Organizational Dynamics* 8, 3 (Summer, 1979): 28–46.

Adizes, I. and Turban, E., "An Innovative Approach to Group Decision Making." *Personnel*, 62,4 (1985): 45–49.

Adizes, I. "Back to Basics: Mutual Trust and Respect and Productivity." *Executive Excellence*, 10, 10 (1993): 11–13.

Adizes, I. "Managing: The Business of Mutual Trust and Respect." *Manage* 45, 1 (1993): 26–28.

Adizes, I. "Twelve Tips on Keeping Your Growing Business at Prime." *Manage* 44,3 (1993): 14–17.

Adizes, I. "Corporate Lifecycles: Entrepreneurship and Integration." In *Management and Entrepreneurship*, the English version, ed. I. Vaji, 168 172. Vol. II. Centar za Management i Marketing, University of Zagreb: Zagreb University Press, 1994.

Adizes, I. "How to Convert a Committee into a Team." *Successful Meetings* 43, 2 (1994): 115–118.

Adizes, I. "Integrating Innovation." *Executive Excellence*. 11, 11 (1994): 12–13.

Adizes, I. "Keeping the Fires Burning [about TQM]." *Manage* 46, 1 (1994): 12 16.

Adizes, I. "Information Superhighway: Overloading Human Potential." *Executive Excellence* 12, 4 (1995): 15.

Adizes, I. "What Comes First? Strategy or Structure?" *Executive Excellence* 2, 9 (1995): 20.

Adizes, I. "Eight Myths [about management]: Getting Right the People Dimension of Business." *Executive Excellence* 14, 9 (1997): 20.

Adizes, I. "Five Myths about Management in the 1990s." *Manage* 48 (July, 1997): 30 32.

Adizes, I. "Looking for Mr./Ms. Perfect: The Search for the Right Professional Manager in a Growing Company. *Progress* 2, 1 (1998): 14–15.

Adizes, I. "Self-Esteem: Who Cares?" *The Adizes Institute Journal of Organizational Transformation* 1, 1 (1998): 7–16.

Working Papers

Adizes, I. Establishing a Program for Arts Administration: Summary of the UCLA Conference and a Report on Implementation. In the *Management in the Arts Research Program Publication Series*, Publication 1. Division of Research, GSM. Los Angeles: UCLA, 1969.

Adizes, I. "The Roles of Art in Post-Industrial Society." Presented at the *Center for the Study of Democratic Institutions.* Santa Barbara, CA: January, 1973.

Adizes, I. "Administering for the Arts: Problems in Practice." *Management in the Arts Program Research Papers*, #15. GSM. Los Angeles: UCLA, October, 1971.

Adizes, I. "A New Framework for Management Theory." Santa Barbara: The Adizes Institute, June, 1987.

Adizes, I. and Haldeman, H.R. "Why Gorbachev Might Fail." Santa Barbara: The Adizes Institute, January, 1988.

Adizes, I. "The Common Principles of Managing Oneself, a Family, a Corporation or a Society." Santa Barbara: The Adizes Institute, September, 1990.

VIDEO

Adizes, I. (1984). *The Adizes Program in Video*. Santa Barbara: The Adizes Institute.

Adizes, I. *Program A: Overview of the Adizes Process of Management*. Set of 3 videotapes. Santa Barbara: Adizes Institute Publications, 1993

 The Adizes Process of Management. 55 min.

 The Adizes Program. Questions and Answers #1

 The Adizes Program. Questions and Answers # 2

Adizes I. *Program B: The Management Process*. Set of 4 videotapes. Santa Barbara: Adizes Institute Publications, 1993

 The Roles of Management. 28 min.

 Mismanagement Styles. 41 min.

 The Structural Causes of Deadwood. 38 min.

 What is a Good Manager? 41 min.

Adizes I. *Program C: Organizational Lifecycles*. Set of 4 videotapes. Santa Barbara: Adizes Institute Publications, 1993

 The Growth Phases of Organizational Lifecycles. 39 min.

 The Aging Phases of Organizational Lifecycles. 38 min.

 Analysis of Lifecycles. 52 min.

 Treating the Growing and Aging Problems of Organizations. 56 min.

Adizes, I. *Program D: Decision Making and Implementation*. Set of 2 videotapes. Santa Barbara: Adizes Institute Publications, 1993.

 CAPI: Predicting Managerial Effectiveness. 45 min.

 The Adizes Process of Decision Making. 49 min.

Adizes, I. *From Entrepreneurship to Professional Management*. Speech to the Council of Growing Companies. Santa Barbara: Adizes Institute Publications, 1993.

Adizes, I. *The Young Company's Lifecycle: Are You Ready for the Future?* Keynote Address to the Inc. 500 Awards. Santa Barbara: Adizes Institute Publications, 1996.

AUDIO

Adizes, I. *Analysis of Management*. 6 audio cassettes. Santa Barbara: Adizes Institute Publications, 1988.

Adizes, I. *Analysis of Lifecycles*. 6 audio cassettes. Santa Barbara: Adizes Institute Publications, 1989.

CD

Caric, N., Horvat, Z. and Vukic, B. *The Adizes Program: An Interactive Compilation of the Writings of Dr. Ichak Adizes and the Programs of the Adizes Institute*. Santa Barbara: Adizes Institute Publications, 1998.

About the Adizes Institute

The Adizes Institute provides organizations worldwide with the managerial resources to achieve extraordinary results while developing and nurturing a constructive, cooperative organizational culture.

Since its establishment in 1975, the Adizes Institute has served hundreds of organizations worldwide, from fledging companies to Fortune 100s, not-for-profit organizations, and governments. Through its network of international locations, the Adizes Institute has provided services to organizations in 45 countries.

The Adizes Institute is the research, publishing, licensing, training, and certification arm for the Adizes® methodology. The Adizes® methodology, developed over the past 35 years by Dr. Ichak Adizes, is a highly evolved proprietary, structured, pragmatic system for accelerating organizational change.

The Adizes Institute is closely associated with the Adizes Graduate School that grants master's and doctoral degrees in the study of Leadership and Change.